DANISH DY

DANISH DYNAMITE

The Story of Football's Greatest Cult Team

Rob Smyth, Lars Eriksen
and Mike Gibbons

BLOOMSBURY
LONDON • NEW DELHI • NEW YORK • SYDNEY

First published in Great Britain 2014

Copyright © 2014 by Rob Smyth, Lars Eriksen and Mike Gibbons

Bloomsbury Publishing plc
50 Bedford Square
London
WC1B 3DP

www.bloomsbury.com

Bloomsbury is a trademark of Bloomsbury Publishing Plc

Bloomsbury Publishing, London, New Delhi, New York and Sydney

A CIP catalogue record for this book is available from the British
Library

ISBN 978 1 4088 4484 7

10 9 8 7 6 5 4 3 2 1

Typeset by Saxon Graphics Ltd, Derby

Printed and bound in Great Britain by CPI Group (UK) Ltd,
Croydon CR0 4YY

To Sepp and the boys of 86, who made football fun

Contents

Chapter 1

Mr and Mrs Bignell

In the 2010s Denmark became one of the world's most fashionable countries. There were myriad reasons for this, from Nordic noir to gastronomy via architecture, craft beer and even knitwear. Football fans of a certain age wondered what took everyone else so long to discover this. In the mid-1980s, Denmark were the most interesting and perhaps the best football team in the world, an almost unprecedented achievement for a country with a population of only five million.

'What Denmark did was amazing,' said Diego Maradona. 'They were like a bullet train.' They made history by playing football from the future: a fast-forward version of the Dutch Total Football that had charmed the world in the 1970s, and with the same unashamedly attacking intent.

Denmark's style made children fall in love with football and reminded adults why they had fallen in love with it in the first place. When the influential British magazine *World Soccer* asked a group of experts in 2008 to select the greatest teams of all time, Denmark's 1980s side were sixteenth on the list – above any side from Argentina, Spain, Germany, Liverpool, Manchester United or Internazionale. The Danish fans gave their team a simple and enduring name: Danish Dynamite.

The team were just as impressive off the field: warm, funny, laid back and approachable – sometimes in four or five different languages. The same was true of their fans, who followed their team abroad in their thousands and extended the mood of innocence with their cheery, peaceful drunkenness that was in contrast to the hooliganism elsewhere during the 1980s.

Around 80 per cent of the population watched a famous match at Wembley, and the players were adored for what they achieved and especially the way they achieved it. Before Danish Dynamite, Denmark for decades had been an irrelevant football country; they were happy amateurs, content with mediocrity, who did not question their place in the wider scheme. That all changed in 1979, year zero for Danish football.

In those days foreign football was only really available during the World Cup, so for those of a certain age Denmark were the first great fantasy team. In the days before the internet and social media, discovering them was like finding a great underground band or art house film. The fact that their story had a bittersweet tang and a doomed innocence only accentuates their alternative appeal. The best stories in life are the ones where those involved don't get the girl, the happy ending or even the Jules Rimet Trophy.

More than three decades later the Dynamite team are still big news – whether it's newspaper tributes when they turn sixty, when songs from 1986 are played on the radio or when toddlers sport the team's kit from the mid-1980s. That kit is a seriously expensive piece of memorabilia from an era that also produced ultra-quotable dialogue from the TV commentator Svend Gehrs and unlikely tributes from obsessive fans overseas. Danish Dynamite is also the name of an award-winning beer made by Stonehenge Ales in Salisbury, Wiltshire, and, in 2010, the Danish embassy in Tokyo arranged for a Japanese pop group to film their own version of 'Re-Sepp-Ten', Denmark's song from the 1986 World Cup.

The team were even special guests at a wedding in another country in 2012. On 10 May, Mr Dave Bignell and Ms Claire Whitehead were married at St Ninian's Church in Douglas on the

Isle of Man. The twelve tables at the reception were named after the Denmark team that played Uruguay at the 1986 World Cup: Rasmussen, Busk, Olsen, Nielsen, Andersen, Arnesen, Berggreen, Bertelsen, Lerby, Laudrup and Elkjær. The starting XI was accompanied by the coach, Sepp Piontek, who naturally took the grandparents' table. Michael Laudrup was chosen for the top table, with Preben Elkjær and Søren Lerby proving especially popular among those who had been told of their character and on-field exploits.

'The team have been a constant reference point in my life,' says Dave Bignell. He is certainly not alone in that.

Chapter 2

For he's a jolly good fellow

The introduction of football in Denmark was half a beat behind the trailblazers in the north of England. It was led by Kjøbenhavns Boldklub (KB), the oldest football club in continental Europe, in 1879. The first football match in Denmark was played in 1883 and six years later Dansk Boldspil-Union (the Danish Football Association, or DBU) was formed. It set up the national championship and provided organisation to a sport whose popularity had been spreading among English immigrants and in boarding schools. The DBU was in on the ground floor as one of seven founder members of Fifa in 1904.

The Danes were handy on the pitch too – an unofficial Danish national team won gold at the 1906 Intercalated Games held to mark the ten-year anniversary of the original Olympics in Athens. After sweeping into a 9-0 lead at half-time in the final, Denmark were crowned champions when their Greek opponents refused to come out for further punishment in the second half.

Two of the early stars of Danish football were Niels and Harald Bohr, siblings who achieved fame in Denmark and beyond as a kind of scholarly version of the Neville brothers in the early twentieth century. Both played for Akademisk Boldklub just north of Copenhagen. Niels was a useful goalkeeper who never ascended to the national side. If you're going to overcompensate for not being an international footballer, you might as well go big. He went on to win the Nobel Prize in Physics in 1922, worked on the Manhattan Project during the Second World War, founded CERN (where the internet was invented), was the first recipient of the Atoms for Peace award and has an element in the periodic table – Bohrium – named in his honour.

His younger brother, Harald, did make it as a Danish international and was also a mathematician of some repute. Rare indeed is the man who can dovetail an international football career with pioneering work in the study of almost periodic functions. He also had a theorem named after him. Harald missed the chance to play in Denmark's unofficial triumph in 1906 as he was helping Niels defend his doctoral thesis, but did play a starring role in Denmark's first official international matches at the London Olympics in 1908. They claimed a silver medal and an Olympic record, walloping France A by a score of 17-1. (They had managed a mere nine goals against France's B team in the previous round.) They lost the final to Great Britain, as they would again in the 1912 Olympics in Stockholm.

Perhaps they would have won in 1912 had Poul 'Tist' Nielsen been fit. He had just begun a career of goalscoring abandon that would make Gerd Müller look profligate by comparison. Nielsen shot KB to six Danish championships and, in a fifteen-year international career, scored fifty-two times in thirty-eight matches. Norway were his bread and butter and on the receiving end of half of his goals – in one game against them in 1917, in which the kick-off was delayed while the Danish left-back and shoe salesman Johannes Hansen was stuck at the hairdresser's, Nielsen struck five times in eleven minutes. When he scored his fiftieth international goal against Belgium in 1924, the Danish goalkeeper Edvin Frigast Larsen ran the length of the pitch to shake his hand and bow before him.

As Nielsen's career wound down, the early burst of amateur success faded. After going out of the 1920 Olympics in the first round, Denmark retreated into international hibernation. They could not afford further attempts at Olympic glory and settled for matches against Finland, Sweden and Norway and the odd friendly with other European nations within easy hitting distance. Elsewhere, the idealistic French football president Jules Rimet launched the World Cup in Uruguay in 1930, a professional tournament to find the best team in the world that would quickly put the amateur Olympic equivalent in the shade. Denmark adhered to their amateur principles and declined to enter.

At the time this attitude was much more in line with their way of thinking. In 1933 the Danish-Norwegian author Aksel Sandemose published his breakthrough novel, *A Fugitive Crosses His Tracks*. Set in the fictional Danish town of Jante, the book identified and explored a social phenomenon across all the Nordic nations that Sandemose called the Law of Jante. There were ten rules in total, all along a similar theme: a warning to the individual from the collective – do not think you are anything special, or that you are in some way better than us. The Law of Jante, or Janteloven as it's known in Danish, is still a hard concept for many Scandinavians to shake. Sandemose had identified the collective pressure on a person to be content with what they had and not to have ambition beyond it.

Denmark returned to international competition at the 1948 Olympics in London, and although they were still more than a match for anyone in amateur football they were soon to experience the impact of the professional game. After beating Italy 5-3 on their way to the bronze medal, ten of the Danish squad were headhunted and signed professional contracts with Serie A clubs. The DBU's strict rules meant that they could never play for Denmark again. It would become a recurring theme.

This dogmatic adherence to the amateur game held Denmark back at a time when the shackles were coming off elsewhere. Neighbouring Sweden, hosts for the World Cup in 1958 and fearing a sub-par performance in their tournament, lifted their restrictions on professional players in 1956 to allow Serie A stars Nils Liedholm, Kurt Hamrin and Lennart Skoglund to play. They helped propel Sweden all the way to the final in Stockholm.

Harald Nielsen was Denmark's star man and the tournament's top scorer in another silver-medal performance at the 1960 Olympic Games in Rome; his performances in front of the Italian crowds secured him a professional contract with Bologna. He stayed for six seasons, twice winning the Capocannoniere for most league goals in Serie A, and was then transferred to Inter Milan for a world-record fee of £300,000. Nielsen repeatedly voiced his frustrations at his suspension but he would never leave the professional shores of Italy, the irony being that his international career effectively ended when he was spotted at the Rome Olympics aged just eighteen.

Denmark reached the semi-finals of the fledgling European Nations Cup in Spain in 1964, but this ostensibly impressive achievement was almost meaningless. The unseeded knockout format put them on very clear water; they avoided the Who's Who of European football and were drawn against the Who? instead. They started by dispatching Malta 9-2 over two legs that, as they were separated by six months, might have caused players on both sides to forget that the tie was essentially over when Denmark initially won 6-1 in Copenhagen. In the last sixteen of qualifying they made light work of Albania, who had only advanced to that stage after Greece refused to play them (the two countries had been at war with each other) and forfeited the match. In the decisive quarter-final against Luxembourg, Denmark were deadlocked at 5-5 after two legs, and in the play-off in Amsterdam eight days later a single strike by Ole Madsen secured a place in the final tournament in the summer of 1964.

The European Nations Cup was still trying to find its place at this point, with many of the major football nations of the Continent still wondering how seriously to take it – West Germany had not even bothered to enter for this edition or the previous one. Spain had withdrawn from the inaugural tournament four years earlier in an ideological huff at the prospect of playing the Soviet Union, who went on to win the tournament. Four years later, the Soviets would be Denmark's semi-final opponents in the Camp Nou, Barcelona. Denmark were swept aside 3-0 and stayed in the same stadium – virtually empty this time – to play the third-place play-off four days later. Although they managed to take the talented Hungarians to extra-time, Denmark lost 3-1. Spain went on to win the title against the Soviet Union (glory outweighing ideology in this instance for General Franco).

Fourth place looks great in the record books but it can't be ignored that, given the format, Denmark's run was laced with the same fortune that occasionally befalls a lower league team in the FA Cup, beating their lessers and equals before they are comfortably dispatched by their superiors. The tournament was at least a success for Madsen, who was the top scorer in the whole competition. After a career spent exclusively in Denmark's lower leagues, he signed a professional contract with Sparta Rotterdam in Holland in 1965 – and was immediately suspended from playing for the national team.

The competition wouldn't have the chance to open up like that again for Denmark as what would become the European Championship quickly switched to the qualifying groups format used in the World Cup. To say that the Danes struggled with this system would be something of an understatement – their maiden attempt to advance from a qualifying group, for the World Cup in Sweden in 1958, ended with them languishing at the bottom of the group, a languish they would come to speak fluently for the decades that followed. In their first nine qualifying groups throughout the fifties, sixties and seventies, they were anchored to the bottom of the group seven times, and in the other two they managed to narrowly edge ahead of the Republic of Ireland and Cyprus.

If amateurism was holding back Denmark they were equally hamstrung by the method with which their players were selected. *Udtagelseskomiteen* (UK) were a panel of representatives from the amateur clubs who selected the team and each had a vote on who would play. The manager sometimes had the luxury of his vote counting extra but he was still at the mercy of the UK, who could change any of his players if they were all in agreement and favoured someone else. Selection meetings were an inevitable series of compromises, traded favours and selections blocked on the grounds of petty club rivalry. A camel is a horse designed by committee, and the UK were helping to keep Danish football in the desert.

Eventually the DBU became tired of losing. They finally relented in 1971 when professionals were allowed back for a tough European championship qualifier away to Portugal. It initially seemed that old amateur habits might be hard to shake. One of the players brought along two right boots for the trip and had to borrow a left one from one of the substitutes, who was forced to sit on the bench wearing his trainers. During the pre-match tactics meeting, one player asked Denmark's coach, the Austrian Rudi Strittich, who exactly Eusebio was. This was perhaps the most startling lack of awareness of one of the greats of the game since an unnamed England player dismissed Ferenç Puskas as a 'little fat chap' in the Wembley tunnel in 1953, shortly before heading on to the pitch to watch said little fat chap orchestrate the legendary 6-3 scudding of his team. The beatings went on for Denmark as they lost 5-0 to the Portuguese.

By 1976 the mantle had passed from Strittich to mutton-chopped idealist Kurt 'Nikkelaj' Nielsen, a former Danish international whose own international career was curtailed in its infancy upon signature of a professional contract with Marseilles. An overweight, avuncular figure popular with both the press and the players, he was employed on a part-time basis for a mere 60,000 kroner (around £6,000) a year. According to the book *Landsholdet*, by Steen Ankerdal, Nielsen didn't even have a home telephone; he could only be contacted by ringing his former club B1901, where his wife would answer on his behalf.

If Nielsen took the job for the glamour, he was badly advised. When he went to Düsseldorf to check on one of his players he told officials at the stadium he was the manager of Denmark. Nielsen expected to be treated like an international dignitary; instead, he was pointed in the direction of the ticket booth. It was possible, though, that he might have been taken more seriously had his chest hair not been poking through the zipper of his tracksuit top. Although the Germans did not take Danish football seriously, Nielsen certainly had lofty ambitions. 'If Denmark can't become world champions with me as manager,' he said, 'we never bloody will be.'

During his three-year reign he oversaw a worldly set of players. Denmark were an international team in more than one sense; his players were scattered across the Continent, getting a head start on globalisation at a time when the vast majority of other nations sourced their players from within. This brought its own set of problems, and the logistics of trying to get the full complement of players in one room together were such that Nielsen complained he had to change his squad as often as he changed his shirt. There was little he could do – players did not have release clauses in their contracts and were scared of offending their employers. The club versus country debate was a divisive issue in Denmark ahead of anywhere else.

The players were super-talented labour and they were going for nothing. DBU rules meant the clubs in Denmark couldn't demand a transfer fee for any of their players, so if any professional club from abroad could agree terms with the player he could leave – a free-market economy with the emphasis on free. In the winter of 1975 two spindly teenage midfielders left the tiny Danish side

Fremad Amager and signed professional contracts with continental behemoths Ajax Amsterdam. Frank Arnesen and Søren Lerby forced their way into the first team shortly after and the ascent continued, with both making their international debuts under Nielsen in the 1977–8 season.

Arnesen and Lerby initially met in opposition when they were told to mark each other at a youth tournament in Vejle. They were close friends, who struck up a bond immediately, but markedly different players. Arnesen was a bewitching dribbler of the highest imagination, proof that there were many ways to skin a full-back. Lerby's trademark was his lung-bursting shuttle runs between the penalty areas, and he was developing into a frightening force of nature in the middle of the park. The two blossomed in Holland. Danish players were a natural fit for the Dutch league, both in their style of play and culturally, given the ease with which the language could be picked up.

Neighbouring Belgium became another haven for the Danish players. Benny Nielsen, an established international, played at Cercles Brugge and RWD Molenbeek through most of the seventies and at both clubs recommended the services of a young midfielder called Morten Olsen. Although he played anywhere and everywhere while in Belgium, Olsen became a linchpin of the Danish midfield throughout the seventies and one of the senior and more serious professionals in the squad. This was slightly at odds with his boyhood idolisation of the wayward geniuses Garrincha and George Best. In light relief to Olsen's hardened professionalism was the charismatic, eccentric goalkeeper Birger Jensen, who played in goal for almost his whole career for Club Brugge, including their defeats in the 1976 Uefa Cup final and the 1978 European Cup final.

At Lokeren there settled – eventually – a precocious and wild young striking talent in Preben Elkjær. He scored with a scissor-kick on his international debut in 1977, and two years later he

11

scored a hat-trick of such intoxicating brilliance against Northern Ireland that their manager, Danny Blanchflower, was moved to call him 'one of the most outstanding talents I have ever seen'. Elkjær arrived in Belgium after a tempestuous year with Cologne in West Germany. His coach, Hennes Weisweiler, had despaired of his zest for after-hours entertainment; Elkjær could not adapt to the German culture of discipline. The mix did not work.

The Bundesliga might have been unsuitable for Elkjær but it housed the two most established talents in Kurt Nielsen's squad. Werder Bremen's Per Røntved was captain of both club and country and under Nielsen became the most capped Danish player. Perhaps his only superior in the position of libero was Franz Beckenbauer, who defined the position, and Røntved was widely believed to be the first choice to replace Beckenbauer should he ever leave Bayern Munich. At Bremen the phrase Verkauf Røntved (Sell Røntved) was popularised as the shorthand solution for their lack of riches compared to their rivals. His personal wealth after signing for Bremen increased beyond his wildest dreams, and he used this to buy a Volvo P1800ES, the same car that he had seen in an episode of *The Saint*.

Among Danish fans and peers he was respected to the point of awe. On one ferry from Denmark to Germany an up-and-coming defender in the 2. Bundesliga called Søren Busk excitedly pointed out Røntved to his underwhelmed wife. Røntved could thwack the ball with such ferocity that in the later years of his career in America he was sounded out as a potential kicker for the Dallas Cowboys. As impressive as Røntved's CV was, however, the biggest star of Danish football was a diminutive forward earning his crust with Borussia Mönchengladbach.

Allan Simonsen arrived in the Bundesliga in 1972 after alerting the German nation to his ability with his performances for Denmark in the Munich Olympics, scoring twice in a famous 3-2 victory over Brazil. Simonsen, a nimble, impish attacker with two right feet, spearheaded Mönchengladbach through the most successful period in their history. They won the Uefa Cup twice (he scored in both finals) and from 1975 to 1977 won three league titles in a row. Although they lost the 1977 European Cup final (in which he scored again) Simonsen had done enough to be awarded the Ballon d'Or as the best player in Europe that year. He is still the only Danish player to win the award. Barcelona had seen enough and signed Simonsen in the summer of 1979. He would go on to score for them when they won the 1982 European Cup Winners' Cup; with that competition now defunct, Simonsen is the only player ever to score in all three different European club finals.

From the outside it seemed an absurd dichotomy that Denmark could have such a burgeoning pool of talent yet deliver international results that, in terms of seeding groups, kept them swirling around in the bowl of chaff occupied in the modern age by the likes of San Marino and the Faroe Islands. Nielsen's first task with Denmark was to reach the 1978 World Cup and he started well with a thumping pair of wins, 5-1 and 5-0. Unfortunately, that only took care of Cyprus, and Denmark were soundly beaten home and away by Poland and Portugal. The clash with the latter in Lisbon descended into comic-book violence, culminating with Røntved chinning a Portuguese player who tried to throttle him. Denmark again missed out on qualifying by a good distance.

A European Championship qualifier with England in 1978, which their coach Don Howe called one of the greatest internationals he'd ever seen, was typical of what was going wrong. Nielsen fielded a side that, on paper, could get a result against any team in the world, particularly in Copenhagen. Eight of the starting XI played with professional clubs in the top divisions in Belgium, Germany and Holland. The crowd were incredible – 'There's a real feeling of patriotism in the night air', the BBC's Barry Davies commented at the time – and Nielsen's team, running with the mood, attacked brilliantly.

They also defended horrendously, conceding four entirely avoidable goals, even if one was ultimately punched in by Bob Latchford. In return, Simonsen scored a penalty that was supplemented by two brilliant strikes from Arnesen and Røntved, but Denmark were never ahead in the game and lost 4-3. In the English press the overriding feeling was that the mighty inventors of the game had played Russian roulette against a bunch of chancers. 'High-wire football – without the safety net,' said the Daily Express. Careless, but nothing more.

Denmark had opened the campaign with a 3-3 draw in Copenhagen against the Republic of Ireland, but, after running the group favourites England so close, they took only one point from their next three qualifying matches. They drew at home to Bulgaria and then suffered on the road, as ever, with defeats to both Northern Ireland and the Republic of Ireland. By the time they hammered the former 4-0 in the summer of 1979 – thanks to Elkjær's hat-trick – they had scored thirteen goals in six matches, many of them spectacular, yet they shipped the same number. More pertinently, they only had four points and would eventually finish bottom of the group again. They clearly had capable players, as they proved when giving England's defence a chasing, so what was going wrong? Perhaps the Danes were the ones being careless.

In an era when tactics and subtle nuances were becoming increasingly important in winning football matches, Nielsen applied his unique brand of lateral thinking to coaching. When quizzed before one match about tactical innovations, he replied simply: 'No, tactically it's still about scoring goals.' Ahead of a match against Iceland the entire training revolved around a warm-up, a short game of eight-on-eight and then some long-range shooting practice while Nielsen sat and watched from a chair on the edge of the penalty area. When Denmark played Italy, Nielsen simply told his players to 'go out there and beat those spaghettis'.

He did at least delegate some of the research on his opponents, once dispatching his assistant Kaj Johansen to Belfast to take notes on the Northern Ireland team. When Johansen returned with four detailed sides of A4, Nielsen walked into the tactical meeting with the players and advised them to play as they always did. These meetings could often take on the tone of a Ray Cooney farce – ahead of one game with Sweden, Nielsen for once comprehensively covered the line-up and tactics before opening up the floor to questions. The players were keen to know why they were only starting with ten players and why the captain, Henning Munk Jensen, wasn't in the team.

If it was enough to drive a man to drink then Nielsen was already in a taxi to the bar. 'He was one who thought you could win a game by having fun the entire time,' recalls the Danish sports journalist Frits Ahlstrøm. In the summer of 1978 Kurt Nielsen called in a small group of players – including Lerby, Røntved and Arnesen – for special training at his old club, Skovshoved. The weather was fine, Nielsen was in a jocular mood and the mildly bemused players went out on to the field and kicked the ball around together in their unique little session while Nielsen headed indoors. Pretty soon he was beckoning them over to reveal the special element of this training.

'We were somewhat surprised when we got to the terrace of the clubhouse,' said Frank Arnesen in the book *Det Bedste De Gav Os*. 'Kurt had gathered a few friends and the table was set with luxurious *smørrebrød* [open-faced sandwiches], beer and schnapps. It looked pretty nice even though Lerby and I, who were used to the disciplined work in Ajax, didn't understand much of it all. But we drank the beers and the schnapps and had a nice day.'

Nielsen was happy to indulge the players, who weren't exactly shy in taking advantage of his leniency. After home internationals the players put the brief into debrief, eschewing any forensic post-match analysis in favour of marching straight to Tordenskjold, a nightclub in Copenhagen that became a bigger fixture for the returning Danish players than the match itself. International games were a stepping stone on the way to the post-match excess. 'Deep down we loved the third half,' remembers Røntved. 'And what was the third half? Well, that meant fun with the boys.' The players christened Tordenskjold 'the Clubhouse'.

Like all good party animals they also took their hedonism abroad, and after a hiding in a World Cup qualifier by Poland in Katowice in 1977 it was Nielsen who led the charge. 'We got plugged 4-1,' remembers the centre-forward Jan Sørensen. 'We should've been cooped up in the hotel for about five hours being told how bad we were but Kurt decided to take us straight to a bloody nightclub for a good time. I look back on those days with a smile on my face. Sometimes it was so ridiculous it was funny.'

Across the Continent, Denmark's players were making their mark in the professional game with the biggest clubs, yet when the time came to return to Denmark or meet up with their colleagues somewhere in Europe they handed in their professionalism at passport control. For the Italians and the Germans an international match was business; for the Danish players it was a beano. They were an international team in name and a pub team in nature, steeped in a quagmire of amateurism in both approach and structure.

It was a delicious irony that booze money should be required to sort the whole thing out, though in this case it started with spirits before moving on to beer. In the summer of 1977, tired of the DBU's dithering, Harald Nielsen and a twenty-six-year-old, upwardly mobile and ambitious entrepreneur called Helge Sander announced plans to set up a professional league in Denmark. There would be a new union, the DPF, and the clubs would receive 20 per cent of any transfer fees. At a press conference announcing this in Copenhagen was a representative from Jägermeister who pledged 250,000 kroner to the cause.

Nielsen and Sander's plan prompted the DBU and specifically Carlsberg into action. In return for their proposed sponsorship deal with the DBU – two million kroner per year for four years, starting in 1978 – the brewery had certain demands. Firstly, the game in Denmark had to allow professional players; they had fought the tide for too long. Although this meant a semi-professional status at best for most clubs the players could at least now be paid, and this nipped in the bud the ambitious and potentially Fifa-provoking plans of the DPF. Prize money would be given to the top teams and the teams that scored the most goals, and it also meant that Danish clubs could now make at least some money through selling their players rather than just waving them off from the door. It was a red-letter day for Danish football, and the root-and-branch reforms didn't end with the league.

'We have asked the DBU to tell us what it costs to get a national team which is among the sixteen best in the world,' said a Carlsberg director when the deal went through. In those days the World Cup was a sixteen-team event, so the inference was clear – every World Cup to date had taken place without Denmark being involved, and the multi-million-kroner investment was to grease the wheels and get Denmark to the next one in Spain. That, however, meant certain professional standards being set, and that meant wholesale change.

With the European Championship out of reach and his contract up in the summer of 1979, the DBU decided to part ways with Kurt Nielsen. The Carlsberg money meant they could now afford a full-time professional coach. The break-up wasn't acrimonious. For his final game in charge against the USSR in June, Nielsen was presented with a bouquet of flowers in the centre circle as a thank you for all his work. He received a standing ovation at the national stadium while the band played 'For he's a jolly good fellow'. They lost the game 2-1 but the match was played in the convivial spirit that defined Nielsen's reign – he even, after a seven-year hiatus, gave a farewell cap to forward and father of two Finn Laudrup.

It would be harsh to remember Nielsen as a failure; he was simply a product of his environment. He was also the man who discovered Morten Olsen and earned the nickname 'the Fisherman' for his ability to dredge up talented young players. He might have failed with his mission to get Denmark to a major tournament but his softly-softly approach had created a great camaraderie among the players. Retaining that while instilling the Carlsberg-demanded professionalism to propel Denmark to España 82 was the onerous task for the new man. He had already been appointed by the DBU and was looking down at Nielsen's final game from the stands of the national stadium. A century on from the introduction of football to Denmark, it was time for something completely different.

Chapter 3

Alemano Bruto

'Have you ever heard the word zombie?' Sepp Piontek asks the question before spiralling into a tale about dead animals, gun-wielding chefs and suspended animation. He is sitting in a roadside hotel near his home in Blommenslyst, Denmark, more than thirty years after and what seems like many civilisations away from where he endured the most unlikely trials and tribulations of a football manager. To understand how Denmark transformed their fortunes on the football pitch, it is necessary to understand what shaped their manager: the war child from Germany who became a revered defensive rock in the Bundesliga and ended up learning from the George A. Romero book of football management in Haiti.

Josef Emanuel Hubertus Piontek, the man responsible for Denmark's halcyon days, was born in the city of Denmark's biggest ever defeat. In May 1937, at the Hermann Göring stadium in Breslau, a German side built around the players who had finished third in the previous World Cup walloped Denmark 8-0. The scoreline flattered the Danes; their best player was the goalkeeper Svend Jensen. When Piontek was born on 5 March 1940 war had diluted the German team, known as the Breslau Elf thanks to their win against the Danes. The Anschluss not only meant the annexation of Austria into the Third Reich, but Austrian players also had to be enrolled in manager Sepp Herberger's squad. What might have made sense as an act of political goodwill proved calamitous for the national team. At the 1938 World Cup in France Germany were knocked out by Switzerland in the first round.

War also left an indelible mark on the young Piontek when Breslau became one of the battlegrounds in the final stand against Soviet forces. His father had been sacked from the postal service because he refused to join the Nazi party and was instead dispatched to the front line in Stalingrad to build barrages. Piontek and his mother were also forced to flee Breslau towards the end of the war when they moved in with his aunt. His mother pulled a handcart with their possessions as they walked past burnt-out houses on their way out of Breslau, but at times the whole situation felt 'like a game' to Piontek. He found model trains and cars left behind by others who had fled; toys he would never have dreamt of playing with. He became friends with a Russian boy who would throw hand grenades into the water and order the German women to cook the dead fish.

When the five-year-old Piontek and his mother returned to Breslau in 1945, they were reunited with his father. Piontek still recalls their first conversation:

Do you remember who I am?

Yes, you are my father.

Polish forces took control of the city (today known as Wrocław), and while many Germans were exiled to Siberia and Kazakhstan, Piontek's family found refuge in Ostfriesland, near the Dutch border. They stayed at a bombed-out castle where Piontek and the other children would search the area for empty ammunition cartridges and eggs to sell.

That kind of entrepreneurship became second nature to Piontek. In an interview in 2005 with the Danish newspaper *Jyllands-Posten*, Piontek told how, as a 10-year-old, he spent his earnings from picking peas on a kilo of bananas and ate the whole lot. It was the first time he had tasted bananas, this exotic fruit he had only read about during the war.

Piontek couldn't stomach another banana for the next twenty years.

Piontek's father was offered a job with the postal service after the war. The family moved into a small house in the town of Leer, where Piontek started playing for local club Germania in 1949. The manager had cast the stocky and staunch Piontek as a striker. It was only when he moved to Werder Bremen in 1960 that the twenty-year-old Piontek was reschooled as a defender. He had been enrolled at an engineering college in Bremen where he passed the entry exam. It was his father's great ambition that Piontek get a degree, but an offer of a professional contract at Werder forced Piontek to choose. Football first, studying later. Football would never let go of him.

He has no illusions about his strengths when reflecting on his playing career. 'I was not technically very good,' he says. 'I was physically very strong, in good condition and I was not afraid of anything.' He made the most of his attributes as part of Werder's *Beton-Abwehr* – concrete defence – where he got a reputation as a no-nonsense enforcer. He knew how to rattle the head as well as the shin pads of an opponent. A brief glance at his perma-frown and squinting eyes put most strikers off a dogfight. One of his first encounters with the Danish language came in a game against Borussia Mönchengladbach. Piontek was due to mark the Danish winger Ulrik le Fevre so he asked his team-mate John Danielsen to teach him a few choice words before the game. 'Le Fevre was playing left-wing and I was right-back,' says Piontek. 'So I told him in Danish when we were standing next to each other: "Hello, Ulrik, I've heard you want to see the hospital in Bremen?" He didn't go in for a tackle, he didn't try to dribble. We are used to this in Germany, it's psychological warfare. Some react.' Two decades later, when Piontek played in an indoor football tournament, a trainee reporter from *Tipsbladet* apparently went flying after a Piontek tackle which indicated time had done nothing to blunt his intensity on the pitch.

Piontek repaid Werder's faith by never leaving the club as a player, tallying up 203 Bundesliga games in a twelve-year career that brought a championship in 1965. When he was called up by West Germany his reputation preceded him. In his first game, against Italy in Hamburg, Ezio Pascutti from Bologna received half an hour of special attention from Piontek before telling his manager: 'I don't want to play against that guy any more.'

Piontek was included in the preliminary squad of twenty-five players for the 1966 World Cup in England. As part of an arduous schedule, Germany travelled to Rio de Janeiro in the summer of 1965, where 140,000 spectators turned out at the Maracanã to see two of the top seeds for the tournament in England. Piontek was handed a prestigious but thankless task. 'I had to deal with Pelé. Nobody could stop him without fouls.' Piontek gave away a penalty for a foul on Pelé, and the press paid particular notice to his uncompromising defending. They called him Alemano Bruto: the brutal German. Piontek's face lights up as he repeats the nickname, and he breaks into a hearty laugh. 'That's not bad, eh?'

Piontek's selection was a significant vote of confidence amid the intense competition for places. He was up against a host of outstanding German defenders, which included Karl-Heinz Schnellinger – the 'Volkswagen' – and Piontek's Werder team-mate Horst-Dieter Höttges. Some of the German players used the media to highlight their commitment and how much they had been grafting in training. Piontek preferred to do his persuading on the pitch. He had already packed his clothes for the journey to London when the German manager, Helmut Schön, cut him at the last hurdle. He never played for Germany again. 'I was so angry that I said goodbye to the national team and took my wife to Sweden and the Italian Riviera.'

When a knee injury ended his playing career in the early seventies, Piontek took over as manager at Werder. At the age of thirty-one, he was the youngest coach in the Bundesliga. He spent the weekdays in Cologne studying for his coaching licence before returning to prepare the team at the weekend. He had been thrown into it, but Piontek had a way of keeping afloat in the deep end, even when that meant picking and choosing between players who had been team-mates for a decade. 'Things like that aren't easy because many were friends,' says Piontek. 'You have to accept that kind of thing or you choose not to do what you do.'

Piontek inadvertently used his time in the Bundesliga to prepare for future employment by drafting in players from Denmark, where the amateur spirit of the international side belied an increasingly talented pool of players. No one was more crucial than Per Røntved, who had moved to Werder after the 1972 Olympics. He had a determination and willpower that rivalled his manager's. The younger players at Werder were stunned when Røntved answered back to his manager. During a training camp, Røntved didn't have anybody to room with so Piontek partnered him with Höttges, whose uncompromising style had earned him the nickname *Eisenfuss* (iron foot). Røntved clearly remembers what Piontek told him: 'Now you can see what it's like sharing a room with an international footballer.' That remark made Røntved more determined than ever to show just how well Danes could play football.

During their training camps Piontek would come around to the players' rooms before they went to bed. Røntved remembers how Piontek would move back towards the window where he ran his hand behind the curtain to check whether any of the players had hidden more than the one König's Pilsner they had been allowed with their dinner. It was only when Piontek was further down the hallway that the players dug out their secret beer stash from the toilet cistern.

Røntved says each of the players was given a short pep talk on the eve of a game. 'He told us to be firing on all cylinders,' says Røntved. He flexes his right arm, holds it close to his chest and makes a quick nudge with the elbow. 'Sepp was that kind of type.'

Røntved makes another elbow nudge. 'He really was a German. He would go forward with his life on the line.'

Werder had finished tenth the season before Piontek took over. They would not improve on that during his four-year reign and were sucked into a relegation battle in 1975, when they survived by one point. Piontek moved to Fortuna Düsseldorf the following season, and told the fans the team were good enough to win the Bundesliga. The early signs were promising. After a 5-2 win over Rot-Weiss Essen in their second game Fortuna were top of the table. Then followed a slump and they finished twelfth. Piontek left before the end of the season. Not even the most vivid imagination would have dreamt up the adventure he was about to embark on.

The German FA had received overtures from the Haitian leader Jean-Claude 'Baby Doc' Duvalier, who wanted a coach from the home of the world champions. The young dictator had taken the reins from his father, Papa Doc, a man responsible for the death of tens of thousands of his compatriots. Haiti had reached the 1974 World Cup, partly because of a group of talented players, partly because Papa Doc had invested money in the team in the sixties – but also because the qualification tournament for the Concacaf federation was held in Haiti, where Baby Doc could wield his power. Haiti stunned Italy by taking the lead in their World Cup opener – the first goal Dino Zoff had conceded in 1,143 minutes, still an international record – but eventually lost the game 3-1. They were then trounced by Poland and Argentina by an aggregate score of 11-1.

Baby Doc had inherited his father's predilection for violence, corruption, voodoo … and football. When Baby Doc came looking for a new manager, Piontek fitted the brief; he was German and spoke French. Haiti caved in to Piontek's financial demands and he went to Hamburg to sign the contract. Then things took a strange turn. When Piontek arrived in Miami to meet the Haitian delegation for the first time, a Yugoslavian man introduced himself as the national manager of Haiti. This contradicted all reassurances Piontek had been given by Baby Doc's negotiators. 'What happened?' Piontek asked his employers. 'You told me you have no coach, but you have a coach with three years more on his contract?' In Port au Prince, Piontek was told to relax, enjoy some time off and watch the league games at the national stadium. After a week he began to wonder where this was all going. Suddenly, the Yugoslavian manager lost his voice. He was told to go to Miami for surgery, but when the visa application fell through he was sent home to Belgrade.

Piontek met the other manager five years later when he went to watch a friendly in Yugoslavia, where the home team were playing Denmark in the qualifiers for the 1982 World Cup. The football association of Yugoslavia had sent a car to pick up Piontek and when the door opened out stepped the man from Haiti. Piontek asked him why he had never come back. 'He told me he went back to Yugoslavia to have a throat operation. He got his voice back and wanted to come back to Haiti but he got no visa – so long!'

Piontek had to pay regular visits to Baby Doc to fill him in on the team tactics and the form of the players. While they talked football, Piontek's wages were being printed elsewhere in the palace and arrived in his hands still wet off the press. Piontek had been forced to adapt to life during the war and coped with the pressure of managing in the Bundesliga in his early thirties, but nothing had prepared him for a culture in which he had to discard his guiding principle. He had to put his rulebook of German discipline in storage. Before the games, the Haitian players would lock themselves in hotel rooms to perform voodoo rituals and drink rum. When Piontek told the team chef that the cooking wasn't up to scratch, the chef pulled out a shotgun.

The chef's death threat wasn't the most bizarre thing Piontek encountered in Haiti. He also saw the practice of spiking drinks with a small amount of poison to induce a state of death-like suspended animation. After being buried alive, victims would be woken up, and the cataclysmic effect of physical and toxicological trauma would recast them as zombies. Piontek couldn't believe what was going on and went to the German embassy to find out whether this ritual could be possible. 'Yes', he was told. 'This happens here.'

Haiti eventually lost to Mexico in the decisive Concacaf qualifier. Piontek had done his best to set up the team for the game, but the players had their own unique spin on preparations by staging an all-night ceremony with a voodoo priest. If Piontek hadn't fulfilled Baby Doc's brief he had at least learned an invaluable lesson that would stand him in good stead the next time he was saddled with a group of international players for whom spirits were an integral part of international gatherings. 'If you have to work there and survive you have to change your mind,' he says about his time in Haiti. 'You cannot try with discipline like in Germany.'

Hamburg's St Pauli district is richer on hedonism than discipline. Yet the prospect of managing the local club must have been akin to taking over a private school netball team after dealing with armed chefs and voodoo people. St Pauli had been relegated to the 2. Bundesliga when Piontek joined in 1978, but his tenure was short-lived. The DBU started to put out feelers for the national manager's job before Kurt Nielsen's contract was up in the summer of 1979. The Danes had taken a leaf out of Baby Doc's scouting book by looking to Germany for their next manager. Even if Denmark were blessed with their most gifted generation of footballers, they needed an outsider to instil the ambition and discipline that could change their fortunes.

Røntved visited Piontek after he returned from Haiti and immediately spotted a difference. 'He could crack jokes and smile,' says Røntved. 'I thought: "It's another Sepp we have here now. All of a sudden he is funny. He couldn't do that in Bremen."' The general secretary of the DBU asked Røntved for his opinion on their list of candidates. 'I said if I have to recommend a manager for the Danish national team I can only, given what I know, recommend Sepp Piontek.'

At the newspaper *Politiken*'s sports desk in Copenhagen, the reporter Frits Ahlstrøm was keen to break the news of the next Denmark manager. 'It became a kind of a puzzle,' Ahlstrøm says. The DBU had initially been in talks with Udo Lattek at Borussia Mönchengladbach, but he wasn't prepared to give up on his family life in Germany. Among the other prospects were Eckhard Krautzen, a relatively unknown German who had been manager of Canada, and Tord Grip, who would go on to serve alongside Sven-Göran Eriksson as England assistant coach. Ahlstrøm had already been given some clues by the DBU – the new manager spoke German and French, was a former international and had worked in another country. Ahlstrøm added the pieces to what he knew from following the Bundesliga, and when he was '99.9 per cent sure', *Politiken* splashed with the news of Piontek's appointment. When the papers hit the press at midnight, the national news agency called the head of the DBU to verify the story. 'If it's Frits, it must be correct,' the DBU replied.

One of the clues Ahlstrøm had been given was that the new manager knew about the mentality of the Danish players. Piontek says today that he knew a lot about the Danish players but little about the Danish mentality. 'I had worked with Danish players in Germany, and we also had to deal with Allan Simonsen, Ulrik le Fevre and Henning Jensen playing at a big club like Mönchengladbach, so why not?' He had the chance to see Denmark play in Copenhagen before he started his new job. He didn't even have to wait for kick-off before realising the size of the challenge he faced. 'Instead of warming up the players were talking to their families. They had brought some liquorice and cheese from Denmark that the players could take back to Europe. That was their preparation for the game! This all had to change.'

Chapter 4

Concrete illness

When a new manager is appointed the focus is usually on his name, not his nationality. That was not the case when Sepp Piontek became Denmark manager. 'Oh no, a German!' was Preben Elkjær's reaction. He was far from alone in his scepticism. In the late 1970s, a Venn diagram with Germany to the left and Denmark to the right would not have had much common ground in the middle. Piontek's nature clashed so intrinsically with the Danish mentality that his eleven-year reign was a balancing act between German yin and Danish yang. It was particularly acute in the early years when results were poor and he struggled to impose the discipline that was second nature to him. 'He was a German, and you know Danes,' says the defender Ivan Nielsen. 'It was a little bit difficult in the beginning.'

The players have different ways of demonstrating Piontek's approach in those early years, whether it's Per Røntved's nudge of the elbow or Michael Laudrup moving his hand up and down in a chopping motion to show Piontek's obstinate nature. The first step towards common ground came with Piontek learning Danish. He had only four hours of lessons and learned the language within two months. Or at least a form of it; his accent was often described as 'circus Danish'.

That circus Danish caused the players much mirth – particularly when, at one of the first meetings, he laid out his mantra: 'motivation, ambition and concentration'. The players found it hilarious, repeating Piontek's words in a hammy accent as pupils might the catchphrase of an eccentric teacher. It took a while but Piontek eventually demonstrated a level of empathy and flexibility that allowed him to get the best out of his team. Never mind losing the dressing room; he would not have found it in the first place had he not been so adaptable. His book of discipline came out of storage when he came to Denmark, but after Haiti it had a few new pages.

'He discovered that being a German in the strictest sense would never work in Denmark,' says the TV commentator Svend Gehrs. Yet part of Piontek had to remain German. He had been given the job precisely because he was German – because he was professional and would improve results. The UK selection committee was disbanded at the end of 1979, with total responsibility given to Piontek, frequently described in the press as the 'dictator' of the national team.

'Never before in the history of the Danish football union has a single man had such a large responsibility for the national team and its results as Piontek has,' said a profile in the newspaper *Aktuelt*. 'The West German – who is big as a Nordic giant, has fists like Thor's hammer and thighs like the mooring bollards that hold Fregatten Jylland to quay in Ebeltoft harbour – is 40 years old.'

Danish football was nearly a century old when it finally embraced professionalism. Carlsberg's money meant that expectations grew almost exponentially, but at first Piontek had to guide the side through thin and thinner. They rounded off an already failed attempt to qualify for Euro 80 that had begun under Kurt Nielsen before starting the qualifying campaign for the 1982 World Cup dismally. Denmark lost their first five competitive games under Piontek, and only an impressive 3-1 win away to Spain in a friendly in Cadiz hinted at a brighter future.

At first Piontek struggled to comprehend how his players were able to treat Kipling's imposters, triumph and disaster, the same.

'That was a sign that he didn't understand the Danish mentality,' says the midfielder Jens Jørn Bertelsen. 'That after a game where we had played *ad helvede til* [like shit] and hadn't achieved a very good result, we could still joke and have fun in the dressing room.' At that stage a highly talented team saw international football as little more than a jolly. 'It was a holiday,' says Nielsen. 'You come home and you have a lot of fun, but you have to play a game before you go out.'

The number of Danes playing abroad created a logistical nightmare. At first Piontek planned to use mostly home-based players. That idea was shelved as soon as he realised how good those playing overseas were; after a couple of months in the job he said there was 'such good material that Denmark could become one of the major forces in Europe'. Piontek estimated that he travelled around 40,000 miles a year to watch his players. 'It might have been more practical,' he told the magazine *Alt om Sport*, 'if I lived in Luxembourg.' Not everyone was unhappy: his parents got to see more of him because he stayed over at the family home in Leer, on the border of Germany and Holland.

In those days, a manager had scarcely any support staff. Piontek's only assistant was the *holdkaptajn* (team leader) Kaj Johansen, an unpaid assistant who used up his work holidays to travel with the team. 'A good man,' says Piontek, 'who never wanted to be important.' Johansen was the guy behind the guy – and to his right in the dugout, puffing away on his pipe, offering counsel and doing all the grunt work. 'When we have a problem we can just turn around and Kaj will fix it,' said Elkjær. 'We can't cope without him.'

Piontek and Johansen often had to deal with unexpected problems. Ahead of a friendly in Prague in 1984, Laudrup went to the wrong airport in Rome and was delayed, while Søren Lerby got lost driving from Munich to Prague. Sometimes they didn't even have the chance to get lost. In the early days of Piontek's reign clubs had no obligation to release their players for international duty. For their first 1982 World Cup qualifier, away to Yugoslavia, Denmark were without two of their best players: Allan Simonsen and Morten Olsen were not released by Barcelona and Anderlecht. When the players did return their heads were often elsewhere: with their clubs, or in the Clubhouse.

Birger Jensen soon found himself in the doghouse. He was the best goalkeeper in Denmark, and made a series of excellent saves for Club Brugge in their 1978 European Cup final defeat by Liverpool, but he was cut loose by Piontek after a few months. Piontek said it was because Jensen lied about his unavailability for a team-bonding camp. Jan Sørensen, the centre-forward who was Jensen's team-mate with Denmark and Brugge, cites an argument after the victory in Spain. 'Me, Birger and Kristen Nygaard were having some food and a glass of wine at around 11.30 p.m. when Piontek said, "Right that's it, go to bed." None of us had a game at the weekend so we said, "We'll just finish the wine and then we'll go up." We stood up to him and that wasn't a clever thing to do. Birger and Kristen never played again, I got two more games and that was it. It had nothing to do with football, he just couldn't stand the sight of me. Birger was by far the best keeper in Denmark and should have been in the team for another six or seven years.'

Jensen, Sørensen and Nygaard may have been symbolic sacrifices. Either way, the players who survived knew that Piontek had a fierce temper. One day a player was twenty seconds late for training because he was tying his bootlaces. Piontek roasted him for three minutes in front of the rest of the squad.

In Jensen's absence, Denmark never had a long-term goalkeeper under Piontek. The role was shared, for the most part, between Ole Qvist, Ole Kjær, Troels Rasmussen and Lars Høgh.

Unlike almost all the outfield players, none of the goalkeepers went to play abroad, although they all had offers. Qvist loved his job as a traffic policeman – he would usually be back at work the morning after an international – and chose to stay at home in

Denmark while Kjær did not think he was good enough. Rasmussen and Høgh did not move for a variety of reasons, from injury to refusal from their clubs to unlikely twists of fate. Høgh was once told by the Boavista coach that a transfer was imminent, and wished that the team would lose their next match so that they would change their goalkeeper and sign him. They lost the next match – but they changed the coach rather than the goalkeeper. Høgh, whose eight Danish caps were spread over twelve years, stayed at his club Odense. A Danish-record 817 appearances and five Goalkeeper of the Year awards were a decent consolation.

Qvist, twenty-nine, made his debut in Piontek's first game, a 0-0 draw in a friendly in Finland on 29 August 1979. The team comprised only home-based players and the XI bore no resemblance to the great side that would emerge: Finn Trikker, Poul Andersen, Ole Højgaard, Frank Olsen, Poul Erik Østergaard and Klaus Nørregaard all failed to reach ten caps. There were two hints of a bright future, however. Klaus Berggreen, twenty-one, made his debut, while the twenty-seven-year-old Bertelsen won his fifth cap. They would become two of Piontek's most trusted lieutenants, tactically astute midfielders who selflessly carried water so that the likes of Elkjær and Laudrup could walk on it.

Bertelsen played as a holding midfielder, a relatively unusual position in those days, Berggreen as a ceaseless worker who, in the words of Elkjær, ran until the sun went down. He was Denmark's unofficial cross-country champion at the age of fourteen. Berggreen was no headless chicken, however, and benefited from playing in Serie A. 'I was educated in the right country,' he says. 'My biggest asset was that I was tactically very strong. I could see where it was going to be dangerous in two seconds' time so I knew where to run. Sepp knew I was doing the running for two people.' Berggreen often seemed to be in two places at the same time. No wonder the official graphic for the Euro 84 match against France had him both in the starting XI and on the bench.

He was in neither for most of Piontek's early years. Berggreen was criticised in the press by his new manager after choosing a holiday with his fiancée ahead of a training camp. After his debut he played only one game in the next three years, but he eventually became one of Piontek's favourite players. Bertelsen and Berggreen were far more concerned with covering blades of grass than filling column inches. Bertelsen was a players' player in more ways than one. 'The others cried when he was injured,' says Gehrs. 'He was the first to be picked by Sepp every time.'

Bertelsen helped tighten up a defence that had often been porous under Kurt Nielsen. In Piontek's second game, a European Championship qualifier at Wembley, Denmark showed considerable defensive discipline during a 1-0 defeat to England – a contrast to the madcap 4-3 defeat in Copenhagen earlier in the group. Two months later they produced an even more impressive performance against Spain, winning 3-1 thanks to two from Elkjær and a rare goal from Bertelsen, one of only two in his sixty-nine games for Denmark. It was also one of only two defeats that Spain suffered at home in the 1970s; the manner and significance of the victory convinced the Danish public that progress was being made.

Denmark did not play again for six months. After a series of summer friendlies, they lost their first three qualifiers for the 1982 World Cup, culminating in a predictable defeat away to Italy. For a team with so many good players it was an unacceptable level of underachievement. It was too much for Piontek. The jaunty atmosphere on the flight home from Italy – Piontek said he felt like he was in a nightclub – made his mind up. He moved the team out of their luxury hotel and into something a little less palatial.

Idrættens Hus. Even the name sounds cold, bleak and forbidding. It had all the warmth and humanity of a prison. After years staying at the delightful Hotel Marina, with its lovely food and view of the sea, this was a significant culture shock. There were no TVs or phones in the players' rooms, and those coming from abroad had to scrabble about for the right coins to call home. The mattresses were on the gossamer side of thin. So was the players' patience. They hated it.

Piontek theorised that hardship would beget hardness. 'I could see that the last thing was not there,' he says. 'That last: you HAVE to do this, you HAVE to qualify. It was something in the Danish mentality.' The players had taken liberties, so Piontek took their liberty away. 'All of a sudden we had to be punished,' says Busk. 'I remember there weren't TVs in the rooms and when you flushed the toilet it sounded like it sucked all the way from below. "Swhooossh", it said. We had become too spoiled so we ended up in the concrete building, which was fine because we shouldn't think that the trees grow into the sky.'

Nor should they think Piontek was born yesterday. Some of the players asked Allan Simonsen, the team's greatest player and biggest name, to tell Piontek he was sick in the hope it would force a move back to Hotel Marina. 'We said to him, "Allan, you have to go down and tell the coach you are ill",' says Elkjær. '"Maybe then we can move somewhere else." So he invented this very bizarre illness: concrete illness.'

Betonsyge, or concrete illness, is something that traditionally afflicts bridges rather than waspish attackers. Simonsen said he had a constant headache and his sense of smell had gone. An unimpressed Piontek told him to go to the doctor. There was only one way the players could get out of Idrættens Hus. 'It was his way of showing us that you cannot just have fun,' says Berggreen. '"I want to see results – if you want nice hotels, make me results".'

So they made him results. In 1981 Denmark won eight of their nine games. They also won four of their last five World Cup qualifiers, although losing those first three group games had left them with too much to do. They might have qualified but for a 2-1 defeat at home to Yugoslavia, when the winning goal came from a dreadful mistake from Røntved. Denmark left their mark nonetheless; they were the only team to beat the eventual champions Italy in qualification or at the World Cup. Eight of the Italian side beaten in Copenhagen played in the World Cup final a year later, including Dino Zoff, Gaetano Scirea, Claudio Gentile and Marco Tardelli.

Italy were well beaten 3-1 on a foggy Saturday night in Copenhagen, with Denmark giving their defence a rare chasing. The first half was goalless, although Denmark could easily have scored three, most notably when Simonsen's glorious volley was spectacularly saved by Zoff. Eventually the libero Røntved sauntered forward to drill past Zoff from a narrow angle. 'I'm just lucky,' he says, watching it thirty years later. 'Zoff takes a step forward to intercept the pass. What's lucky for me is that I hit it with the outside of the foot so it goes in between the post and his legs. It was a shot.'

Italy's raggedness was reflected two minutes later. A comical flying handball from Antonio Cabrini should have led to a penalty but the referee awarded a free-kick. No matter: Frank Arnesen drove through the wall and into the far corner.

When Francesco Graziani made it 2-1, there were twenty-one minutes remaining. Denmark's subsequent nervousness reflected the subconscious belief that the natural order was about to be reasserted, with Italy likely to equalise and maybe win the game. This was the psychological rubble Piontek had to sift through. 'When you lose, lose, lose all the important games for the last forty years,' says Elkjær, 'it's difficult to believe you actually can beat the great teams of Europe.'

Elkjær was involved in the goal that helped them finally beat one of those great teams. He led a counter-attack with Simonsen in the eighty-seventh minute and, after Elkjær went down in the box, Lars Bastrup rammed home the loose ball before the referee had time to decide whether it was a penalty or not. Bastrup and Simonsen threw their arms around each other before falling over, still clinging to their clumsy embrace.

It's impossible to overstate the significance of the victory. 'That was the start of everything, because then the players realised that all the shit they blamed Piontek for, it worked,' says Gehrs. 'They saw that, somehow, this bloody German might be right!'

Victory was celebrated at Tordenskjold, the Clubhouse, where the only thing that had an ice bath was the champagne. Piontek had, for the first time, imposed a curfew – a generous 2 a.m., with a fine of 200 kroner (around £20) for every five minutes a player was late. At 2 a.m. he sat on the stairs of the team hotel, where they stayed on the evening of the match, with a checklist of those due to return. As Piontek's watch ticked on, so he started ticking.

At 2.07 a.m. a group of players arrived in a series of taxis, blaming their lateness on the drivers. A few were still missing, and as the clock moved towards 3 a.m. and the cartoon clouds gathered above his head, Piontek decided to drive to Tordenskjold.

When he entered the nightclub he stomped towards the dance floor, every step turning a few more heads. He found a group of players, some of whom he had ticked off on his checklist an hour earlier; they had gone straight out of the bedroom window and back into town. One was slumped on a black leather sofa with his arms round two girls. Another, not realising he had been seen, hid in the toilet until Piontek knocked on the door and told him to come out. A third player was in the middle of a slow dance when he felt a tap on the shoulder. As Piontek tells the story, he closes his eyes and makes a dreamy face, lost in lust. 'He had not seen me, but perhaps she knew me or could see there was something wrong. Then he opened his eyes: "Nej nej nej!"'

It became famous in Denmark: the night Piontek literally pulled the players out of Tordenskjold. The identity of the third player is the subject of omerta, even thirty years later. What goes on at home stays at home. Whoever it was, he paid his fine of 2,500 kroner, as did the other players there. Such fines became the norm in the first few years; an anecdote in the book *Landsholdet* suggested that, on one occasion, Elkjær pulled out two 500-kroner bills and paid his upfront because he knew he'd be late.

Piontek created *bødekassen* (the penalty box), in which players' fines were kept. It swelled. The money was put to good use: Piontek bought presents for players on special occasions, such as when they had a baby or reached a landmark of twenty-five or fifty caps. The gifts ranged from the expensive to the absurd. When Elkjær turned twenty-seven in 1984, he received a copy of *Ugens Rapport*, the porn magazine in which he had a column, a packet of cigarettes and a lighter. 'In the beginning we had good gifts, lamps that cost 8,500 kroner,' says Piontek. 'At the end, there was only chocolate.'

The players knew that if they continued to err they would get the Birger Jensen treatment. They soon began to make curfews almost all of the time. A combination of fines, good results and increasing respect for Piontek helped change the culture of the team. 'Trust is okay, but control is better,' laughs Piontek. Better still was a combination of the two. 'He found the right balance between being the hard man and the soft man,' says Berggreen. 'Everything Sepp did was 100 per cent correct – the only thing that wasn't, because he didn't know it yet, was the training at the World Cup. He has a lot of humour. That's why he had success, because we had so much fun. At the same time he taught us to concentrate and to focus.'

Sometimes Piontek was inadvertently funny, usually because of his accent, but even when the players laughed at him they also laughed with him. 'If you had to make a speech to two hundred people he is number one in Denmark for me, because he has so many funny stories,' says Berggreen. Ivan Nielsen calls him 'the funniest guy I know'.

On one occasion, ahead of a game against Romania, Piontek asked for help so that he could show the players a video of the Romanians' free-kicks. Elkjær came to his rescue and sat down. As Piontek started to address the room, everyone burst out laughing; Piontek was about to admonish the team when he turned round to see a porn movie on the screen. 'That was later,' says Elkjær. 'The first couple of years nobody dared to do that! But as we began to win the atmosphere was different. When he noticed that now they are serious, now they want to win, now we have a great team, he could relax more and he showed also his funny side. At the start he wasn't funny. We taught him to be funny!'

Elkjær was the cheekiest character in the team, a softly spoken alpha male with an infectious slow laugh. During his time with Cologne, he was confronted by his manager, Hennes Weisweiler, over a visit to a nightclub. 'I have heard that you were spotted with a bottle of whisky in your hand,' fumed Weisweiler. 'Wrong,' deadpanned Elkjær. 'It was two bottles.'

In the mid-eighties Elkjær was the world's best centre-forward; he finished runner-up in the Ballon d'Or in 1985, third in 1984 and fourth in 1986. He also won the Bronze Ball at the 1986 World Cup. Elkjær was determination personified, and his seemingly endless lung capacity – one Spanish newspaper described him as 'the human locomotive' – is even more amazing given that he was a chain smoker; he would often sit at the back of a bus, having a sneaky cigarette like a school kid. Elkjær and Piontek were an odd couple who squabbled like an old couple. 'In the beginning I had a lot of fights with him,' says Piontek. 'Sometimes I could have killed him.' He was somewhere between problem child and teacher's pet, and as time went on his friendship with Piontek became stronger. Now Piontek is closer to Elkjær than any other player in the team; the two regularly go on holiday together with their wives.

On the field Elkjær nagged away at defenders constantly, inverting the relationship between defender and attacker and never giving opponents a moment's peace. Often he would go on me-against-the-world runs, notably for famous goals against Belgium in 1984 and the USSR a year later. He had his own signature manoeuvres: thrusting out his arm like an American footballer running back to hold defenders off, dainty chipped finishes, and a variation on the Cruyff turn that he learned while watching children playing football on the beach during a holiday in Barbados.

That trick was proof that Elkjær was not just about power. He had wonderful balance that meant he could ride challenges or withstand their impact; he was also a thoroughly decisive finisher, capable of deftness or brutality. Few goalscorers have such an impressive, varied showreel. He was the red-blooded, blue-eyed boy of any team he played for: unfettered and immensely popular with fans because of his talent, attitude, charisma, single-mindedness and confidence. He preferred Coca-Cola to alcohol – 'I wasn't interested in drinking' – and says he has never had a beer. But he was invariably the life and soul of the party.

As a teenager he was wild, rebelling against authority, particularly during a difficult year in Cologne when he encountered a culture of discipline that he could not comprehend. The label of *gadedreng* (street urchin) irked him, although it was hard to resist after certain incidents. He allegedly slapped a ball boy in Cologne, and when he was sent off in a Danish youth cup final for sarcastically applauding the referee he kicked the bumper off a Beetle.

Elkjær changed when he met his future wife Nicole at a nightclub in Lokeren, Belgium. Within a year they were married. Elkjær is a textbook example of why so many football managers implore their players to settle down. Nicole, a Catholic, would light a candle before each of his games. Elkjær kept his cheeky side, and his furious will to win, but after meeting Nicole he saw the world through different eyes. Family was now the most important thing. 'We are building a house for Nicole and the dog,' he said in 1983. 'The new house is going to be really nicely decorated but also costs a fortune. The idea is that there will be a hair salon, bedroom and horse stables in one building. Doesn't that sound lovely?'

Elkjær, sometimes inadvertently, helped Piontek understand the Denmark team. Just as Piontek changed them, so they changed him. He married his second wife, a Dane called Gitte, in 1988; two years earlier he said he had a 'German passport and a Danish heart'. He has now lived in Denmark for almost half his life. 'Sometimes I feel Danish,' he says. 'It's fifty/fifty. Serious problems, I think in German; easy problems, I think in Danish.'

By 1982 he was starting to think increasingly in Danish. The side had missed out on the World Cup – Elkjær, on holiday in Sicily with Nicole, had to rent a television from a local shop so that he could watch the tournament in his hotel – but ended the campaign so strongly that they had little to fear, even when they drew England in the qualifiers for the 1984 European Championship. 'There was a whole new mentality and discipline within the team, without it curbing the joy of playing,' says Bertelsen. After three often trying years, Piontek had a team he recognised.

Chapter 5

De Vlo effect

Denmark's qualifying campaign for the 1984 European Championship kicked off in September 1982 in a group that was far from easy. While Luxembourg didn't present much of a problem the group also contained Greece, who had qualified for the previous European Championship in Italy. Hungary were just back from the World Cup having been knocked out in the first round despite a record 10-1 win over El Salvador. Then there was England, a reawakened international force, with their club sides having won the last six European Cups. Denmark had never beaten them in professional football, and the European Championship only allowed the group winners to advance to the exclusive eight-team tournament in France.

In the build-up to the opening qualifier with England in Copenhagen, one word recurred in the English press to describe the Danish team: mercenaries, a reference to many of the Danish players having the temerity to leave their own shores to earn a living. This missed the point entirely. The Danes were the soldiers who came back home, and what they brought back benefited everybody.

The players were hired to go overseas but, unlike some Englanders on package holidays in mainland Europe at the time, they were learning, and when they had to 'fight' for their country they could apply their knowledge gained overseas to great effect.

Competing in the leagues of Italy, Belgium, Germany and Holland created a melting pot of styles and ideas that would eventually make their brand of football unique. The clearest influence came from around five hundred miles south-west of Copenhagen courtesy of Johan Cruyff and Ajax of Amsterdam.

The impact of Holland's Total Football has been so profound that it still resonates today in the players who graduate from La Masía, the youth academy, to play for Barcelona. The first team to drink in the influence beyond the borders of Holland was Denmark, with four of their players having direct access to the well. After spells in Spain and America, Cruyff returned to Ajax as an adviser in 1980 and eventually laced up his boots again a year later. Once again Cruyff cast his spell on the club and in particular the young recruits Frank Arnesen, Søren Lerby, Jesper Olsen and Jan Mølby.

Cruyff was the ultimate sensei for a young footballer, broadening and blowing their minds in equal measure. Olsen in particular struck up a great understanding with his mentor, cemented in one legendary penalty in 1982 against Helmond Sport. Cruyff rolled the penalty sideways a couple of feet to Olsen, who accelerated into the area as soon as the ball was played. As the goalkeeper came off his line, Olsen passed it back to Cruyff, who struck it into an empty net. The referee knew the rules; so did Cruyff and Olsen, who had used a brilliant ploy to turn a penalty kick into an open goal. It was a rare act of audacity that took a deceptive amount of skill and nerve, as a botched tribute by Thierry Henry and Robert Pires for Arsenal in 2005 would prove. When asked who cooked up the scheme, Olsen just laughs: 'Well, who do you think?'

Olsen blossomed into one of the most gifted players in Europe. In Holland they called him De Vlo – the Flea – though the Fly might have been a better description, such was his innate gift of buzzing around the pitch while skipping over tackles and changing direction with the ball. Another nickname, the Untouchable, characterised his meteoric rise as he won the championship in his first two seasons with Ajax. He wouldn't be Denmark and Holland's best kept secret for long.

A week ahead of the match with England in Copenhagen, Olsen fired a warning shot just over their border against Glasgow Celtic. The throw-in from the left was innocuous enough, straight to the feet of Olsen in the unfamiliar blue away strip of Ajax. In one sweet movement he turned his marker. With a shake of the hips and some delicate touches he beat two more players before placing the ball into the net. It was one of the great European Cup goals of the decade. Later he tortured Celtic again, escaping down the left to set up a goal for Lerby with the help of Cruyff. Many at Celtic Park would have waited all their lives to see Cruyff in the flesh, but they left that night talking about Olsen.

While Olsen's performance captivated Scotland, it seemed to pass almost entirely unnoticed just to the immediate south. The England national team were preparing for the upcoming qualifying match under new manager Bobby Robson. They came back from the World Cup in Spain unbeaten – England were only knocked out in the second group phase – and the new captain Ray Wilkins claimed they could win the 1986 World Cup. The match was also a mere four months on from the conclusion of the Falklands War, and Bobby Robson ramped up the jingoism by saying there was 'no difference in fighting for your country and playing for your country'. The fighting-for-your-country element was taken a bit too literally by some of England's supporters; thirty were jailed ahead of the match for rioting and later deported. Hooliganism was making England fans the pariahs of Europe – the tragic nadir of Heysel was just three years away – and the night before the England–Denmark game they booed the black players in their own under-21 side.

Despite their problems off the pitch, England were supremely confident ahead of this fixture. Sepp Piontek was without Morten Olsen, Allan Simonsen and Arnesen through injury, although

Robson had generated controversy by ending the international career of Kevin Keegan. Even in a post-Keegan world the English media were expecting Hungary to be the main threat in the group. Although a few referenced the 3-1 win over Italy or even the 4-3 in Copenhagen in 1978 as evidence of the Danes' ability, there was barely a mention of their players in the build-up. They were expected to be little more than makeweights. 'The finals in France are nearly two years away,' wrote David Lacey in the *Guardian*. 'Now is the time for a little fun.' They might have identified the Danes as mercenaries but it seems little research had been conducted into their qualities as footballers.

In Copenhagen there was something in the air as the match approached kick-off. The atmosphere was incendiary, and not just because some Danish and English fans had clashed around the town during the day. Wilkins said after the game that he had never played in a more hostile atmosphere, and there was a genuine feeling that this campaign could be different. 'The belief in the team at that stage was really high,' remembers Jesper Olsen. 'We didn't fear England because we were happy that we could handle their style and system.' Piontek handed a debut to the twenty-one-year-old goalkeeper Troels Rasmussen of Aarhus GF. In his first test of the game he did well to save a Trevor Morley shot but the rebound fell straight to Trevor Francis who put England 1-0 up after seven minutes.

What would normally instil a library-like hush on a boisterous home crowd did nothing of the sort. Denmark had been the better team even in those embryonic stages and should have had a penalty almost immediately afterwards when Russell Osman hauled down Preben Elkjær. Even with the hand of fate apparently against them there was a sense that Denmark, on this night, would not be denied. Olsen brought a great save out of Shilton, and twice Elkjær blasted good chances high and wide. With his pace he was pulling the defenders, and particularly Osman, all over the pitch.

There was no let-up in the second half. Denmark put England on the rack and manacled them to it. Early in the half Elkjær hared into the penalty area and was clearly fouled by Kenny Sansom, but the Dutch referee, Charles Corver, waved play on while simultaneously receiving a choice volley of words from Lerby. Corver was having quite the year for missing the glaringly obvious. In his previous international, the World Cup semi-final between West Germany and France, he overlooked Harald Schumacher's flying assault that knocked Patrick Battiston unconscious and took out three of his teeth. In the Copenhagen frenzy a canister of tear gas was thrown on to the pitch. The game was stopped for a few minutes, but the break failed to dull the intensity.

In the fifty-sixth minute the pressure finally told as a frazzled Osman lunged straight through Olsen in the penalty area. Even Corver couldn't miss that one and Hamburg's Allan Hansen placed his spot-kick into the top corner. The game was on now. Olsen soon found Elkjær, who improvised a double-take-inducing piece of skill to create another chance. Elkjær, on the right of the box, let the ball run through his legs and then, in one mesmeric movement, turned 180 degrees and flicked the ball away from Osman with the outside of his left foot to go clear on goal. This reverse Cruyff turn left Osman with twisted blood and those watching with twisted minds. It needed another save from Shilton to prevent one of the goals of the year. Elkjær was torturing Osman, who could scarcely have conceived a more harrowing nightmare had he eaten two kilograms of the most pungent blue cheese before retiring to bed. England were fading badly. Yet when the one-way traffic briefly changed direction, Denmark conceded a needless corner. Francis bundled the ball over the line again to restore England's lead.

So far, so familiar. On this night, though, whatever fate threw at Denmark they were determined to catch it and throw it back.

Lerby had already put in a shift more commonly associated with the pacemaker for a long-distance world-record attempt. In the last minute he pushed his body through another off-the-ball run into the penalty area, pulling back the curtain and leaving the stage free behind him for Olsen.

'It opened up,' Olsen says. 'That was the way I played, very direct.' If it felt simple, it looked sublime. Olsen sashayed into the vacuum created by Lerby, away from Ricky Hill and around Osman before daintily skipping over Terry Butcher's sliding tackle to advance into the penalty area. As Shilton flew out, Olsen calmly rolled the ball through a tiny gap between the keeper's arm and torso. 'You couldn't have written a better script if you'd wanted to,' says Olsen. 'To score an important goal in a European qualifier, against England, all those things … it just happens like that sometimes, doesn't it? Great timing, I suppose.'

The stadium erupted in delight, no more so than in the commentary box. 'I'm stunned, but I have to present our new star player: Jesper Olsen!' said Svend Gehrs. 'Here he outwits four defenders and Shilton. Presenting Jesper Olsen!' The final line became the title of a book and the commentary, along with the goal, went into Danish folklore. Gehrs would follow the rise of Piontek's team and mark the big moments with memorable phrases that were repeated in playgrounds and workplaces across Denmark like lines from a cult sketch show.

It was incidental that Olsen's goal only secured a draw rather than a victory. A point earned and also a point made; there had been a small yet seismic shift in the landscape of Danish and world football. 'Last, last, last minute,' says Piontek, thumping the table to emphasise exactly what saloon the Danes had been drinking in. 'If Jesper Olsen does not score the goal we cannot get a point. If we do not get this point we will not qualify for France, and if we do not qualify for France we will not qualify for Mexico.' De Vlo changed the course of football history.

The English media preferred to give their own players a coating for being subjected to such a runaround by a team of supposed inferiors. Underneath the predictable headlines of RUBBISH and ENGLAND'S SHAME, Piontek's opposite number gave a more accurate account. 'It would have been a travesty of justice if we had won,' said Bobby Robson. 'Denmark were brilliant. I did not see many better teams in the World Cup finals. We were overrun in midfield by a team who did not have a single bad player. Peter Shilton played marvellously. It was as if they had twelve to our eleven. The draw was a bloody good result and we should be grateful for it.'

Bloody good results were on the way for Denmark. Over the next year they showcased both their evolving brand of attacking football and a resilience that was lacking pre-Piontek. In their next qualifier against Luxembourg they bounced back from conceding a shock second-half equaliser to win 2-1 thanks to Klaus Berggreen's first international goal. In April 1983 a towering header from Søren Busk in the last quarter of the match grabbed a crucial 1-0 victory at home to Greece. 'I was so high up that I had ice on my forehead when I came down,' he says. 'I headed it with such force that I have had a headache ever since.' More late goals – perhaps the most important calling card of sides with great team spirit – followed six weeks later against Hungary in Copenhagen. With the game locked at 1-1 in the last ten minutes, a leaping header from Jesper Olsen – of all people – and a Simonsen penalty put Denmark at the top of the group. England had dropped a point at home to Greece four weeks earlier. It was building towards a decisive match at Wembley.

As Danish fortunes changed so did Piontek's team. Per Røntved retired from international football just short of his thirty-fourth birthday after the match against Luxembourg in November 1982. Piontek had to replace not only his captain but the libero who organised the team. The solution was a man only seven months younger than Røntved.

Morten Olsen was an easy choice as captain. His approach and application served as an example to a squad that needed the occasional reminder of what they were gathered together for. 'I think I've drunk one beer with Morten,' says the defender Ivan Nielsen. 'Morten was very serious about his game. Even warming up he was running, running, running, while the other guys were standing around.' When Olsen spoke everyone listened. He could hush a room full of players just by walking into it. 'He was very important for the team because he was very serious, like me,' said Piontek. 'He's more German than I am.'

Beyond his natural desire to be the best footballer he could be, there were other reasons for Olsen's intensity. In the summer of 1978 his girlfriend was travelling on a ferry with her mother and sister. She left them to go on deck for some air. It was the last time anyone saw her; a body was never found. Olsen later acknowledged that it had a huge effect on his career and life.

Olsen spent the majority of 1982 out of the game with a severe shin injury at an age when such an extended absence frequently ends a career. When he returned for Anderlecht, the manager, Tomislav Ivić – a significant influence on the Danish players both in Belgium and earlier at Ajax, who was later on the short list to succeed Piontek – decided to protect the legs but retain the influence of Olsen by dropping him back to the sweeper position. It was a resounding success. Olsen could read a game as if he had written it himself.

He later coached Denmark for over a decade. Before that he was effectively Piontek's manager on the pitch. 'He was the man who gave the small instructions: bom, bom, left, right, bom, push forward,' says Per Frimann, who played with Olsen for Denmark and Anderlecht. 'His vision of football was so clear. He was looking after his own game and ten other people's games. People usually have enough on with themselves. That kind of guidance was very special.'

Piontek lifted the Anderlecht idea of using Olsen as sweeper. And that wasn't the only thing he adopted. Both Olsen and Busk were advocates of a pressing game and a cavalry-charge offside trap that became ultra-fashionable later in the eighties through Arrigo Sacchi's AC Milan, an idea Piontek weighed up and soon implemented. Many of his key players had gone abroad while they were young enough to pick up and retain good habits, creating a unique microclimate for Piontek. There was also a near-perfect balance between young players, those at their peak and senior professionals that drew a harmonious line through the whole squad.

Throughout 1983 Piontek pulled all these elements together to form a system that would propel Denmark forward in international football. It is never easy to trace the precise evolution of tactics, but Piontek has a strong case for being the inventor of 3-5-2 in its purest sense. This essentially involved, with a full bill of health, Morten Olsen as the all-seeing eye in the sweeper position with Busk and Nielsen deployed just in front of him to cling to the opposition forwards like wet shower curtains. Bertelsen and Berggreen would patrol the midfield. Bertelsen would cover for others and do the simple things well; Berggreen would link defence and attack like a metronome, using his tactical experience gathered from Serie A to put out fires before the matches had been struck. From that base the attacking players could search and destroy, and to pick a combination of five from Arnesen, Lerby, Olsen, Mølby, Elkjær, Simonsen and Michael Laudrup was what managers refer to as a nice problem.

The 3-5-2 system was only a basis for negotiation. This was Jackson Pollock football, with players encouraged to go where their instinct took them. At times it might have been easier simply to list their formation as 10. 'Tactically it was a strange team we had,' says Laudrup. 'Sometimes we played with the left-back and no right-back. On the right we had Klaus Berggreen, my friend from Italy, and he was always joking: "Why do I have to play full-back, midfield and winger?" Sometimes I dropped into midfield, sometimes it was a 3-6-1, sometimes it was a 4-5-1, sometimes a 3-5-2. Organisation is important, but the players' quality – and their knowledge of each other – is so important as well. Nowadays you see Barcelona, and I don't know if you know what system they play. I certainly don't. Sometimes they play 3-7-0, sometimes they play 2-4-4.'

This system was part plan, part necessity. An immutable truth when assembling a football team is to utilise the best players you have; the formation and tactics will work themselves out from there. The Danish squad was top-heavy with attacking players, so Denmark had to play aggressively. What else could they do?

If they ever played their way into trouble they were always willing to try and play their way out. No international team has ever had so many fleet-footed dribblers. And not just in attack. Morten Olsen would often run with the ball from his own penalty area, setting everything in motion and turning the maxim of defending from the front on its head.

'We had a lot of street footballers,' says Morten Olsen. 'As a coach it is important that you have these kinds of players, and that you allow them to make mistakes.' Piontek was willing to take the risk, not least because he had the insurance of Bertelsen and Berggreen. It was a cocktail of individualists who made goals and headlines, and the quiet men who ran what Busk calls the 'sour metres' when the other team had the ball. 'Sour metres, Buski?' sniffed Elkjær when the idea was suggested to him. Piontek wanted Elkjær to conserve his energy for when he had the ball. 'Sepp was good because he had the right system and the right players,' says Berggreen. 'He knew he had a lot of players not running so much to defend. Preben and Michael, if they have to work hard then they cannot use their quality, so it's okay if they don't work hard as long as they make goals.'

The system might have had echoes of Total Football from the seventies, and there is little doubt about the debt owed to Cruyff,

Johan Neeskens, Johnny Rep et al., but the Danes stood on the shoulders of these giants to take their skill and flexibility and combine it with the robust athleticism demanded of footballers a decade further on. The game, and particularly the pace of the game, had changed. Piontek's system was played at more beats per minute than Total Football, making it at once both derivative and thrillingly futuristic. The Danish players were quick enough but it was their change of pace that set them apart, both individually and collectively, with slow-rumbling attacks often building a sudden and devastating momentum. After years of experimenting, Piontek had found the formula to turn Denmark into a potent force in international football. A good manager is a chemist; Piontek was an alchemist.

Bobby Robson was in attendance to check on their progress in Copenhagen in September 1983 when Denmark took on France in a friendly ahead of the crucial return with England at Wembley just two weeks later. The spine of the Danish side was missing – no Morten Olsen, Bertelsen or Elkjær, nor Arnesen because of a long-term knee injury – and France were resplendent with the players who had carried them to the brink of the 1982 World Cup final: Battiston, Maxime Bossis, Dominique Rocheteau, Alain Giresse and the European Footballer of the Year-in-waiting, Michel Platini. Even though Platini would score, he was overshadowed by a young talent also registered to Juventus.

It was mere confirmation. The word was already out on Michael Laudrup; foreign clubs had been after him since he was thirteen. 'You get a player like Laudrup every fifteen to twenty years,' Piontek says of the diamond that fell into his lap. Laudrup scored on his international debut in 1982 against Norway, also his eighteenth birthday. His rise was unstoppable and he began attracting covetous glances from all over Europe, with a move to one of the giants of the Continent a case of when rather than if. His family had to get a secret phone number when journalists and agents bombarded them with calls after midnight. When that number leaked out, they just pulled the plug at bedtime.

Laudrup nearly ended up joining the great Liverpool side of the early eighties. They all but signed him from Brøndby in 1983, with a deal agreed and Laudrup photographed in a bowler hat and Liverpool shirt. The move fell through when the club asked Laudrup to accept the same money for four years rather than the original three. Later that summer he signed for Juventus. Only two foreigners per side were allowed in Serie A so he joined Lazio until he was ready to supplant either Platini or Zbigniew Boniek. It would not be long.

In Copenhagen he struck two beautifully crafted goals as Denmark handed France their sole defeat in 22 matches between August 1982 and May 1985. Laudrup's strikes took his tally to six in just five internationals and helped Denmark run out 3-1 winners. A despairing yet futile tackle left Laudrup hobbling as he scored his second goal. Piontek promptly substituted him, keen to wrap Laudrup in cotton wool for the game against England. The Danes had shown enough and no one understood this better than the watching Bobby Robson. 'It was chilling to know that the team which played so well to beat France will be improved for the Wembley game,' he said. 'They gave us the runaround a year ago while against France they confirmed the quality of their players. It is wonderful that a little country can produce such players. They now have a formidable team, one of the best I have seen for ten to fifteen years.'

It may have been subconscious, it may have been throwaway, but ten years earlier would take in the Dutch Total Football side. Fifteen would include what, in terms of both aesthetics and achievement, most regard as the greatest international team of all, the Brazilians of 1970. If Robson was using these teams as his barometer of comparison it was lavish praise for a nation that had yet to finish even second in a qualifying group. Whatever he meant there is no doubt that the purest of football men was struck, both smitten and fearful, by what he had seen.

It had taken four years but everything had fallen into place – the manager, the focus, the system and, finally, Laudrup completing a twenty-four-carat golden generation of players. What they needed now was the breakthrough.

Chapter 6

Twin towers

In the twentieth century England lost only three competitive matches at Wembley against sides from continental Europe. None of the players involved in those victories will ever run out of things to tell their grandchildren. Wembley was the home of football, with the aura to match. That aura was even greater in Scandinavia. Most of the Denmark team who visited Wembley in 1983 grew up watching a live match from the Football League every Saturday as part of the TV show *Sportslørdag*. As well as the main game, goal updates were announced with a sudden DONG!

In the Laudrup household it was one of the highlights of the week; the young Michael would excitedly scribble down the scores as they were donged in. There were only a few channels available. On one Saturday afternoon in 1981, alternative programmes included *Liberalism or Marxism?* and *Stamps – not just for collectors*. 'Believe me, Sheffield Wednesday against Stoke could be a great Saturday afternoon,' says the reserve midfielder John Lauridsen. 'The greatest game I ever saw was Manchester United 3 West Brom 5 in 1978. A few years later I played against West Brom in a friendly. It was a great feeling. I loved West Brom because of that game.' At times more than 30 per cent of the population would watch a match from the Football League on Saturdays; more than 80 per cent watched the match at Wembley.

The stirring win over Italy in 1981 could conceivably have been a one-off. Wembley, however, confirmed the burgeoning perception that Denmark were now one of international football's best teams. When Piontek is asked what was the team's most important victory, he answers instantly. 'England, 1-0. If you beat England in qualification, at Wembley, you can see the capacity of the team.'

It established what would become a theme of the decade: beating a football superpower for the first time in a generation, or, indeed, ever. That Denmark team took the whole country on a vicarious voyage of discovery; they were and still are subject to the peculiar kind of goodwill, gratitude and unconditional love that occurs when you are exploring new territory. After decades of defeat, most Danes greeted the results with sweet disbelief.

'Everything that happened in those years was new and therefore can never be repeated,' says Svend Gehrs. 'We were beating nations that we had never even been close to scoring against. It was history; every single game made history.' The overstatement is understandable. Nielsen puts it another way, raising his hands triumphantly above his head and shrieking 'Yay!' to reflect the national reaction to every victory. 'It was so easy for us – we were playing teams we had never beaten before. It was a big party the whole time.' Few yays were as great, or as grateful, as the one after Wembley.

There were only two weeks between the win over France and the match against England. That was more than enough time for the 'chilling' victory over France to impact. One thing reduced the temperature in England even further: the reports that Laudrup, the best teenager in the world, might not even be picked, such was the Danish wealth of resources. 'Well, they can only pick eleven, can't they?' said England manager Bobby Robson. 'If they don't want him, I'll have him.' Had Preben Elkjær not been injured in training the day before the match, Laudrup probably would not have played. Piontek said Laudrup had 'a little bit of Franz Beckenbauer and a little bit of Johan Cruyff'. This was the man likely to start on the bench.

There aren't many defenders in the 1980s and 1990s who would have been pleased to go up against Laudrup, but Russell Osman might have been one. Laudrup's presence meant the absence of Elkjær, who had given Osman a torrid night in the first fixture. Osman can be forgiven for not buying into the romance of Danish Dynamite; this would be the last of his eleven England caps. Elkjær and Laudrup were not the only ones for England to worry about. All of Denmark's attacking players were in form – not least Jesper Olsen, who, four days before Wembley, inspired Ajax to a stupendous 8-2 destruction of Feyenoord. Rinus Michels, the godfather of Total Football, called Olsen's performance 'one of the greatest I have seen in my years of football'.

Robson had been in football for thirty-three years but rarely had he been as tetchy as he was in the build-up. It was a reflection of the game's significance and his frustration that the rest of England didn't realise just how good Denmark were. He said he had watched them 'more than any other opposition for a single game in my managerial career' and, while his judgement was correct, he went too far in sharing it with others. A problem shared was not a problem halved. 'Every one of them could play for a top English club and they are easily one of the top four international sides in Europe. Where are England? I'll tell you on Thursday morning.' Robson's comments numbed his own players into subservience. It didn't help that England were without their best player, Bryan Robson.

Denmark were a point behind England but with a game in hand. A victory would give either side control of the group. Bobby Robson broke the habit of a lifetime of England managers by delaying the announcement of his team. In those days it was the norm to name the England side thirty-six hours before a home game; ahead of the first match in Copenhagen, more innocent times, Robson even named it three days before kick-off. 'Managers have the right to do what they want,' he said. 'It's not my job to fill

Wednesday morning's papers.' It was a legitimate tactic, validated by its subsequent widespread adoption, but at the time it sent the message that England were running scared. Piontek, by contrast, cut an intimidatingly relaxed figure. He had been throughout the extended build-up: at a lunch in London a month before the game, with Jesper Olsen struggling through injury, he joked about putting a half-fit Olsen on the bench 'to create a little fear for Bobby Robson'.

Denmark had not been without fear before the game – this was England, at Wembley, in a probable group decider – but their poker face was so superior that nobody realised. 'You can bluff,' says Morten Olsen, 'but you must have the class to bluff.' Ultimately, England's opposition fright was greater than Denmark's stage fright. That opposition fright increased after fifty seconds of the game. Laudrup ran on to Allan Simonsen's long pass, slipped past the goalkeeper Peter Shilton and hit the side netting. 'I was twenty metres ahead of the defenders,' says Laudrup. 'I had too much time to think, much too much.'

So had England before the game. The ease with which Laudrup's chance was created accentuated all their pre-match fears, and they performed with a caution that verged on cowardice. Denmark had the better of the first half, keeping the ball with relative ease, although it was largely sterile domination. There were very few chances in the entire game. But Denmark were just a little bit surer, a little bit smoother. A little bit better. The game was low on entertainment but it had the unique tension you see when an established team comes up against a superior upstart.

That superiority was underlined shortly before half-time when Denmark took the lead with a penalty from Simonsen. It was ostensibly an ugly goal – a cross, a handball, a penalty – but a closer look shows that it had all the hallmarks of Denmark's version of Total Football. A slow-slow-quick attack, involving thirteen passes, crescendoed until Laudrup duped Terry Butcher on the right and put over a cross that was handled by Phil Neal. It was the first time an Englishman had touched the ball in over a minute. By that stage Denmark had four men against three in the box – one of whom was the centre-back Søren Busk, given licence to wander forward in open play. Without his presence the goal would not have happened. He challenged Neal, the ball cleared them both to reach Simonsen, and the off-balance Neal handled the ball.

Just in case the significance of the penalty was not obvious, Lerby started shaking Simonsen's head like a child trying to get the last coin out of the piggy bank. Then Lerby stood with his hands behind his own head in anguish.

'I knew what it could mean for Danish football,' Simonsen says. 'I always took penalties for my clubs and for Denmark. Normally I was never nervous but when I put the ball on the spot my hands were shaking.' Simonsen ran up. And. Time. Stood. Still. Before he stroked it calmly into the net.

Denmark protected their lead in the second half, keeping England at arm's length with little trouble. 'We were very well organised and disciplined,' says Jesper Olsen. 'Tactically we were fantastic.' England were reduced to confused endeavour and thud-and-blunder. They did not even have a shot on target until injury time. As Denmark kept the ball in the seventy-fifth minute, the home crowd chanted: 'What a load of rubbish.' Denmark's attack lacked focus in the second half; their concentration was on defending their lead. This, more than any of Denmark's major victories, was a game for the defenders. They seemed to appreciate the symbolism of victory at Wembley more than anybody. Nielsen calls it 'the temple', Busk 'the mecca'.

Nielsen and Busk were Denmark's own twin towers: tall, imposing, mustachioed centre-backs. They roomed together for a number of years and Nielsen talks of a telepathic understanding on the field. Their physicality was such that it's natural to think of them as the bouncers of the side, yet they did not quite fit the profile: they picked up only three yellow cards and no reds in 112 games for Denmark. Their fellow defender Morten Olsen was booked only once in 102 appearances. And they could play. 'They were very good on the ball,' says Per Frimann. 'They were street-football players.' Nielsen had played midfield and Busk used to be a forward.

Both were quiet, laid-back characters. One day Busk saw something flapping in the curtain of their hotel room and was loath to check what it was. 'So I tell him "Ivan, Ivan, wake up. There is something in the curtain." He gets up, the big guy in his briefs and bare stomach. He shakes the curtain and closes the door and then he goes back to sleep. Turns out it was a tiny bat. Bloody hell. It was lying on the terrace outside and Ivan just went back to sleep. He didn't give a toss. That's typical Ivan. Nice and easy.'

Just about the only time he was unsettled was in Moscow when the pair found cockroaches in their liquorice. 'We couldn't sleep,' says Busk. 'They were crunching in the liquorice. That was too much for the big guy. Luckily it was after the game so we had had some beers.'

Nielsen is a man of simple pleasures: a drink and a smoke at the end of a hard day's graft. He loved smoking so much that he made sure the allowance of it was written into his club contracts. He certainly knew how to stub out attacks. Nielsen was extremely quick for someone 6ft 4ins, had spidery legs that could win the ball from improbable angles and was comfortable enough to play at left-back and maraud forward. He even took the third penalty in a European Cup final shootout in 1988.

'You cannot imagine how good Ivan was,' says Klaus Berggreen. 'He had such long legs. He and Søren don't need to talk to the press or go on television, they're just relaxed. Good boys.' The defence was sometimes seen as the weakest element of that Denmark team, but that was more than a little harsh. Denmark conceded 123 goals in 115 games under Piontek, a fine record for such a brazenly attacking side. They did not have a glass jaw, only an exposed one.

The only time Busk and Nielsen left their keeper Ole Kjær exposed at Wembley was in injury time. A loose ball broke to the substitute Luther Blissett, whose close-range snapshot was brilliantly saved by Kjær. As with Jesper Olsen's goal against England earlier in the group, this was another moment of immense significance. 'If this ball goes in we don't go to the European Championship in 1984, and if we don't go to France we don't go to the World Cup in 1986,' says Piontek. 'In one second' – he clicks his fingers – 'everything has changed.'

Not least Kjær's life. From now on it would be defined by that save. The credit was partially shared with his mother-in-law – before the match at Wembley she added a Velcro strap to his gloves – and with Piontek, who met him the week before the game so that he and Kjær could practise with the same ball that was to be used at Wembley. Kjær later had the chance to go to England, but turned down a move to Sunderland. 'Honestly,' he says, 'I wasn't good enough.' It was a rare example of somebody telling himself not to give up the day job, so Kjær stayed as a part-time keeper who worked in a sports shop in Esbjerg. He was back in the day job thirty-six hours after Wembley, just in time to be accosted by hungover Danish fans arriving home on the ferry.

Eleven seconds after Kjær's save, the game was over. 'Denmark has created an international football sensation!' said Gehrs on Danish TV. You can often gauge the significance of a sporting moment by the reaction of those involved. When the final whistle blew, there were no choreographed celebrations. The Denmark players leapt on the spot or raised both arms so high that it strained the sinews or ran around in a daze, unable to work out what to do.

A famous evening was shared with around 15,000 Danish fans at Wembley. 'When we came out on to the pitch at the start I looked to the left and the first thing I saw was that everything was red and white,' says Simonsen. 'That was beautiful. It's a lovely memory to have.'

After the game the Danish fans took off their scarves and stayed away from landmarks such as Trafalgar Square, fearing reprisals for the trouble in Copenhagen a year earlier. Red and white was in evidence on the ferry home, both in clothing and song. Two weeks before the match, the newspaper *B.T.* arranged a competition for the best Danish football song or slogan. The winner, among more than two thousand entries, was Søren Bo Andersen, from Vesterbro in Copenhagen. He received 2,500 kroner, a golden football and an additional 1,000 kroner for every goal Denmark scored. The winning chorus – 'We are red, we are white, we are Danish dynamite' – was to accompany the team's success. Danish Dynamite became their trademark. When he was asked why the chorus was in English, Andersen said: 'The English fans at Wembley should be able to understand it. Also, a football chant sounds best in English. It had to be something with red and white. Then I just had to find a word that rhymed with white. It really wasn't that hard.'

Nor, in the end, was winning at Wembley. In Denmark the victory was greeted with a mixture of disbelief and joy. THE BRITS GOT BUMPS IN THEIR BOWLER was the headline in *Alt om Sport*. 'To conquer the English lion in its own cave is unusual,' wrote Frits Ahlstrøm. 'To pull its teeth out – one by one – as the Danish Vikings did with their clever, coldblooded, disciplined and concentrated performance is even more remarkable.'

Bobby Robson dismissed Piontek's suggestion that England were frightened, describing it as 'a load of nonsense', but changed his mind as the dust settled. 'I put the Danes on a pedestal and, in so doing, knocked our own confidence so that we failed to show our innate qualities,' he said in 1986. The defeat sent English football into one of its periodic bouts of soul-searching. 'SEND FOR

CLOUGHIE' said a *Sun* editorial. 'We were not just beaten by tiny Denmark, we were MURDERED. Outclassed for skill. Hopelessly left behind for confidence, guts and, above all, national pride. Our pampered near-millionaires were taken apart by a team that included a part-time shopkeeper. Denmark with its 5,000,000 population is best known for bacon and blue cheese, sex and the little mermaid statue. We are the oldest soccer country in the world.'

Robson, only a year into a job that this fiercest of patriots craved, offered his resignation, which was rejected. A few years later he wrote: 'Whatever I may or may not achieve in my football career, the blackest day will remain 21 September 1983.' Denmark had turned the world of English football upside down.

Denmark now needed four points from the last three games to qualify for Euro 84. After a 6-0 win at home to Luxembourg, in which Laudrup scored his only Denmark hat-trick, they lost 1-0 in Hungary despite dominating the game. Although Elkjær was omitted, with Piontek unusually wanting to play a little more cagily, Denmark could have been 4-0 up at half-time. Berggreen had a goal wrongly disallowed for offside; Simonsen chipped just wide after a twinkling run from inside his own half; another Simonsen burst ended with the goalkeeper Attila Kovacs saving his shot by sitting on the ball; and finally Denmark could have had a penalty when Simonsen was clumsily challenged by Ferenç Csongrádi.

The pattern continued after half-time. Laudrup, as at Wembley, went round the keeper only to hit the side netting. Then the hero of Wembley, Kjær, was at fault for the goal that gave Hungary the lead, with Sandor Kiss beating him at the near post. Denmark's attacks became increasingly desperate, with Kovacs's save from Laudrup the closest they came to an equaliser. 'Our nerves began to show for the first time,' said Piontek. He was also unimpressed with the Spanish referee Emilio Mura, who allowed a number of excessive tackles on Jesper Olsen in particular. 'There are not enough words for me to express what I think about this referee.'

Denmark's fate remained in their own hands. All they had to do was win a tricky match away to Greece to clinch qualification. 'I am certain we will win,' said Piontek. With Laudrup absent, Simonsen started despite heel and knee injuries. 'I must bear any pain,' he said. Piontek told them to play watchfully for the first twenty minutes. Elkjær, who had not started in England and Hungary, so nearly managed to follow orders; he got to sixteen minutes and then scored a majestic solo goal. He received a pass from Simonsen forty yards out, slowed down to draw the defender Petros Michos towards him and then burned him off with an exhilarating change of pace. Moments later he was into the area, from where he dinked the ball over Georgios Plitsis.

The second goal, which all but clinched Denmark's place at Euro 84, came shortly after half-time from Simonsen. Berggreen beat two players on the edge of the box and played an almost tender through pass. The weight was such that Simonsen did not have to break stride before striking it into the corner. The goal that finally took Simonsen to a major tournament would be his last for Denmark.

There was no danger of Greece scoring twice. The rest of the match was played out in a wonderful mezzanine between unspoken confirmation of success and joyous actuality. With a couple of minutes remaining, Piontek demonstrated his softer side by replacing Simonsen with Frank Arnesen, who had not played for Denmark for sixteen months because of a series of injuries. In injury time, Gehrs implored Kjær to kick the ball as long as possible. He didn't. But moments later the whistle had gone. 'Make sure you sit down comfortably or go to the window and shout your joy to all who pass by,' said Gehrs. 'There will definitely be a party here in Athens, I guarantee that, and maybe also at home on the streets of Denmark.' It was both the fulfilment of a dream and a beginning: Denmark would be one of only two sides to play in every European Championship from 1984 to 2004. The other was Germany.

As the Danish-German Piontek fought to suppress a smile, the players ran towards the fans, throwing their shirts into the crowd en masse. This was not the kind of night on which you worried about a cold torso. Or cared about going flying, as a Danish cameraman did when he fell comically over an advertising hoarding while snapping a topless player. Moments later the players formed a circle and gave Piontek the bumps. The rest of Denmark contented themselves with goosebumps.

When the stadium had cleared, and with Greek folk music playing jauntily in the background, Gehrs gathered the goalscorers Elkjær, his hair drenched in sweat, and Simonsen for a pitchside interview. As the camera crew prepared, Gehrs expressed paternal concern for Simonsen.

'It's getting cold for your injury.'

'No, that's okay.'

'I guess that doesn't matter ...'

'No, that doesn't mean a thing. It's holiday time now.'

Small talk has rarely been so poignant. After that there was a small pause, with Simonsen's face glazing over for a couple of seconds. This was the precise moment the achievement sank in. 'Bloody hell it's nice,' he said to Gehrs, who smiled and shook his head gently. When the interview began Simonsen – who had won the Ballon d'Or and scored in a European Cup final – said it was the greatest moment of his career.

It was the same for all the other players. They went to a restaurant in Athens to celebrate, eating roast beef, prawns and cake. With Kjær and Busk approaching their twenty-fifth game and Simonsen his fiftieth, Piontek needed some money for the penalty box. 'All players who go to bed before 1.30 a.m. will get a fine,' he told *Ekstra Bladet*. 'This time the clubs must understand if the players return tired. We will only get a result like this once every twenty years, and this time we should be allowed to party all night. Nobody's going to hear from me if we don't even get to bed before the plane departs.'

The anti-curfew was diligently upheld by the players. Denmark flew home the following day, some nursing the happiest hangovers of their lives. A perfect year was completed when *World Soccer* voted Piontek Coach of the Year. But there would be a bumpy road ahead before the plane departed for the European Championship in France.

Chapter 7

The sparrow and the shadow

It was only six months after the glory days of Wembley and Athens but the Danish press were already jumping ship. Denmark had lost 2-1 to Spain in a friendly and the newspaper *B.T.* didn't mince its words: 'Just stay home from France!' Per Høyer Hansen, an acclaimed writer from the weekly sports paper *Tipsbladet*, was more eloquent, if no less scathing: 'The Danish football crowd has to get used to the fact that the Euro-euphoria of the autumn has become a heavy depression, which could very well culminate in France.'

Before the Spain debacle a depleted Denmark side lost 6-0 in Amsterdam, the biggest defeat under Piontek. It left six nails in the coffin of Ole Kjær's international career, but the consensus was that such a freakish defeat could be written off provided the slate was wiped clean against Spain. Without Morten Olsen, Frank Arnesen and Søren Lerby, the team trudging out for the warm-up at Estadio Luis Casanova in Valencia wasn't quite vintage Dynamite. The list of absentees had prompted Piontek to call up the centre-forward Mogens Hansen from Næstved in the Danish first division. Hansen was so bowled over by the selection that he thought it was an April Fool's joke. 'It's got to be a lie,' he told *B.T.* 'Can Sepp really use me in such fine company? Yes, well in that case it's about seizing the opportunity.'

A call-up from Piontek was a rare opportunity for players in a league that was one of the weakest in Europe. The four Danish clubs in European competition in 1983–4 all bombed out in the first round with an aggregate score of 26-5. Hansen didn't seize his opportunity and neither did the rest of the Denmark team. It wasn't so much the scoreline against Spain that riled reporters; it was the Danes' unusually cagey and defensive first-half performance. Høyer Hansen described it as 'depressing and most insultingly pussyfooting'. It wouldn't be the last time misery stole the headlines after a date with Spain.

Piontek said the team had been 'completely headless' and lambasted Laudrup, who was substituted at half-time, for failing to progress as a player during his time in Italy. The other managers preparing for Euro 84 licked their lips. The German coach, Jupp Derwall, called Denmark an overrated team and Belgium's Guy Thys said that 'the Danes were not interested in playing football – probably because of the big defeat against Holland'.

That the Danish press were also critical was the result of expectations that had continued to grow since Piontek transformed the team. If every nation beaten and every goal reached was uncharted territory for the players, this evolving fairy tale was also a new reality for a Danish press previously used to picking through the scraps of failure. Niels-Christian Holmstrøm, who captained Denmark for three games in the seventies, wrote on the eve of the tournament in France that no other sports team in the country had been exposed to this kind of hero worship or frenzy: 'Not since the years during and just after the Second World War has a similar national cohesion and sense of identity been facilitated by a gathering of athletes.'

A 1-0 defeat to Czechoslovakia in May was merely a 'fall forward', said *Tipsbladet*, but the squad was starting to take shape. The legends of the fall were back, except for Jesper Olsen; he was in Frankfurt receiving specialist treatment for an ongoing ankle injury. Piontek kept his promise to the club managers and took off Lerby, Morten Olsen and Allan Simonsen at half-time. By that stage he had seen forty-five minutes of football that appeared to have won over the sceptics. 'Just go to France after all,' backtracked *B.T.* 'Forget the disappointments in Holland and Spain. The Euro 84 team is good and breeds confidence as long as all the big guns are lined up.' Few people expected one of the big guns to be their goalkeeper, but Ole Qvist became one of the stars of the European Championship in France.

Qvist wore gloves of a different kind when he worked as a motorcycle officer in Copenhagen. The police force was proud to have an international goalkeeper among its rank and file and happily allowed him unpaid leave to play for Denmark. In a team brimming with world-class players who were hailed as superstars in Europe's biggest clubs, the goalkeeping post was a domain reserved for the domestic amateur.

Some journalists campaigned for the reinstatement of Birger Jensen, but Piontek was not for turning. He decided to give his three regular keepers a trial run in their friendlies during the spring of 1984. Kjær never played for Denmark again after the 6-0 drubbing in Amsterdam while Troels Rasmussen suffered an ankle injury against Sweden a week before Euro 84 kicked off. It cleared the stage for Qvist, who didn't fluff the audition. 'Without Qvist's four brilliant saves in the second half we would have lost,' said Piontek after the 1-0 win against Sweden.

Denmark played their last friendly two days later in Copenhagen against Bulgaria. Some people claimed the players were being overworked in order to milk the team's marketability – if Denmark had made the final the team would have played seven games in twenty-two days – but the country was now gripped by Euro fever. Even the politicians gearing up for the European parliament elections tried to pander to the zeitgeist, with the Social Democrats running an ad in the sports pages: 'The European Championship yesterday, the European Community tomorrow – are you a conservative or a social democrat?' An election poster for the

Danish Agricultural Association tried a similar tactic: 'The Euro 84 squad has been picked ... on Thursday the EC squad is selected. Put your cross by a team-mate.'

It would have been a clean sweep of seats in Brussels had Danish Dynamite been on the ballot paper. The ubiquitous players appeared on stickers, stationery and chocolate boxes, and signed autographs for adoring crowds at the Copenhagen department store Magasin. The only place you had trouble spotting them was on primetime TV talk shows, where the strict non-commercial rules of the national broadcaster Danmarks Radio clashed with the DBU's request for players to appear in Carlsberg-branded clothes. A report in *Tipsbladet* estimated that the players made 100,000 kroner (£10,000) each on the collective sponsorship deals, without counting their individual engagements. Preben Elkjær put his time before the training camp to good use: in one day alone he played tennis with Søren Busk (he won in two sets), modelled the latest Nike collection in a photo shoot and posed for a trim at a hair salon.

The excitement also spread to the small town of Jouy-en-Josas, south-west of Paris, where the players were staying for the opening game. Staff at the modest three-star Hôtel Valbievre ('You can hardly fit four people for a game of poker,' noted a Danish journalist inspecting the rooms) were looking forward to the return of M. Piontek. 'He is a friendly and charming man,' cooed the receptionist. When Piontek requested English breakfast instead of croissants, the chef didn't pull out a shotgun. 'The Danish footballers can have exactly what they want,' he said. 'I also like bacon and eggs in the morning.'

While the Danish press went into overdrive, devoting daily supplements to the minutiae of the players' form, diets and leisure activities, questions remained over how a footballing nation with no real tournament pedigree would cope in France. They were one of the fancied teams, but the calamitous start to the year had not

69

gone unnoticed with the bookmakers. They were 10-1 to win it – fifth out of the eight participants – while *The Times* pitched them as the Cinderellas of the tournament: 'Will they blossom or crumble?'

If the previous European Championship was anything to go by, this probably wasn't an occasion for Cinderella. The tournament in Italy had been dominated by defensive play, with an average of under two goals per game. The official West German account called the tournament 'a hideous disfigurement of football'. That was the winner's report.

In 1984 the format changed to include semi-finals, and pundits were further buoyed by the prospect of seeing the Ballon d'Or winner (Michel Platini) facing Simonsen, number three on the list, in the opening match. Simonsen wasn't the only household name around Europe. Denmark's twenty-man squad contained fourteen overseas-based players; the other seven teams had only five between them. 'Denmark and France represent a hope for the future,' wrote Høyer Hansen. 'The French through ball-playing as refinement and entertainment for the masses, and attack as the best defence; the Danes through their belief that the optimistic outsider still has a chance when fantasy and tactical discipline reach a greater whole.'

In the training camp before the tournament, Arnesen had a dream in which a half-empty stadium in Paris watches Jesper Olsen hit a screamer that goes in off the underside of the crossbar. One-nil Denmark. When dreamland Arnesen comes on in the second half he runs on to the pitch without boots and plays in bare feet for ten minutes. It wasn't the kind of dream that would have sent Arnesen to the chaise longue for a session with Freud but rather the result of pent-up excitement that was bubbling over. Arnesen's presence in the squad was a joyous surprise after two years of injury problems; he had all but given up on the idea of going to France.

On a sunny Tuesday evening in Paris, the collective dreams of a nation were about to be realised. Two hours before kick-off most of the ten thousand Danish fans with tickets to the game had already pitched up at the Parc des Princes stadium. They were rewarded with a line-up that was probably the strongest in Denmark's history: Qvist – Busk, Morten Olsen, Nielsen – Arnesen, Berggreen, Bertelsen, Lerby, Simonsen – Elkjær, Laudrup. It was the only time these players would ever start a match together.

In the commentary box, Svend Gehrs was making final preparations. When he came on air to introduce the game he described 'a strange tingling sensation' that he hadn't felt since he watched Denmark play in the final of the 1960 Rome Olympics when he was twenty years old. Among his viewers back home were the Danish royal family and the consort's French relatives visiting for his birthday. The chef at Fredensborg Castle had been asked to prepare an early supper – turbot and venison – so that the young princes and the French contingent could follow the game.

The royal visitors from the Gironde would have been pleased by the opening exchanges. 'Oh dear, our players are so nervous,' said Gehrs, when Qvist dived at the feet of Bernard Lacombe to prevent an early goal after the lively Alain Giresse had bamboozled the Danish defenders. The Danes eventually found their width going forward, but any attacking ambition was offset by caution and respect for the French favourites and the occasion. In the opening forty-five minutes Platini rarely touched the ball thanks to a straitjacket by the name of Klaus Berggreen.

Berggreen knew Platini from Serie A and told Piontek that man-marking was the only way of containing the French captain. The night before the game, Berggreen was playing billiards at the hotel when Piontek popped by to tell him that he was the man to handle the job. It was the kind of assignment that intrigued and excited Berggreen, whose iron-lung capacity was matched by his love affair with running. 'If you want to have success you have to specialise,' he says. 'It has always been easy for me to run.' During laps in training, he would run on the outside of his team-mates to gain the few extra yards that would pay off in matches where stamina was the crucial factor. Even now, in his mid-fifties, it is a big part of his life. 'I get crazy when I cannot run. I need it, and I love it.'

No matter where Platini went, Berggreen stuck to his heels like an eager puppy. When a free-kick was awarded on the edge of the Danish penalty area and Platini looked to catch out the defenders with a quick move, Berggreen sniffed out the plot and played the ball out of danger. When a tackle was timed with raw intent and perfection for the umpteenth time, Gehrs said: 'And Berggreen ... the shadow.'

A shadow was cast over the game, and the whole tournament, with two minutes left of the first half. Simonsen and Yvon Le Roux slid in for a loose ball near the centre circle. Players and the fans in the stadium that day still talk about the sound. It sounded like a branch breaking in a tree. Then there was a wall of gasps. Simonsen's left leg collapsed under him and *spurven fra Vejle* – the sparrow from Vejle – fell to the ground.

'It's going to be the game of my life,' Simonsen had told reporters before the game. The tournament in France provided another chance for him to play on the biggest stage, but this time with his country. Despite masterminding Barcelona's European Cup Winners' Cup final win over Standard Liège in 1982, Simonsen drew the short straw in a ridiculously competitive threesome with Bernd Schuster and the newly arrived Diego Maradona for the two available places. A baffling move to English second division club Charlton Athletic followed ('Charlton was not the world for Allan Simonsen,' says Piontek. 'He needed a team that was technically good, and he goes to Charlton!') before returning to his childhood club, Vejle.

International anonymity in the Danish first division didn't affect Simonsen, as his third-place finish in the previous year's Ballon d'Or showed. He looked as relaxed and confident as any of his team-mates in the build-up to Euro 84. This was the moment for which he had waited his entire career. A couple of weeks before leaving for France he had even appeared on a sketch show where a comedy duo, *Øb og Bøv*, pretended to injure his leg after celebrating a goal. Simonsen told the newspaper *Aktuelt* that he never felt afraid on the pitch. 'If you want any hope of making it in top football, you have to concentrate 100 per cent, and then there is no time whatsoever to feel fear. I don't feel fear, but I'm careful because I know what can happen with the legs if I don't get away in time.'

After Simonsen's collision with Le Roux, play went on for another thirty seconds before Qvist picked up the ball and booted it out of touch. Elkjær had rushed over to his long-time room-mate and immediately gesticulated wildly towards the bench with the desperation of a man who had seen something no one else had seen. 'I had seen something similar with one of my team-mates in Belgium,' he says. 'I heard the sound – I had heard it before – so I knew exactly what was wrong.' When the medical staff came on, Elkjær turned to Jean Tigana and made a hand gesture that simulated a twig breaking in two. Arnesen folded his hands behind his head and stared at the ground as he walked away. Simonsen knew immediately it was broken. 'I don't remember what else I thought,' he says. 'You have so much pain that you can't really think.'

Simonsen suffered a clean break to the shinbone and was replaced by John Lauridsen. The journalists' focus switched from filing half-time updates to penning what most feared would be tributes marking the end of a glorious career. 'Let me just confess that I'm writing these lines with tears in my eyes,' wrote Knud Lundberg, a journalist who had represented Denmark in three different team sports. 'He is the Danish footballer I rank highest among all those I have met, as an artist and maybe also as a human being. His unusual ability is in sharp contrast to his modesty. He is, despite his exploits on the biggest arenas, almost shy when he is celebrated. Sure he likes the applause, sure he enjoys feeling how much the fans appreciate him and his art, but he is reluctant to talk about it and he never seeks the limelight.'

France pushed forward at the start of the second half. It opened up space for the Danes and it took a deceptively magnificent save from Joël Bats to turn Elkjær's deflected shot round the post. Berggreen kept his iron grip on Platini, but as soon as the shadow faded the French captain found space. Cruelly, the goal came after yet another interception from Berggreen. Having won the ball from Platini, he tried to go past Tigana near the halfway line and was dispossessed; suddenly, for the first time in the game, Platini found himself out of his marker's reach. Moments later Giresse's through ball towards Lacombe was intercepted by the sliding Ivan Nielsen, who inadvertently tripped the covering Søren Busk in the same movement. The ball broke to Platini, whose mishit shot struck the head of Busk as he fell. The deflection left Qvist with no chance.

'If there hadn't been so many photographers standing behind me I would have lain down and cried,' Qvist said after the game. The goal was the only blemish for him in a commanding performance that made a mockery of any doubters. After the tournament, Queens Park Rangers were among the clubs that showed an interest in signing Qvist. He never spoke to them. 'I had my job here,' he says almost thirty years later, sitting at the headquarters of the Copenhagen traffic police. 'I knew it was what I was going to live off for the rest of my life.' Out in the corridor hangs a small sign that his police colleagues put up: 'Boulevard le Grand Qvist'. Nobody here would ever forget his moonlighting in Paris. When the Danish team landed at Copenhagen airport after the 1984 tournament, Qvist was greeted by motorcycle policemen who lifted him up on their shoulders and carried him across the tarmac.

Berggreen should have had a penalty after the goal and Giresse squandered a huge chance, but the final act belonged to the madness of Manuel Amoros. The French defender had already sparked fury after hacking down Elkjær in front of the Danish bench, but his retaliation after a foul by Jesper Olsen was a rush of blood that owed as much to slapstick as it did to bar brawling. The side of Amoros's neck landed on the ball when he fell forward. As the two players sat on the ground with their legs tangled, Amoros first took aim at Olsen by tossing the ball at his face. When that missed, he leaned over and landed a perfectly timed headbutt.

Lauridsen, who was right next to the two players, stretched his arms out in incredulity and looked at the referee with the demeanour of a man who had just lost faith in humanity. Elkjær stormed towards Amoros pointing his right index finger while Lerby's pro-wrestler stare did its best to prove that looks could actually kill. After the sending-off, Amoros took a seat among the substitutes. This breach of regulations was one insult too many for Gehrs: 'He is not allowed to sit there,' Gehrs fumed. 'He must go. He must be removed completely from the playing field. Thank you and goodbye.'

Gehrs's broadside at Amoros masked a general exasperation at the end of a game in which Denmark proved they were equals of France. 'We'll see you in the final,' Giresse told Lauridsen when they swapped shirts. A seething Lerby stormed off the pitch shaking his head, while Berggreen and Qvist headed for a post-match interview. 'I feel bloody sorry for you boys,' Gehrs told the players, who were still in their kit, banging the studio chairs in frustration. Before the live feed came on, Berggreen waved three fingers in Gehrs's face. 'Platini touches the ball three times in the whole game. And then he scores with a lousy shot.'

Thirty years on, Berggreen's lingering frustration has been tempered with admiration for an opponent who went on to score nine goals in five games and win Euro 84 almost on his own. 'Platini was fantastic,' says Berggreen. He gets up and leads an invisible dancing partner with his hands to show how he struggled to keep Platini on the right side of him. 'He was so intelligent. His movement was always diagonal, so that he could always keep me behind him. That was the best tournament he ever had. He was so strong – and he was also fucking lucky.'

Chapter 8

The *roligans*

There are two pictures taken during the European Championship in France that sum up the story of the *roligans*, the Danish fans who supported their team throughout the eighties. One shows a bare-chested man lying on his back in a field, below a signpost for Lyon, with a Danish flag covering his face from the sun and a bottle of beer resting on his exposed paunch. The other shows two lookalike Danish fans, both wearing jaunty hats, jauntier smiles and a T-shirt sporting the Danish flag. They are chatting to an old French lady who looks intrigued and charmed.

For much of Euro 84, France became a colony of Denmark. Around 30,000 Danish fans travelled to support the team. *Rolig* is the Danish word for calm and the *roligans* were seen as the antidote to the widespread hooliganism of the time: shiny, happy people, dressed in red and white, many with their faces painted. They defied the rules of biology: the more they drank, the happier they became. It was during Euro 84 that they first came to Europe-wide attention, and later that year the *roligans* won the Unesco Fair Play trophy.

Ib Thage, Jan Madsen and Søren Bernstorf Hansen, three old friends from an insurance company, were among those who made the journey to France. They met Benny and Lars, a butcher and a policeman, on the bus and ended up going round France with them. The company they had booked the tour through went bankrupt halfway through the tournament. No matter. They switched to the Holiday Inn and were pleasantly surprised to find the Denmark players were also staying there for the third group game against Belgium.

'I didn't see a single fight in France, not a single one,' says Hansen. 'And we were drunk and silly at times, but nothing happened. It was just a good atmosphere the whole way through.' Thirty years on, the five men still meet up on the pretext of a game of cards. Until recently one of the highlights of their meeting was playing audio clips of Svend Gehrs's most famous commentaries from the eighties.

'You can't but love this horde of red-and-white-clad Vikings, who, singing and drunk on happiness, march out with unsteady gait, swimming eyes and dreamy gazes,' said *L'Equipe*. 'World champions in sympathy.' They were easily recognisable because of their painted faces and cheery demeanour. Later on many of the Danish fans embraced the *klaphat*: the red and white baseball cap with two strings below the chin which, when pulled, made the hands clap on top of the cap. The *klaphat*, which was developed by two students at the Copenhagen Business School who had been inspired after watching a Mickey Mouse cartoon, sold hundreds of thousands, was exhibited in a museum and has even been the subject of a few court cases concerning copyright.

Nobody was in danger of copying the *roligans*, a unique group who became a huge part of the landscape wherever the Danish team travelled in the eighties. 'It was a strange feeling,' said a report in *Tipsbladet*. 'Only when Denmark were knocked out did people return to normal. Until then they walked around in a weird, tense haze, which wasn't just caused by the consumption of brewery products. They were in a strange dreamlike condition and couldn't focus on anything but football.' And yet they didn't take it too seriously. 'The Danish *roligan* has a completely special weapon against violence – namely the gallows humour and the self-irony,' wrote Bente Holm Kristensen, who had researched the behaviour of the fans.

Some people think the *roligans'* self-deprecating image was an odd contrast to what was happening on the pitch. In his acclaimed book *Tynd Luft* (Thin Air) about the 1986 World Cup, the Danish author Joakim Jakobsen suggests that the folksy *roligan* culture represented the polar opposite of the illustrious and ambitious football the team were playing. 'The *roligan* uproar seemed like a culturally conditioned panic reaction,' he wrote, 'which tried to make us incapacitated again.'

The present stars mixed happily with the *roligans*, regularly wandering outside the hotel for a chat and to sign autographs, occasionally sharing a beer. 'It started at Wembley but France was when we realised something was going on here, something special,' says Klaus Berggreen. 'We saw twenty-five or thirty thousand Danes and thought "What is going on?" You got so excited and so ready to fight that even if you were tired you did not feel it. You were so boosted.'

A similar injection of strength came from the bond between the squad members themselves. Almost all of the players agree that their unusually strong team spirit was one of the main reasons for their success. 'When you're good together you do more for each other on the field,' says the defender John Sivebæk. 'It was just a group of people who went very well together, and we still have that when we meet each other now.' Like any workplace it was not entirely harmonious – one player had a particular bee in his bonnet about the way another slurped his soup – but they were certainly closer than 99 per cent of football teams. 'It was one for all and all for one,' says Frits Ahlstrøm, who was Denmark's press officer for much of the 1980s. 'It's something you often say, but here it was reality.'

That unity was evident after the France game, when Piontek allowed the team out in Paris with their wives and girlfriends until

2.15 a.m. before the team headed to Lyon. 'This was also their last *udgangstilladelse* [exit permit] during this tournament,' Piontek told the newspaper *Aktuelt*.

Just as on the field, the Denmark team had a balance of contrasting yet complementary characters off it. The irrepressible Preben Elkjær and the 'Ajax clan' of Jan Mølby, Frank Arnesen, Søren Lerby and Jesper Olsen gelled with more languid types like Søren Busk, Ivan Nielsen and Jens Jørn Bertelsen. Another player specialised in opening beer bottles with his eye sockets. 'We enjoyed each other's company even though we were completely different types,' says Busk. 'We accepted each other and we were a bunch of boys who took the piss and told jokes. There was a fantastic unity in the team.' The former Scotland striker Steve Archibald famously said that team spirit 'was an illusion glimpsed in the aftermath of victory'. He had obviously never had a night out at the Clubhouse.

The team spirit was evident in how often rivals for the same position, or spiritual opposites, shared hotel rooms. The goalkeepers regularly did so, as did Mølby and Bertelsen. Elkjær was great friends with Simonsen – one a chain talker from the big city, one a softly spoken, gentle soul from Vejle. 'Preben was the type of guy who would keep talking and tell stories,' says Busk, who later roomed with him. 'And then he needed a fag in between and I used to say, "Preben, this is the last one because we have to sleep now". "Yes, Buski, just one more story."'

Nothing demonstrated their unity quite like 'Song For Allan', the unashamedly cheesy folk song that the players sang for Simonsen on national TV. The idea came from the press officer Ahlstrøm when he found out that the team's French security guard, Charly, was an accomplished guitarist. The players had already sent flowers and a case of wine, but wanted a more human demonstration of their sympathy, respect and even love. 'He was their idol,' says Ahlstrøm.

The idea of 'Song For Allan' did not impress everybody. 'You will sing?' spluttered Piontek. 'You cannot sing!' Arnesen was a very good singer; the rest were best heard in the shower. Piontek often liked to complain in a pantomime manner. 'I knew a no from Sepp was not necessarily a no,' says Ahlstrøm. 'He always reacted that way.' Ahlstrøm wrote the song in Danish, English and French and invited a TV station to film it. The players stood in a garden behind a bed of flowers to sing the song; the natural performer Arnesen relished it the most, demonstrating some Cliff Richard-style swing kicks during the second and third chorus.

Denmark loved it and so did Piontek. 'They were prepared to make fools of themselves to show Allan they were thinking of him,' he says. 'I could see that now they were a team.' Gehrs concurs. 'It even impressed Sepp, because he realised what was the strength of this team – that they were friends, deep, deep, deep in their hearts.'

It is easy to see what Bertelsen means when he describes their performance as hopeless, but in a different sense few songs have been so full of hope and generosity of spirit. That generosity of spirit was also manifest in their dealings with the media. Very few sides have been so open. There were two main reasons for this: the players' innate personability and the work of Ahlstrøm, who was the DBU press officer and sports editor of *Politiken*. 'Can you believe that?' he says. 'It could never happen today.' Ahlstrøm later went on to be chief media officer for Uefa.

'We were very accessible to the media,' says Elkjær. 'Today it is difficult for the media to approach the players. We liked to have visitors from the press.' The players were as boyishly excited about their success as everyone else, and as such enjoyed talking about it. Ahlstrøm says the players and journalists were friends.

The mutual respect was such that the players could trust the media not to report anything too salacious or private. In France the players were available to the media for an hour each day, regularly staying beyond the allotted time if they were mid-interview. There were no velvet ropes surrounding the team.

They certainly knew how to laugh, particularly at themselves. 'Song For Allan'; Morten Olsen break-dancing during a chat show; Lerby and Jesper Olsen in tuxedos and white gloves, warbling diabolically alongside the Dutch singer Willy Alberti; Busk and his family advertising knitwear; Simonsen being shot by a sniper during a match in the film *Skytten*. They may have been superstars but they were not unreachable. They were easygoing, natural and men of the people.

They spoke the language of many people, too. Some of the players were fluent in four or five languages – Danes usually learn English and German or French in their youth – and were thus a foreign media man's dream. 'They were magnificently accessible,' says the Sky Sports commentator Martin Tyler, who was invited to join the players at Tordenskjold after the 2-2 draw against England in 1982. 'They had no fear of the media. It was hard not to be in their camp. It really tested your objectivity, because you could talk to them at any time.'

They were just as good with local fans, signing autographs with RSI-inducing enthusiasm and patience and handing out items of kit. Then there was Piontek: occasionally spiky, but for the most part honest, charismatic, holding court almost regally. 'He is a journalist's as well as a player's dream,' said David Miller in *The Times* during the 1986 World Cup. 'The man's relaxed, realistic adjustment to the demands of his job is reflected in the worldliness of his players.' Even when he was in one of his moods, he was thoroughly compelling.

Piontek was briefly in one of those moods ahead of the second game of Euro 84, against Yugoslavia in Lyon. Uefa's executive committee had rejected the DBU's request for a replacement for Simonsen. Piontek called the decision 'unfair and indecent' and threatened to pull Denmark out of the tournament. 'I wanted to rattle the old men in Uefa,' he said. 'They have to wake up.'

On the day before the game, the team bus went on a breakneck 80mph drive from the hotel in Lyon to the training ground in order to meet the precise schedule. *B.T.* reported that a lively match ensued, with Jesper Olsen – of all people – sliding into some rash tackles and Lerby reacting angrily when Richard Møller Nielsen, the under-21 coach, judged that his shot had not gone between the two jumpers that passed for goalposts: 'Are you watching at all?' screamed Lerby.

The failure to score goals, valid or otherwise, was on Danish minds before the game. The press highlighted their recent drought, with only three in six games in 1984. 'I wish there was a bit more co-operation between Preben Elkjær and Michael Laudrup,' said Piontek, 'but I will not try to change Preben Elkjær's style of play, because that will break his rhythm, and we can't afford that.'

The ability to stop goals was an issue, too. Ole Qvist badly bruised his thumb during a mock fight in training, Ole Kjær had an argument with Arnesen that almost boiled over, and Troels Rasmussen had still not recovered from his pre-tournament injury.

The other Rasmussen, Ole, was brought in for the injured Simonsen to give extra support against the magnificent Safet Sušic. Simonsen was not in the team but they were still on his mind, and he on theirs. 'I hope they will get a telegram from me today,' he said in a column for *B.T.* 'I would have sent it two days ago but I was so tired and sad that I fell asleep.' The hospital had to lock the door to ward number eight, such were the numbers of people wanting to visit Simonsen. 'I hope you all understand this, as I need a bit of quiet,' he wrote on the note that was put on the door of the ward.

Denmark met Yugoslavia on a boiling Saturday evening in Lyon. Ib, Søren and Jan brought two cases of Kronenbourg into the match; the beers almost fermented in the heat. Yugoslavia had also lost their first game, 2-0 to Belgium. Denmark knew a second defeat would take their destiny out of their own hands. They were nonetheless relaxed before kick-off, with Laudrup, Elkjær and Bertelsen idly playing keepy-uppy in the centre circle before the game. There was nothing so languid once the game started; the pace was demented and unrelenting.

The Danes put on what was almost an Allan Simonsen memorial performance, a 5-0 victory that was their first at a European Championship or World Cup. It wasn't as one-sided as the score suggests; the goalkeeper Qvist was one of Denmark's best players and was applauded into the dressing room after the game. The match was so open that it might have come from the 1950s. Had all the clear chances on both sides been taken, it would have finished 14-7 to Denmark.

Denmark took the lead in the eighth minute when Arnesen beat Ljubomir Radanović and put in a cross that was fumbled into his own net by the goalkeeper Tomislav Ivković. The goal was nonetheless credited to Arnesen. It was a cathartic moment for a player who had had such severe injury problems that he played only two minutes for Denmark between May 1982 and May 1984.

Injury problems were a recurring theme of Arnesen's career, but he still played fifty-two times for his country. As a winger he beat defenders with an urgent, pitter-pattering run and an array of unusual tricks; he was equally effective as a playmaker and performed with the authority of somebody who had no doubt as to how good he was.

Lerby was blessed with similar conviction. With Yugoslavia consistently troubling Denmark down the right after Arnesen's goal, Lerby took matters into his own hands. He shouted at the left-back Ole Rasmussen, waved him to the other side of the field and then decided to take care of Denmark's left flank himself.

Even Lerby relaxed a little when Denmark went 2-0 up in the sixteenth minute. Elkjær set off on a storming forty-yard run down the left before coaxing a near-post cross towards Laudrup.

He flicked the ball deftly on the volley over the advancing goalkeeper with the outside of his foot, and although it was going in anyway Berggreen ran the ball into the net from a yard out. Those two celebrated this goal together; the rest of the team ran straight to the man who had made it, Elkjær.

Yugoslavia were so overwhelmed in midfield that their manager Todor Veselinović substituted an exasperated Mehmed Bazdarević after twenty-three minutes. It was partially successful: Yugoslavia could not stop the stream of Denmark chances, but they managed to create plenty of their own. Qvist made four point-blank saves, including two in thirty seconds from Zlatko Vujović in the second half. Denmark could certainly not feel safe at 2-0. They had a number of chances to extend the lead before Arnesen did so from the penalty spot after a foul by Ivan Gudelj on Laudrup. Denmark, lost in the sheer fun of the match, had no inclination to declare at 3-0.

For all their individual talent, Denmark had a glittering portfolio of team goals throughout the 1980s. The best might have been the one that put them 4-0 up against Yugoslavia. Morten Olsen scooped a nonchalant pass to Elkjær, who beat a man and played in Berggreen on the right. He crossed to Laudrup, who controlled the ball and then carefully, almost lovingly, teed up Elkjær to place a first-time shot into the net. This was the co-operation that Piontek wanted from his two strikers.

The fifth goal, two minutes later, came from the substitute John Lauridsen, who placed a superb curler into the far corner from twenty yards before running over to celebrate pointedly in front of Piontek. In a different era Lauridsen would have been a regular. He was the darling of his Spanish club Espanyol, where he played for six years and won the Uefa Cup. He is still nicknamed Señor and retains a Spanish twang in his accent.

There were six minutes remaining after Lauridsen had put Denmark 5-0 ahead. In that time they could easily have scored three more. Busk thumped an immense header just wide from the left side of the box, Laudrup overhit a cross to Elkjær, who would have had a tap-in, and then played a delicious scooped-through pass to Berggreen, who missed another great chance. It was one of the first sightings of a skill that would become Laudrup's trademark.

Piontek was so thrilled after the match that he gave the translator the night off and addressed the press in Danish, German, English and French. It was not such a pleasurable experience for the Yugoslav manager Veselinović, who was admitted to hospital suffering from stress after the match. 'He could not endure what was happening on the pitch,' said the team doctor.

At the hospital in Aarhus, Simonsen needed an injection after instinctively kicking every ball during the game. Lyon was certainly alive and kicking after the game. An entire street of bars ran out of beer, so the *roligans* broke the habit of a lifetime by drinking wine.

Denmark's win equalled the biggest margin of victory in the European Championship. There have been four five-goal victories in over fifty years. Two of them came on the same day; that afternoon France had thumped Belgium 5-0. It should be remembered as one of the defining matches of the era, yet it has been relegated to the second tier for one simple reason. An even more memorable match took place three days later.

Chapter 9

'If I had a gun ...'

Economics may have turned Anderlecht into Champions League group stage cannon fodder now but back in the mists of time they were one of the best teams in Europe. They reached three European Cup Winners' Cup finals at the end of the seventies, winning two and also landing two European Super Cups. In the eighties they switched their sights to the Uefa Cup, winning it in 1983 and narrowly missing out on retaining it just prior to Euro 84 with a penalty shootout defeat against Tottenham Hotspur. The bulk of the team were Belgian internationals, topped off with a select group of Danish stars known as the Anderlecht Five – two rising young players, Per Frimann and Henrik Andersen, who were not yet developed enough to make the Denmark squad; Kenneth Brylle, a forward who scored in the 1983 final; Frank Arnesen, newly arrived from Valencia; and Morten Olsen, the captain and sweeper.

There have been many international teams composed almost entirely of players from a dominant side within its own country but no club had ever imposed such an influence on two opposing sides as Anderlecht did when Belgium met Denmark to decide which team would qualify for the semi-finals along with France. There were eight Anderlecht players in the Belgian squad. Six of them – Georges Grun, Frank Vercauteren, René Vandereycken, Erwin Vandenbergh, Walter De Greef and Enzo Scifo – were in the starting line-up to play Denmark. The rest of the Belgian team was drawn from the Jupiler League, and Denmark's XI also included Preben Elkjær, Søren Busk and Jens Jørn Bertelsen, all based in Belgium. The mystique of the unknown that usually accompanied international football was nowhere to be seen. Familiarity overshadowed the game; the contempt was in the post.

The match had been a topic of much discussion in the Anderlecht dressing room since the draw was made. As the game approached, the kidding stopped. 'It's amusing right now, but I doubt that any of us think that it is amusing when it gets serious,' Olsen told *Alt om Sport* prior to the tournament. 'It can't be very nice having to battle against your club mates for something as attractive as the European Championship. Think about how good our relationship is with each other day in and day out.' Elkjær, reflecting on the match, puts it more succinctly: 'You just can't lose a game like that.'

Belgium, as their recent international form suggested, were tough opposition. In 1980 they reached the final of the European Championship, only losing to West Germany in the dying seconds. Although they went out in the second round of the 1982 World Cup they caused a sensation in the opening match by beating the defending champions Argentina. Belgium had uncovered their own golden generation of players who had been expertly moulded into a force under the long-term stewardship of Guy Thys. Their results at Euro 84 had mirrored Denmark's up to this point. They had beaten Yugoslavia and lost to France, but Belgium's victory over Yugoslavia was not as emphatic as Denmark's. More damagingly, while Platini was largely kept on the leash by Berggreen he ran riot against Belgium in Nantes, scoring a hat-trick in France's 5-0 victory. He would ultimately score another hat-trick against Yugoslavia to win the group for France, so the game between Denmark and Belgium was for second spot.

With goal difference heavily in their favour, Denmark only needed to draw to advance. The fact that they were in uncharted waters was not lost on the Belgian players. 'The Danish players will be exposed to a physical and mental pressure that they haven't experienced before and there is no guarantee they can handle it,' warned Vercauteren ahead of the match. The game would take place in Strasbourg in the Alsace region of France, a territory fought over by and divided up between the various imperial rivals of Europe for centuries – quite an appropriate location given what would follow. Denmark went into the game unchanged from the Yugoslavia match. With the sun going down, the game kicked off.

Before long, it all kicked off.

So who does start a riot? When it's an angry, faceless mob involved it's always impossible to tell; when there are twenty-two footballers with numbers on their backs it's a little more obvious. The first foul of the game after thirteen seconds was innocuous enough, but the second one really put the heat into the evening. Elkjær was visibly worked up for this one. Charging around the pitch like a particularly incensed bull in the first minute, he caught Vandereycken with a stray arm and the two immediately squared up to each other. Vandereycken, with a combustible temper never far from the surface, was off, and packed an impressive amount of hard-man posturing into the opening seven minutes. After his contretemps with Elkjær he went in late on Søren Lerby and fronted up to him. He then switched his sights to the much less menacing target of Michael Laudrup. Vandereycken planted the full set of studs of one boot on Laudrup's shin and then had a wild hack at him moments later. The referee disciplined no one and the mood was set.

One man was not surprised at how the match played out. Frimann, who had missed out on Denmark's squad while recovering from injury, watched the game at his brother's house. He did not just see the aggression coming – he had seen it before in training. 'I expected it to be a little bit nasty,' he says. 'The culture and mentality at Anderlecht were that you played really hard in training

– we had a very good training team. It should be tough and it was tough, so I was not shocked. We had our share of fights in training. That Anderlecht team was very competitive and had the sort of winning mentality I had never experienced in my career before. And everything started with the training.' It was business as usual when the players arrived back for the new season at Anderlecht a month later. 'People liked the idea of conflict,' says Frimann, 'and that the dressing room would be a disaster. But it was okay.'

When any match descends into a brawl any chance of a decent game of football usually goes out of the window. Almost all of the famous dust-ups of the international game – the Battle of Santiago in 1962, or the 2010 World Cup final in particular – stunk the place out as football matches. That wasn't the case here; after a particularly brutal opening the game morphed into one of the greatest in the history of the European Championship. A genuinely brilliant football match and a stripped-to-the-waist set-to were gloriously entwined. As the saying goes, in the middle of it all a football match broke out. And what a match.

Denmark, clearly nervous in the opening exchanges, could be forgiven for thinking that this wouldn't be their night. Within a minute both Elkjær and Arnesen had decent shouts for a penalty turned down. Elkjær's was the clearest – he was fouled by the Belgium goalkeeper Jean-Marie Pfaff, who then gave him an earful and suggested he had dived. Their relationship already had a back story: Pfaff played for Lokeren's hated local rivals Beveren and their previous exchanges at club level had not exactly been Christmas cards. Belgium rubbed salt in the wounds with two brilliant goals. Firstly, a pirouetting half-volley by Jan Ceulemans put Belgium ahead. Soon afterwards a thunderous long-range thump from Vercauteren flew over a flailing and powerless Ole Qvist with numbing certainty.

As Belgium had a two-goal lead, carte blanche to be as savage as necessary and the safety net of endlessly passing the ball back to Pfaff as an option, it looked a monumental task for Denmark to recover the situation. The players had to stand up and be counted, and one by one they did. In such circumstances it's often vital to hit back immediately. Within a minute of Vercauteren's goal, Laudrup released Elkjær into the area. Cutting back on to his right foot, he crumpled under the mildest of challenges and the referee awarded a penalty. It was Andrex-soft and in the post-match interviews Pfaff complained to Danish reporters that Elkjær was the world's biggest actor. Given the ones not awarded earlier in the game, no one in red cared. Arnesen thumped it in with some venom to give the Danes a lifeline going into half-time.

Next up to the plate was Qvist. His air of calm certainty came in handy straight after half-time, as Vandenbergh broke Denmark's high offside line to go through one on one. In this game of chicken he waited and waited and Vandenbergh flinched, shooting low to the right. An instinctive save by Qvist with his foot prevented a certain goal.

Sepp Piontek decided with half an hour left that he had to go for it. In a move that would prove to be the same ace he held up his sleeve throughout the time he managed Denmark, he took off a full-back to put on a forward, with Ole Rasmussen making way for Brylle. It was an instant success.

Later in life Brylle acquired Belgian nationality and in Strasbourg he bit the hand that would later feed him. With his first touch of the game – and his first in a major tournament – he headed an Arnesen cross into an unguarded goal, bringing Denmark level and, more importantly, putting them in the semi-finals as things stood. Arnesen was having a great game, torturing some of his Anderlecht colleagues with his dribbling. Vandereycken was Arnesen's room-mate at Anderlecht and had urged him to get fit in time for the tournament. Now he tried to remove him from it.

On the right touchline Arnesen received the ball, clocked that Vandereycken was approaching fast and took evasive action.

Vanderycken had decided he was going to get something in this tackle, though, and clobbered Arnesen on the same knee that had sidelined him for such lengthy spells and on which he had, as everyone at Anderlecht well knew, recently had two operations. 'I guess he had become tired of me running past him all the time,' Arnesen later told *Tipsbladet*. It was a dreadful foul, born purely of frustration, and all the aggression that had simmered through the game suddenly came to the boil. Lerby and Ivan Nielsen made a beeline for Vandereycken to share their thoughts with him but there was general astonishment at which man got his retaliation in first.

'In this kind of game you are not friends any more,' says Morten Olsen. Although on good terms with Vandereycken, he went crazy at him. Olsen sprinted thirty yards to get in his face and shove him to the floor, before gesticulating wildly at the prone midfielder about just what the hell he was thinking. This was no minimal contact followed by a RADA-style audition that you see today. Vandereycken was genuinely bounced away from the incident like a Wild West drunk being hurled through the saloon bar doors. 'If I had a gun,' Olsen said in the documentary *Og Det Var Danmark* (And it was Denmark), 'I'd have shot him.'

The reaction still surprises Olsen. 'Nowadays I would surely get a red card,' he reflects. 'It was a human reaction.' That one of the game's abiding gentlemen lost it so spectacularly said everything about the match, and also revealed a hidden and rarely spoken truth about the team. Affable everymen and media-friendly they may have been, but these were serious professionals with spines of titanium. If you thought you could bully this team off the park you were dreaming.

While heads were going on the Belgian side, all the Danes needed to do was keep theirs to make the semi-finals. Vandereycken dumped Arnesen again and Scifo threw the ball at him, but the Danes refused to react. The final twenty minutes were played out in an almost suffocating pressure. The *roligans*, with a near monopoly of the tickets in Strasbourg, were deafening in willing their team to the finish line. The Belgians pushed on, becoming more and more desperate, but could not create a clear chance. In the eighty-fourth minute Nielsen won yet another header on the edge of the Danish area and sent the ball twenty-five yards to Elkjær. A game dominated by players from Anderlecht would now be settled by one from Lokeren.

From his own half Elkjær turned and assessed the Belgian defence. His intent was clear; he would simply run through whatever was in front of him. Laudrup was with him but Elkjær was oblivious, and as a gap opened up between Leo Clijsters and de Greef he hammered on the accelerator. Clijsters got a toe to the ball and it ricocheted off de Greef, but Elkjær got it back under control and nutmegged de Greef to put himself clean through on Pfaff. Where Vandenbergh had flinched in a similar situation, Elkjær was coolness incarnate, caressing a gentle chip over Pfaff and into the net.

Pfaff booted Elkjær high on the thigh as he went past. Elkjær could hardly have cared less: he ran off and celebrated with an unorthodox, clumsy forward roll, joy plastered all over his face. There was enough adrenaline coursing through him to override any pain. 'Unbelievable!' cried Svend Gehrs in the commentary box. 'That man is fantastic!'

When Elkjær jogged back to the centre circle the pain kicked in. 'In the moment he did not realise what had happened,' Piontek says. 'But then after the big celebration he was "Aargh! My leg, my leg!" He had five stud marks in his leg from Pfaff. I said, "You have to move. If you stop it will get worse." Then a few minutes later the game was over. That goal was world-class, fantastic.' Belgium were spent, and when Scifo blasted a shot over the bar near the end Lerby punched the air towards his own bench in celebration.

The referee blew the final whistle soon after and the game was over – 3-2 to Denmark, who were now in the semi-finals. No side has ever come from further behind to win a match at the European Championship. Four days earlier, Denmark had equalled the biggest margin of victory at the tournament when they pummelled Yugoslavia, a record that still stands. Records were falling to Denmark and fans in Europe were falling for them. In Denmark, unconditional love had long since been established. At the final whistle, Gehrs captured the charm of the Denmark team and the mood of the Danish nation when he spoke of 'this team of super indomitable optimists'. The physical and emotional strain of the match was such that most of the players were too shattered to wheel themselves out in front of the media. Only Jens Jørn Bertelsen was able to push himself through it. 'I thought people went at it a bit too hard occasionally,' he told Gehrs. 'It was definitely not a friendly, if you could have expected that between two teams who knew each other so well.'

In mid-flow Bertelsen stopped the interview to send a message back home. 'There is something that falls close to my heart, which is that we miss one of our steady guys down here and we think a lot about him at home – about wee Allan who I'm absolutely sure would have loved to have been here. We send our regards to him.' Gehrs joked that Allan had probably poured himself a decent glass of wine on his sickbed to celebrate. 'I think he should do that because he has been part of this,' said Bertelsen. 'And I also think we'll do that tonight.' Wouldn't they just.

Accounts vary as to what happened next, as tends to be the way when substantial quantities of drink are consumed, but one thing we know for certain is that the players were given the evening off after the match to unwind at the hotel. The players happily mingled with the fans there – Ib Thage and his travelling companions enjoyed drinks with their heroes while Arnesen sat at the bar, strumming away on a guitar to entertain everyone. With a 5 a.m. curfew set by Piontek, their scheduled breakfast was pushed back until midday and lunch served at five in the afternoon.

The story of the 'third half' was leaked in *L'Equipe*, to Piontek's chagrin, but he did not deny it. 'There is no point in sending the players to bed at 1 a.m. after such a big game, than rather, say, 5 a.m.,' he told reporters. 'That's fine by me. It's also okay if they drink five, ten or fifteen beers and smoke some cigarettes. The players just have to keep the agreements. And if that means breakfast at eleven, then they have to show up. And they did. What's upsetting me is that foreign journalists are snooping around our hotel and searching for "scandals".'

Some would say a fountain of ale would be the last thing a professional footballer needed after such a match, though if you'd lived on your nerves for the entirety of those ninety minutes in Strasbourg you might think it was the first thing required. If ever there was an occasion where a Danish international side had earned a third half, this was surely it.

The afternoon after the night before, with Danish players nursing sore heads and digesting a very late lunch, thoughts turned to who would be their semi-final opponents. Group A had been a box of fireworks in terms of goals and entertainment but Group B, contested by West Germany, Romania, Portugal and Spain, was a far more prosaic affair. Denmark would have to face the group winners, and as the clock ticked down to the last ten minutes in both the goalless West Germany versus Spain and Portugal versus Romania matches, the equation was simple – West Germany were top with four points, Spain were through on goal difference even though they were level on three points with Portugal, and Romania were bottom of the group on one point. As things stood, it looked as if Piontek was guaranteed a chance to prove himself against the country of his birth.

It was a daunting prospect. Not only were West Germany the reigning European champions but they had reached the final in five of the last six international tournaments they had contested. Their biennial knack of turning in superhuman performances at the big summer tournaments was legendary. The 1984 incarnation wasn't a classic West German side but that scarcely ever seemed to matter. They were the bête noire of the beautiful team – Hungary 1954, Holland 1974, France 1982 – and now Denmark were in their sights.

Then things changed. In Nantes, Portugal suddenly took the lead to leave the prospect of drawing lots with West Germany for the group leadership. Spain, now on their way out, had to gamble everything. They sent their giant centre-back Antonio Maceda into the attack for the final few seconds, and launched a hopeful cross into the penalty area. Maceda connected perfectly to send a flying header through Harald Schumacher for a goal that shook the Continent. There was no time to respond. From nowhere, Spain had won the group, Portugal were second and West Germany were out.

The tournament was blown wide open. Some big teams had failed even to qualify – Italy, USSR, Holland, England – and now the defending champions were gone. Piontek's date with West Germany would have to wait. Instead it would be Spain in Lyon. A nemesis had entered the fairy tale.

Chapter 10

The first time

Modern football is a simple game. Twenty-two men chase a ball for ninety minutes, and in the end Spain win. It was not always thus. Before their breakthrough at Euro 2008, Spain were, along with England, the biggest joke among the major football nations. At every tournament they would be touted as dark horses; almost every time they would fall at the first significant hurdle.

In the forty-four years between winning Euro 64 and Euro 2008 they won just four knockout games at European Championships and World Cups. Two of those were against Denmark. Since their meeting in the semi-final of Euro 84, Denmark have played Spain eleven times, losing eight – and a ninth on penalties – and winning only one. 'Spanish football has given me so much in terms of club level and what I became,' says Michael Laudrup, who starred for both Barcelona and Real Madrid, 'and it has taken so much from me with the national team.'

When Denmark meet Spain nowadays, the whole country assumes the position behind the sofa. Yet in 1984, they were thrilled to be meeting in the semi-finals. Spain were more renowned for thuggery than tiki-taka; their side included Andoni Goikoetxea, known as the Butcher of Bilbao, who broke Diego Maradona's ankle and then put the offending boot on display at his house in a glass case.

Spain were fortunate even to be at Euro 84. In their final qualifying game they needed to beat Malta by eleven goals to qualify ahead of Holland. Incredibly, they won 12-1, with nine of those goals in the second half. Denmark lost the friendly in Valencia two months before the tournament, but that team contained only five of the XI who would start in Lyon. With a full-strength side, and all things being equal, they would beat Spain.

'Now we are in the final!' read the front page of *B.T.* three days before the match. 'Spanish international football,' said Morten Olsen in the same paper, 'has rarely had much to offer in the big tournaments.' This was not just the Danish view. In England, *The Times* match preview said: 'By the end of the weekend, Europe should have the final it has always desired – France v Denmark. It is highly unlikely that even a better Spain would remotely trouble Denmark, who are a frightening force.'

The superstitious watched the draw to see who would wear their home kit. Spain won, which meant Denmark would have to play in white. They had not lost in red throughout qualification for the Euros or at the tournament itself; they had not won in white for almost two years.

Denmark had a number of injury concerns after the bruising contest with Belgium. Morten Olsen had problems with his lip, groin, leg and elbow. Frank Arnesen's knee was still troubled by the kick from René Vandereycken, while Preben Elkjær had a thigh strain. A first European Championship semi-final was not the kind of game where you gave your excuses to the manager, however, and they would all start. As would Michael Laudrup, who had to miss the family's midsummer bonfire party. Elkjær decided not to interrupt his preparation by flying home for the funeral of his grandfather, whose death he had not been told about until his wife Nicole came to the dressing room after the Belgium game.

Piontek made one change from that match, bringing the twenty-two-year-old John Sivebæk in to replace Ole Rasmussen, almost ten years his senior, on the right. Sivebæk was the only Dane to play in the European Championship in both 1984 and 1992, a dynamic wing-back and one of the quiet achievers of the team. He went on to win more Danish caps than anybody bar Morten Olsen and Michael Laudrup and spent a year at Manchester United. During Euro 84 he was still at Vejle, one of only six home-based players in the squad.

Denmark's start to the match was such that they could have been forgiven for thinking fate was on their side. Their first attack, in the sixth minute, led to a goal from Søren Lerby. Arnesen clipped a flat cross towards Elkjær on the penalty spot; he strained his neck muscles to flick a superb header on to the crossbar and Lerby rammed in the rebound with glee.

Denmark might have gone 2-0 up a few minutes later when Arnesen was taken down in the penalty area by Julio Alberto. The referee, George Courtney, gave nothing. It was a weirdly recurring theme of Arnesen's Denmark career; a clear foul in the area, sweet FA from the referee. A few minutes later Arnesen's chipped backpass, lofted breezily over the head of the striker Santillana, reflected his and Denmark's confidence.

The first half was largely uneventful thereafter, with only a dramatic early save by Ole Qvist from Francisco José Carrasco worth discussing at half-time. The first and second halves made chalk and cheese seem like siblings. After the break there were a series of great chances at both ends. Denmark could have secured a place in the final before the hour. Arnesen hit the post; Lerby hit a tired shot at Luis Arconada after marauding through the defence; Arconada made a superb double save, first from Elkjær and then from a deflection off Antonio Maceda; and fourteen seconds later, after an insouciant square chip by Arnesen on the left wing, Lerby lashed a shot fractionally wide.

Then it was Spain's turn. When the Danish offside trap failed and Señor ran through on goal, Qvist charged from his line to make an outstanding save, almost identical to the one he had made at a similar stage against Belgium. His performances in particular are a compelling response to the argument that, had Peter Schmeichel been born ten years earlier, Denmark would have won a major tournament. 'At Euro 84 we had a fantastic goalkeeper, maybe the best in the tournament,' says Elkjær. 'Ole Qvist was unbelievable. I wouldn't say we failed to win anything because of our goalkeepers.'

One of the reasons they didn't win Euro 84 was Spain's clever use of substitutes. They had an uncapped twenty-year-old Emilio Butragueño on the bench, but went with the dangerous, leggy forward Manuel Sarabia, who was used as an impact substitute throughout the tournament. Within a minute of coming on, his cross was flicked wide from four yards by Santillana. In the sixty-seventh minute Sarabia slithered through the Danish defence before driving a shot against the post. For the next ten seconds Denmark were hanging on for dear life until Søren Busk's desperate tackle deflected the ball to Spain's unlikely goalscoring hero, Maceda. He slammed it into the corner.

There was a brief lull as both teams adjusted to the changing circumstances; then, in the last six minutes of normal time, Denmark had four great opportunities to reach the final. Elkjær, eight yards out, stabbed just over on the turn after a fine run from the substitute Jesper Olsen. Elkjær then sliced a shot wide after a storming run infield from the right, and had another shot blocked desperately by Salvador García. In the final minute, the increasingly brilliant Laudrup shimmered infield from the left and hit a long-range shot that was wonderfully saved by Arconada, sprawling to his left. The resulting corner ended with a desperate scramble yards from goal. 'We were the better team,' says Jens Jørn Bertelsen. 'We had loads of chances.'

At the start of extra-time, a tired slip from Ivan Nielsen allowed Santillana through on goal, and Qvist roared off his line to make an even better save than the first. Lerby gave himself cramp by running three-quarters of the length of the field to deny Carrasco a certain goal after another dangerous run from Sarabia. At the other end a cross from Sivebæk was headed towards the far post by Klaus Berggreen. As the ball bounced up both Elkjær and Arconada went for it with a flying kick. Elkjær got there a fraction before the keeper, who blocked his shot. Both followed through into each other. Arconada needed treatment; Elkjær's shorts were ripped at the back. 'I had some very big stripes on my bum after the game,' says Elkjær. As if the brutish treatment of man-markers was not enough in the 1980s, Elkjær also received stud marks from goalkeepers in consecutive games.

Elkjær had been booked earlier in the game. *The Times* called referee Courtney's performance 'a traffic-warden's orgy': he showed nine yellow cards – there had been only two in the Belgium match – even though there were no particularly malicious tackles by the standards of the day. Jesper Olsen, Maceda and Rafael Gordillo all received cards that ruled them out of a potential final. So did Berggreen: he received two yellow cards for pulling back players, the second right at the start of the second period of extra-time to reduce Denmark to ten men. It was at best a pedantic decision; a nonplussed Berggreen took almost a minute to leave the field. His disappointment at being banned from a possible final was tinged with relief that he would not have to take a penalty if it went to a shootout.

It shouldn't have gone that far. Elkjær's low free-kick was saved by Arconada, who got straight to his feet to dive in the other direction and make an outrageous save from Nielsen's follow-up. Nielsen walked away with his hands over his mouth, his knees buckling in disbelief.

Even with ten men, Denmark pushed for the win. When the sweeper Morten Olsen went off injured with seven minutes to go, he was replaced by a striker, Kenneth Brylle. It was a dual-purpose substitution: to win the game in extra-time or to have an expert penalty taker on the pitch. Lerby dropped into defence like a mother protecting her cubs. The game went to penalties.

There had been no practice in training from Denmark. At that time there had only ever been three penalty shootouts in the World Cup, Copa America and European Championship combined; they were a sufficiently rare occurrence that they did not occupy pre-match thoughts as they do nowadays. Jesper Olsen, Brylle, Lerby and Laudrup agreed to take penalties, but none wanted to take the fifth kick. 'I had only Preben Elkjær,' says Piontek. 'I said, "Preben, you have to take number five." "Yes! No problem. I'll take all five!"'

The first four penalties were scored comfortably by Brylle, Santillana, Olsen and Señor. Then it was the turn of Laudrup. He had taken penalties before, but 'never in that way'. Even for the world's most talented twenty-year-old footballer, it was scary stuff. He decided to change sides as he walked from the centre circle, something he vowed never to do again after his kick was saved by Arconada. He was given another chance when Courtney ordered a retake because Arconada had twitched a muscle before the kick was taken. It was a technically correct but ridiculously officious decision.

Now Laudrup had to decide what to do with his second chance. He theorised that Arconada would think that, because of his inexperience, he would change sides. So he went to the same side and scored. As did Santiago Urquiaga, Lerby – who thrashed a ludicrously unsaveable penalty into the top corner – and Victor.

At 4-4 it was the turn of Elkjær. He strolled towards the penalty spot like a man popping out for a pint of milk. 'I had never missed a penalty, I'd scored eight for my club,' he says. 'No, no problem. But of course it's a big responsibility. You are a young man and you know all of your nation is watching and hoping. But I was not particularly nervous.'

As Elkjær shaped to shoot to his right, his peripheral vision spotted Arconada moving the same way. It was too late to change sides, so Elkjær adjusted his shot. 'That's why I put it a little further and a little bit higher,' Elkjær laughs. 'And it was too high.' He passed the ball over the bar. Three decades on Laudrup, Lauridsen and Ole Kjær independently make the same joke. 'They are still looking for the ball.'

Qvist ran straight over to Elkjær and promised he would save the next penalty to keep Denmark in the tournament. Elkjær trudged back to the centre circle, his bare backside visible after the earlier clash with Arconada. He was used to showing his cheek, but not like this.

Clothing was also a concern for Sarabia, the man who was to take Spain's fifth penalty. He was so nervous that he got to the penalty area before realising he still had his tracksuit top on. Qvist had plenty of time to consider how precisely he would make good his promise to Elkjær. But Ole couldn't stop the olés; Sarabia rammed the penalty into the corner. Qvist had made so many one-on-one saves in open play during the tournament, but he could not win the formalised one-to-one contest. 'I was never very good at penalties,' he says. Denmark were out. Spain had only led their opponents in the tournament for fourteen out of 390 minutes; all that mattered was that they were in the final.

After the game Elkjær was cornered by sympathetic Danish journalists and scarely had room to light his cigarette. It was a devastating blow to Denmark – one fan threw his TV out of a third-floor window – but not everyone was exactly shattered by the defeat. 'In many ways we are happy not to be in the final,' Carl Nielsen, the head of the DBU, told the *Daily Telegraph*. 'We would rather be remembered for the exciting finish to our game against Spain than for a poor performance with a below-strength team watched by millions.'

Piontek was thinking in Danish after the game. 'We should be happy we didn't reach that final,' he told *Aktuelt*. 'After two hours of a gruelling semi-final, and with a team that was already more tired than the opponent, it could have been the big collapse.' Lerby, by contrast, was furious with suggestions that it was best Denmark didn't make the final.

They would have been without the suspended Jesper Olsen and Berggreen, and also the injured Morten Olsen. They would have needed somebody to mark Platini. But France had only beaten Portugal in the last minute of extra-time in their semi-final, and perhaps peaked in the group stage. They went on to beat Spain 2-0 in the final, but it was a nervy game.

Time has made the near-miss even more acute. Three decades on, Laudrup, Busk, Gehrs and even Piontek all agree that this was the one that got away. 'I think we were better than Spain that night,' says Laudrup. 'France looked tired in the semi-final against Portugal and they were a little lucky with the first goal in the final. Yes, I think we could have been European champions in 1984.'

A weary team went back to the hotel to reflect on all they had achieved in a life-changing fortnight in France. 'We couldn't get really drunk,' said Arnesen in the book *Vejen til Mexico*. 'We couldn't at all. We tried to sing a bit once in a while but not a damn thing happened.'

Some went down to mix with a group of Danish fans camping outside the hotel. The players were less comfortable with the idea of a party upon returning home. A horse-drawn carriage ride through Copenhagen's pedestrian street and a reception at Carlsberg had been planned. 'Now the party is over,' said Morten Olsen. 'We can't take any more. I sincerely hope that people will respect that.' The public gives what the public wants, however, and although there was no Carlsberg reception the team were greeted by three thousand people at the airport. It took Laudrup fifteen minutes to get from customs to a Jaguar waiting for him outside. The players received one last souvenir of their summer romance: a girl in the north of Denmark lovingly prepared 200-page albums of newspaper cuttings for each of the twenty-man squad and sent them to the DBU after the tournament. In the nicest possible way, the players were now public property.

Chapter 11

Poster boys

One day in Copenhagen, some graffiti appeared posing the question: 'What if Jesus comes back?' Before long, the obvious response was scrawled underneath: 'We'll just move Elkjær out wide.' Preben Elkjær's European Championship ended in personal disappointment but the euphoria of the experience as a whole created a new era of optimism and interest in Danish football. No one embodied this quite like Elkjær.

As a youth player Elkjær wore free boots supplied by Patrick but later switched to Nike. As his fame grew, Elkjær became the poster boy for Nike in Denmark, and at their behest travelled to a factory in England to help develop new ranges of boots. They had little experience in making boots up to this point and in the meantime Elkjær had someone paint the famous swoosh over the top of other manufacturers' versions. Other endorsements followed and in one magazine advertisement he seemed to be attempting a product placement world record by sitting on a Mustang outside Burger King, in a pair of Nike trainers, advertising Toms Chokolade.

There was also media work and in addition to columns for the magazine *Billed-Bladet* and the newspaper *Ekstra Bladet* he also had a stint writing for the pornographic magazine *Ugens Rapport*, a sideline as bizarre then as it would be now. Elkjær embodied the rising confidence of Danish football and a career that had once threatened to get away from him was now flying. He had an amazing spell at Lokeren, where he became an instant hero. He scored a hat-trick on his debut in the Belgian Cup to turn a 3-0 deficit into a 5-3 victory and in the two years leading up to the European Championship he scored four times in a game on four separate occasions. Elkjær wasn't enamoured with all aspects of his burgeoning fame. He told *Alt om Sport* that he was worried his rising profile might make him a target for burglars. After a spate of robberies near his home he decided to sleep with a shotgun next to the bed to protect himself and Nicole. 'Should there be a mysterious rumbling at night-time, I will be there with the loaded shotgun,' he said.

His performances in France introduced him to the world. It became abundantly clear during Euro 84 that Lokeren couldn't possibly hang on to him any longer and that Elkjær – like several of his team-mates – would be on the move.

For Jens Jørn Bertelsen there was little other choice. His club, FC Seraing in Belgium, were on the point of bankruptcy. In keeping with his low profile he transferred to FC Rouen to spend a season in a doomed fight against relegation in France's Championnat, and his inter-railing around Europe's smaller clubs would continue in 1985–6 when he moved on to FC Aarau in Switzerland. It's an anomaly that Bertelsen was considered indispensable by his team-mates and Piontek yet crept under the radar of all the big European clubs. Perhaps he went abroad too late – he was thirty before he arrived in Belgium – but like Morten Olsen he was enjoying an Indian summer to his career.

It wasn't hard to notice Jan Mølby, a huge presence in the Ajax midfield. Although there were several roadblocks to his route into the Denmark team his abilities had not gone unnoticed at Liverpool. The European and English champions were left with a considerable gap to plug in their midfield when Graeme Souness left for Sampdoria in the summer of 1984. They contacted Mølby for a week of trials in August; it was perfectly timed as he had just fallen out with the coach at Ajax. Liverpool liked what they saw and Mølby signed a three-year contract, which they rushed to the Football League in a taxi to register him in time for the opening game of the season at Norwich City. Rooming with Kenny Dalglish, language was initially a problem. 'He was very friendly even if it was a bit hard understanding his distinct Scottish accent,' Mølby told *Alt om Sport*. Mølby was much more accommodating with making his own accent understandable in his new home, famously developing a unique hybrid of Danish and Scouse dialects to the amusement of fans everywhere.

The standard of his football was not to be sniggered at, and in the 1985–6 season he was a key figure in Liverpool's only Double. Despite his success on Merseyside, Mølby's international career never truly got going. He took Bertelsen's place for a brief spell in the year before the Mexico World Cup, and Piontek considered him as an option to cover for and eventually replace Morten Olsen as sweeper.

The trail from Amsterdam to the north-west of England had been blazed earlier that summer when Jesper Olsen, in one of the high-profile transfers of the close season, signed for the comatose giants of English football, Manchester United. This had rumbled on through the entirety of Euro 84, with United waiting to see if Olsen's ankle would hold up after all of his problems earlier in the year. Ron Atkinson had found out he was a United fan and met him at Amsterdam airport at the conclusion of Euro 84 to discuss the transfer. With professionalism paramount in pulling off what was something of a coup given Olsen's reputation, Atkinson walked into the meeting flying low. 'It was embarrassing,' Atkinson would later tell *Alt om Sport*, 'but I stretched out my hand to Jesper and said: "You are welcome in Manchester. We don't pay that much but we have a great time."' The sum of £350,000 changed hands and Olsen entered the rough-and-tumble world of English football.

'It was very different from what I was used to with Ajax,' Olsen remembers. 'The English have a lot more games, high balls and a different way of playing, and they didn't have as many foreigners in the UK at that time. It was difficult to adjust in some ways but I learned a lot in other ways.' In his first season Olsen won the FA Cup, the first Dane ever to complete that particular dream of schoolboys and lovers of English football in Denmark.

The biggest transfer of a Danish player that summer was conducted at the European Championship. In the wee hours after the Belgium game, with all manner of officious characters patrolling the hotel corridors and making arrangements, Elkjær's future was decided. As a child he had holidayed in Italy several times and now an extended visit was on the way. He was recruited to add a dash of foreign glamour to Hellas Verona, a small club in a northern Italian city more synonymous with Shakespeare plays than football. Hellas had never won anything in their entire history – but Elkjær soon got to work on that.

To suggest that Serie A in 1984–5 would be difficult would be like advising Edmund Hillary that Everest has a few hilly bits. Juventus were the reigning champions, with most of the Italian World Cup-winning team plus Michel Platini and Zbigniew Boniek; they still couldn't find a place for Michael Laudrup, who was again farmed out to Lazio. Arriving in the same summer as Elkjær were Karl-Heinz Rummenigge at Inter and the Brazilian Socrates at Fiorentina, and in the biggest transfer of the summer Napoli broke the bank to bring Diego Maradona to town. Every team was intent on getting maximum value from their quota of two overseas players and it only heightened the level of competition.

The games themselves were tight to the point of being claustrophobic. Throughout the season the watertight *catennaccio* defences kept the average of goals per game to just two, and one in every six matches ended 0-0. For new arrivals from abroad the pressure wasn't confined to the pitch either. 'We were so loved, people loved the foreigners,' remembers Klaus Berggreen, who played at both Pisa and Roma. 'It was so important for Italy to have foreign players but there was also enormous pressure. At Roma we lost a match and Boniek was not playing as well as he could and not doing his best. When he went outside after the game they'd burned his car.'

Berggreen was the first Dane to go to Serie A after the Italian FA lifted the blockade on overseas players in 1980. Inter had a look at him but feared he wasn't a big enough name to impress their fans so he signed instead for Pisa in 1982, becoming one of an elite band of foreign nationals in Italy's top division. The experience was invaluable, both for Berggreen and for Denmark. He became physically stronger and quicker and also developed a greater tactical awareness. When he arrived in Pisa he was finishing his dissertation in economics. The media called him *Dottore*, one of only two doctors in the league along with Socrates.

He started well, singled out by some members of the Italian national team as the best foreign player in the league in his debut season, and the perks were numerous. Pisa paid for his phone bills to Denmark and any parking tickets, and when he scored in his first three games a group of fans turned up at his house with a layer cake and a bottle of champagne. He is revered in Pisa to this day, immortalised in a pizza called the King Klaus and in a famous picture in the club museum that shows Berggreen in the heat of battle with a torn shirt. That photograph made its way into a tattoo on the forearm of one particularly zealous fan. 'Sometimes,' says Berggreen, 'I meet people who know more about me than I do.'

In Serie A some people had known a little more than they should about the destiny of certain games. The *calcioscommesse* betting scandal had rocked Serie A in 1980 and after a series of punishments for clubs and players in Italy it was decided that, for the first and still only time, referees would be appointed at random rather than by a designated panel in the 1984–5 season. Against this backdrop, Hellas Verona won the title.

The impact of the random selection of referees is debatable, but that of Elkjær on that season is not. He was not even the highest scorer in the team yet so iconic were some of his goals and performances that he has become the one player synonymous with an achievement that is the equivalent of, say, Stoke City winning the English Premier League. His equaliser in Bergamo against Atalanta sealed the *Scudetto* and there were crucial momentum changers against Udinese and Roma, but his most famous effort, the one that made everyone believe, came just five weeks into the campaign against the mighty Juventus.

Elkjær was scampering down the left wing towards the end of the match when he lost his right boot after a tackle from a Juventus defender. He cut into the area, past another defender, before passing the ball into the net with his bootless foot to seal a 2-0 victory. His sponsors in Oregon might have frowned upon Nike not getting the final touch, but the fans in Verona couldn't have cared less – Elkjær had won their hearts for ever and it was still only October. They christened him Gol-kjaer and the *gol senza scarpa* passed into folklore in Verona, becoming the defining image of an incredible triumph.

Elkjær's *Scudetto* would prove to be merely one triumph in a period of stunning success for the overseas-based Danish players. Between them Elkjær, Laudrup, Allan Simonsen, Mølby, Jesper Olsen, Frank Arnesen, Søren Lerby, Ivan Nielsen, Søren Busk and Morten Olsen won a staggering seventy-nine major trophies abroad, including forty league titles and four European Cups. They were the definition of winners, amassing a hoard of treasure more commonly associated with the crew of a pirate ship than a group of footballers. Berggreen managed to win Serie B during a brief hiatus there with Pisa and only Bertelsen and John Sivebæk failed to pick up a medal with an overseas club – though tragedy and fortune would later throw Sivebæk the most impressive triumph of all at international level.

The squad players also flourished abroad, with Kenneth Brylle, Per Frimann and Henrik Andersen all complicit in Anderlecht's domestic and European success even if they usually couldn't break into the Denmark team due to the competition ahead of them. Even the discarded players were picking up medals. The unwelcome Birger Jensen kept goal in numerous league and cup triumphs for Brugge while Lars Bastrup and Allan Hansen, deemed surplus to requirements in 1983, picked up European Cup winners' medals that year with Hamburg. The Danish players were an embarrassment of riches for Piontek and amassed the very same with their clubs. As a collective they were about to go after the biggest prize of all.

For a European audience nothing evokes the magic and mystique of a World Cup quite like one held in the Americas. Late-night kick-offs, crackly commentary from across the Atlantic and a searing afternoon sun that casts huge shadows of the stands over sections of the pitch make it unlike a World Cup back in the Old World. The 1986 edition would be returning to Mexico, scene of perhaps the greatest ever World Cup in 1970 when Pelé and Brazil ran riot in the Jalisco and Azteca stadiums.

It should have been in Colombia, awarded the right to host in 1974, but the tournament had now expanded to twenty-four teams and the logistics and economics of staging the event was beyond them, a portentous sign of the road Fifa would ultimately head down; nevertheless the grandeur of the World Cup still held firm in 1986. It remained the highest level of football on the planet. Neither Piontek nor Denmark had ever been to a World Cup, but with the infectious momentum generated since Wembley in 1983 it seemed impossible that the party would stop now. It wasn't just the players who didn't want the music to end.

'After the European adventure everybody wanted to go,' Jesper Olsen recalls, 'not only as players but our supporters were very into that whole thing at the time too, so their experiences in the European Championship in France made them want to go and have another trip abroad. It was amazing the amount of people that were interested in us on the back of that tournament.' To secure those holidays for the nation Denmark would first have to negotiate a qualifying group containing Norway, the Republic of Ireland, Switzerland and the Soviet Union.

The campaign kicked off against Norway in September 1984 at a packed national stadium basking in the afterglow of the great adventure in France. The returning heroes put on a show for their audience, with Elkjær curling a twenty-yard shot into the top corner to win the game. They were, however, developing a curious habit of creating a slew of great chances and missing them, a trend that would continue throughout the qualifying campaign.

This wayward finishing would haunt them in their next match away to Switzerland, played out on a bobbling sand dune of a pitch in Bern. Mølby, Elkjær and Busk, the latter with the simplest of close-range headers, all managed to twang the post. At the other end Switzerland converted one of their few chances, with Umberto Barberis lashing an unstoppable half-volley past Ole Qvist for a victory entirely against the run of play. The early stages of Group 6 were characterised by eyebrow-raising results – the Republic of Ireland beat the Soviet Union and then in turn lost to Norway, the same Norway who had held the Soviet Union a week earlier. Denmark had the chance to assert some control in Copenhagen against the Republic of Ireland in November. A month shy of a third-place finish in the Ballon d'Or, the man of the moment was the match-winner again.

The opening goal of the game was textbook Elkjær. Picking up a loose ball in the middle of the field with only David O'Leary to beat, Elkjær flew past him with his head back and arms flailing

113

like Eric Liddell in *Chariots of Fire*. Then, as his flat-out sprint took him into the right side of the area, he drew out the goalkeeper Seamus McDonagh, composing himself enough to lift the equivalent of a dainty bunker shot over the goalkeeper. It was similar to the goals against Greece and Belgium – delicate skill at devastating speed and after a long run with the ball.

Straight after half-time Elkjær added another. This time it was an ensemble piece. It began as far away from the Irish goal as possible, near the corner flag on the left side of the pitch. Morten Olsen dribbled across his own area and split the Irish team open with a pass inside his own half. Sivebæk hurtled forwards and transferred the ball to Laudrup, who skipped past his marker and crossed to Elkjær. With his back to goal he chipped the ball into position and hooked it home to complete a mesmerising goal. From the root to the fruit the goal took thirty seconds and spanned the entire length of the pitch. When describing just how good it was in a post-match interview, Elkjær let out a giggle of embarrassment. It was understandable; Denmark were playing so well at this stage that you couldn't help but be swept away by the joy of it all.

After those two stunning goals Lerby barnstormed his way into the area to add the final goal of a 3-0 win. It was a nice goal but rendered positively moribund by what had gone before. One final cavalry charge up the pitch by Laudrup and Elkjær, batting the ball back and forth to each other like an eighties tennis arcade game, resulted in Elkjær shooting narrowly wide and just missing out on one of the most impressive hat-tricks of all time. For the crowd's pleasure Elkjær collapsed into a forward roll of mock frustration before bouncing back up to his feet.

'On the way to sunny Mexico, away from cold Denmark!' said Elkjær after the game when he was asked if the result made the team optimistic about reaching the World Cup. The high hopes were shared by Carlsberg, who agreed to invest another six million kroner in sponsorship to help propel the team across the Atlantic. No one knew where this whole thing was going or where it would end, particularly with Elkjær in this form. The trajectory only seemed to go upwards.

Chapter 12

'The game'

The neon thermometer in Copenhagen's City Hall square was heading towards minus twenty degrees on a Thursday evening in February 1985. Most people were tucked up on the sofa watching the ten o'clock news or the latest episode of *Cagney & Lacey*, which was showing on Swedish TV. In the western suburb of Valby, a group of beanie-hatted men started to form a line outside a corner shop. When the shopkeeper came in at six the next morning, the queue was six hundred people long and stretched down the street.

Of the international matches for which the shop was selling tickets, the 5 June World Cup qualifier against the Soviet Union in Copenhagen was the one that caused fans to brave the elements. Tickets were gone within minutes of the shop opening, and the owner eventually pulled the phone line out of its socket to stop the incessant ringing. The DBU reckoned it could have sold 150,000 tickets for the game.

If that winter night was strictly for the hardest core, the whole country was talking about the game in the days leading up to kick-off. Some footballing nations instilled a rare sense of occasion in games. Sweden – the rivalry; England – the trailblazers; USSR – mystery and inevitable defeat. The newspapers were having a jingoistic field day. Cartoon Vikings wielded their swords against bears draped in the hammer and sickle. The headlines went along the same theme: LET'S SKIN THE RUSSIAN BEAR. THE BEAR IS GETTING A POUNDING.

Tipsbladet went as far as printing a warning to its readers: 'In the next couple of weeks leading up to the Russia game you will be exposed to a lot of nationalistic crap in assorted newspapers and magazines – some of it is pretty stupid, while some is actually thought through and pretty funny.' Perhaps they were alluding to the opposite page where the same paper was selling a *Datski Dinamit* T-shirt with a cartoon-like 'boom' on the front. The game was played a few months before *Rocky IV* premiered in the US, but the Denmark fans had already been sold the image of a Soviet team spearheaded by Ivan Drago setting out to crush the Danish Balboas.

It was fighting talk from a nation that rarely troubled the front line during the Cold War. Despite being a founding member of Nato, Danish defence and foreign policy in the eighties became shrouded in what was known as the 'footnote policies'. The parliamentary majority didn't approve of the government's support of the US and the escalating missile programmes, so the foreign secretary, much to his chagrin, had to go begging Nato for opt-outs. Some diplomats mockingly spoke of Denmarkisation as the notion of getting a free ride while the rest of Nato got the rounds in during the arms race.

Not that most *roligans* turning out for the game were too worried about what the new Soviet leader, Mikhail Gorbachev, was up to or what Ronald Reagan really meant when he said that 'we've come a long way since the decade of the seventies'. Many things had changed since the previous decade, but predicting a Danish defeat against the USSR was as safe as houses. Denmark had never beaten the Soviets, losing eight consecutive games since 1956 and conceding thirty goals along the way. Tommy Troelsen, who had coached the Denmark under-21s and was now co-commentator alongside Svend Gehrs, had scored when Denmark lost 3-1 against the USSR twenty years earlier. Back then these games were foregone conclusions. 'With us training two nights, from 7 p.m. to 8.30 p.m., during the week as preparation, the game was already lost beforehand,' Troelsen told *Tipsbladet*. 'The Soviet Union was a footballing giant then and now they are once again fighting to reach the elite.'

The Danish football association had staged a warm-up game against East Germany. It wasn't quite the equivalent of getting the theatre understudy on stage for the preview, but it was a chance for the Danes to pitch themselves against an Eastern European nation they had never beaten. Even if East German glory had faded since they picked up Olympic bronze, gold and silver at three consecutive Games between 1972 and 1980, they were still an imposing challenge for a Danish team who hadn't played together for six months. That fact made it even more baffling for the journalists who filed match reports deciphering an impressive 4-1 victory to Denmark. It prompted the East Germany manager, Bernd Stange, to tell Sepp Piontek: 'That kind of team I have never played against before – that wasn't football.' It wasn't veiled criticism from Stange; he just hadn't seen anybody play the game with such skill and flair.

'The players moved for each other in almost blind understanding and the passes fell with precision,' Per Høyer Hansen wrote in *Tipsbladet*. 'They worked with a flowing rhythm, also without the ball, and there were almost no internal misunderstandings. The explanation for delivering such a homogenous effort after such a long break is basically that each individual player on the Danish team has such high international standard. Players of that calibre almost don't need any time to find the common ground, which sometimes makes football pure artistry.'

The East Germany game also marked the return of Allan Simonsen who, since his injury, had only played a friendly in Honduras with a Denmark team made up of domestic players. He was presented with flowers before the game to mark his fiftieth appearance for Denmark, but Simonsen's emotions told the story of a much more epic struggle. 'What none of us have dared hope for has happened,' Morten Olsen told Simonsen in a speech after the game. 'You are back.'

Not only was Simonsen back, his assist for Michael Laudrup's opening goal was so sublime that it was hard to believe he had been away from top-level international football for eleven months. He scooped down a long ball from Søren Busk with the softest of touches, readjusted his stance, and then played Laudrup through on goal with the outside of the right boot. Simonsen was never quite the same player again after the injury in France, but his technical class was permanent.

While Denmark dispatched East Germany with ease, the USSR regained momentum in the qualifying group by beating Switzerland 4-0 in Moscow. Switzerland had been the only team in the group not to drop a point but they were annihilated by a USSR team who had five shots on target in the first half and scored four. The Swiss defending bordered on self-destruction, but the intricate link-up that catalysed the fourth goal in particular was a study in attacking football. This Soviet team was far detached from any crude stereotypical view of an Eastern European football machine. Michael Laudrup uses the phrase 'Total Football' to describe how they played. 'They had people running all over: they were all strong, they were all fast, they were all good technical players. They did not have a star player but it was top quality.'

Their manager, Eduard Malofeyev, had an appreciation for free-flowing football that was pure perestroika compared to his predecessor, Valeri Lobanovskyi. In Rinat Dasaev – known as 'The Iron Curtain' – they had one of the best keepers in the world.

Expectations for the Soviet game a week later were already occupying the Danish journalists who travelled to Brussels on 29 May to cover the European Cup final between Liverpool and

Juventus. That evening, thirty-nine people died and any footballing expectations were supplanted by anguish and desolation. 'The Cup of Death' was how Juventus defender Antonio Cabrini labelled the trophy his team won after the game had callously been allowed to go ahead amid the shadow of human trauma.

The mayhem in the terraces of Heysel still loomed large a week later in Copenhagen, but football somehow managed to engineer its own response. Gehrs says that anybody involved in football should be forced to watch Denmark's game against the Soviet Union: 'One week before football died. The week after it stood up from the grave.'

You couldn't have staged a more remarkable contrast. Copenhagen was bathed in generous sunshine while a carnival atmosphere raged among the fans. It was the first time in several years that a home game of any importance had been played in the afternoon. 5 June was *Grundlovsdag* – Constitution Day – in Denmark. It was no longer a public holiday, but most people were allowed to finish work at midday. Many gathered at Fælledparken next to the national stadium where rallies took place. This year some speeches had to be brought forward so the rousing words wouldn't get drowned out by the sound of merry *roligans*. Even a strike at the Carlsberg brewery failed to dampen the mood, the pumps in the stadium being refilled at the last minute with supplies from the Belgian brewery Palm.

Idrætsparken, Denmark's national stadium, was inaugurated in 1911 when a select team of Copenhagen footballers played against Sheffield Wednesday. More than 230 internationals were played there until the early nineties when the stadium was torn down, rebuilt and renamed Parken. Even now that the old wooden boards have been pulled up and the executive box seats have been padded, nothing comes close to rivalling the atmosphere of *Grundlovsdag* in 1985. Inside the stadium, a sprawling sea of red and white

A man of his time: the avuncular, likeable Kurt Nielsen was Denmark's manager before Sepp Piontek.

Sepp Piontek, sitting right, managed Haiti – where his salary was usually fresh off the press – before taking over Denmark.

Reservoir Danes: Frank Arnesen, Søren Lerby, Allan Simonsen
and Preben Elkjær strut their stuff during training for the
World Cup qualifier against Yugoslavia in 1981.

Scouting missions to Anderlecht were a blessing for Sepp Piontek, with four of his far-flung squad based there. From left: Kenneth Brylle, Morten Olsen, Sepp Piontek, Per Frimann and Frank Arnesen.

'Ajax clan' members Søren Lerby, Jesper Olsen and Frank Arnesen play to stereotype ahead of the crucial match at Wembley.

And a football nation is born: Allan Simonsen scores at Wembley to secure the breakthrough victory for Danish football.

The team celebrate in Greece after sensationally qualifying for Euro 84 at England's expense. Clockwise from left; Ivan Nielsen, Jan Mølby, Søren Busk, Jens Jørn Bertelsen, John Lauridsen and Ole Kjær.

A Roligan takes a well-earned break from the festivities in France. Next stop – Lyon.

© PER KJÆRBYE

'If I had a gun …': Morten Olsen, Denmark's manager on the field, almost came to blows with his Anderlecht teammate René Vandereycken during Denmark's fractious 3-2 victory over Belgium at Euro 84.

Preben Elkjær misses the crucial penalty against Spain in the Euro 84 semi-final, his agony not the only thing laid bare to the world.

An unusually strong team spirit was one of the features of the Danish Dynamite era.

Preben Elkjær Larsen
Danmark

ElkjAir: Denmark's star striker became Nike's poster boy during the mid-80s.

Dodo and the Danish
team at the recording
of Re-Sepp-Ten, their
1986 World Cup
song. It became the
biggest-selling single
in Danish history.

Altitude and attitude:
Denmark's training for
Mexico gets serious.

He-Man: Søren Lerby, the hard man of the side, played without shinpads – even against Graeme Souness. The 1-0 win over Scotland in 1986 was Denmark's first game at a World Cup final.

The Danish players were at ease whether lounging by the pool or talking to the media – even at the same time.

Roliganexpressen, an old London double-decker bus which housed a group of Danish fans during the Mexico World Cup and was later converted into a greenhouse.

Good friends and roommates Michael Laudrup and Klaus Berggreen model their sportswear on Roliganexpressen.

The XI who trounced South American champions Uruguay 6-1 at the World Cup – and provided the names for the tables at a wedding on the Isle of Man 26 years later. Back row (l-r): Frank Arnesen, Søren Busk, Michael Laudrup, Søren Lerby, Henrik Andersen, Preben Elkjær. Front row (l-r): Morten Olsen, Troels Rasmussen, Klaus Berggreen, Jens Jørn Bertelsen, Ivan Nielsen.

© PER KJÆRBYE

With only thirty seconds remaining, and after a week of personal trauma, Frank Arnesen is needlessly sent off against West Germany. There may be trouble ahead…

Jesper Olsen reflects on the infamous backpass which catalysed Denmark's shocking exit from Mexico 86.

Put your hands together for Sepp Piontek: a nation pays thanks as Sepp leaves his post after eleven incredible years.

The hard work continues even though the playing days are over for Ivan Nielsen, who now runs a plumbing business with his son.

formed in the stands long before the 4 p.m. kick-off. Many of the 45,700 spectators had rushed to take up their spots as soon as the gates opened. The head of security had been on tenterhooks since events in Brussels and his team checked every splinter, sprocket and railing before the game. The only things bursting were bladders.

Ib Thage was among the fans who crammed in on the main concrete stand where there was no seating. 'I didn't dare go to the toilet,' says Thage. 'People just stayed on the spot. It is the kind of game that for many football fans still stands as "the game".' The spectators, many decked out in candy-coloured horizontal stripes and with their faces painted red and white, knew something was afoot. They dared to hope that the fairy tale of Wembley and France might just be about to get rewritten with an even more glorious apogee on their home turf.

'If we have a secret weapon then it's our fans,' Piontek told Danish TV before the game. 'They give the players the feeling that "you can't play a bad game, you can't leave us hanging with all the joy that we bring".' At Hotel Marina where the team gathered in the days before the game, hundreds of fans turned up to follow every move in training. The players and Piontek signed autographs as they talked to the press, while Preben Elkjær had to change from boots to boat shoes on the side of the pitch to get away quickly from the crowds. When the players arrived at Idrætsparken on the day of the game, they saw how this special bond with the fans had sparked an electric atmosphere.

Gehrs was just as awestruck when he took his seat in the commentary box. 'Under these conditions it must be a good game,' he says. 'It would be an insult not to try to make it a feast.' He remembers the pitch being far from perfect when he played in Idrætsparken as a youngster ('There was no grass at all'). As the nation gathered in front of their TVs on *Grundlovsdag* to hear him guide them through the game, Gehrs described it as a billiard cloth: 'This pitch encourages lovely football.'

Nobody wanted to miss a beat – especially not Gehrs's employer, the national Danish TV broadcaster Danmarks Radio, which had taken some flak after viewers missed Elkjær's goal against Norway in an earlier qualifier. *Tipsbladet* reported that this time DR had placed a record five cameras around the pitch. This included one behind the goal that was equipped with a slow-motion machine that made it possible 'to quickly replay an exciting situation, hopefully several goals'. One of the first things the cameras zoomed in on was the marching band playing the Danish national anthem, '*Der er et yndigt land*' (There is a lovely country). Except for Frank Arnesen and Morten Olsen, none of the players sang along. Olsen later told DR he could feel the shivers running down his spine. 'When you are standing there listening to forty-five thousand singing the national anthem, then you get the famous lump in your throat. I think that is one of the best ways to set you up for the match. Especially because many of us don't live in Denmark, I think we feel more Danish than the ones who do.'

To complete the extraordinary mise-en-scène, Piontek had lined up what was one of the strongest starting XIs during the World Cup campaign: Qvist – Busk, Morten Olsen, Nielsen – Jesper Olsen, Berggreen, Bertelsen, Lerby, Arnesen – Laudrup, Elkjær. The last name, which normally struck fear among Serie A defenders, caused a sigh of relief among the Russian delegation and the manager. When they saw the Danish team sheet in the changing room, they noticed a glaring omission. There was no Preben Larsen.

It was as if Preben Elkjær Larsen – as his parents had christened him – knew about this farcical faux pas as he waited alongside Laudrup in the centre circle to kick off the game. Elkjær fidgeted, looked around the stadium and muttered a few words before breaking into a wide grin. On a day when Denmark was blessed by a footballing god and intoxicated by replacement lager, the partnership of Laudrup and Elkjær reached an apex that would be admired far beyond the terraces.

Football used to be about scoring one more goal than the opposition; nowadays it is about conceding one less. Games have to 'settle in' now while coaches prioritise caution and control. Nobody had to 'settle in' that Wednesday afternoon in Idrætsparken. Arnesen pre-empted a relentlessly pulsating encounter when he broke down the left wing within thirty seconds to win a free-kick on the edge of the Russian box. The Russian attacks kept rolling in waves that slammed into the Danish levee, while Søren Lerby, the Danes' chief conductor, went back into his own half to set up his darting runs through midfield. While most of the players headed off on their summer holidays after the game, Lerby was heading to the airport so that he could get straight back to training before Bayern Munich's league decider three days later. It was not the last time he would jet off quickly on Bayern's behalf.

The first major chance of the game fell to Jens Jørn Bertelsen, who found himself one on one with Dasaev on the left side of the Soviet penalty area. This was strangely unfamiliar territory for the industrious defensive midfielder. He recalls the 'fierce chap' who stood in front of him. 'Yes, yes, there should have been a goal all right,' he says. 'I remember having way too much time in that situation. Most players would score in the far corner so instead I thought, no, you are not going to do that, you want to try squeeze it into the near corner.' Bertelsen squeezed the ball well outside the left post and collapsed to his knees in anguish.

On the quarter-hour mark, Klaus Berggreen dispossessed Oleg Protasov in front of the Danish goal. After a clever bit of interplay between Bertelsen, Lerby and Arnesen, Berggreen got back on the ball and released Bertelsen just outside the right side of the Soviet penalty area. Via Laudrup, the ball ended up with Elkjær who got a lucky pinball rebound between two Soviet defenders. As he took aim at goal, Gehrs anticipated the plot. 'And Elkjær ... Now he scores.'

Elkjær's low diagonal drive into the bottom of the right corner was his twenty-eighth international goal. A few minutes later and he had reached twenty-nine. Igor Belanov was chasing down a ball when Ole Qvist clearly used his hands outside the Danish area. Instead of a Russian free-kick, a long ball ended up with Elkjær. After an initial fumble, Elkjær made the simplest and most lethal of touches: surrounded by three Soviet players, like a lone gunslinger in a hostile saloon, he gently poked the ball with his right foot before making a sharp burst forward past Tengiz Sulakvelidze on the left. His shot was as opportunistic as it was brilliant. 'A completely crazy angle to shoot from' was the verdict from Gehrs, while Troelsen hailed the moment as 'Elkjær in a nutshell'. Elkjær later told DR: '[The angle] was just as tight as for everybody else. At that point, I believed I was all on my own so I had to shoot. I also think the keeper made an error at that goal ... and I thank him for that.'

On the Soviet bench Malofeyev smelled something rotten in the state of the Denmark team. Elkjær, the Trojan horse, had been Larsen all along. Sulakvelidze said he was blamed for failing to mark the player nobody knew was going to be on the pitch. The Soviet players backed Sulakvelidze, but he had already been made the scapegoat in a report sent to the Soviet sports committee in Moscow. 'Even if I got a better rating for my performance than the other players, the game had serious implications for me,' Sulakvelidze told the Danish broadcaster TV3+ in 2006. He didn't play for the Soviet Union for another year after the unfortunate case of mistaken identity in Copenhagen.

Revved up by Elkjær's double, the crowd in Idrætsparken was rocking. Berggreen, could see his team-mates' lips moving but all he could hear was the chorus of 'Dan-mark, Dan-mark' echoing around the ground. 'I've never played a match where you couldn't talk to each other on the field,' says Berggreen.

The USSR threw on the defensive midfielder Andrei Zygmantovich, which created more space as chinks started to appear in the Danish armour. Protasov wrestled past Busk on the edge of the Danish penalty area. 'All of a sudden he spins around on a plate and whacks it into the top corner,' says Busk. He creates a launchpad with his hands as he describes Protasov's goal. 'Bang!'

Yuri Gavrilov and Sergey Gotsmanov saw shots ricochet off the post either side of Protasov's goal as the ceaseless intensity of the game started to take its toll. 'The tempo was crazy,' says Busk. 'The tongue was hanging out of the mouth all the time. We were driven into the highest gear. You had to be alert constantly.' The Danes regained some control in a ferocious first half when Dasaev had to stretch to keep out Lerby's dipping shot and Berggreen's glancing header from the ensuing corner.

The Danish dressing room at half-time looked like a post-marathon paramedics tent. Players were lying on the floor out of breath, not understanding the freight train of a game that had just hit them. They grabbed their tea and water but could barely speak. 'I was so tired,' says Laudrup. 'It was hot, it was 5 June. "Ouch, we have to play forty-five minutes more like this? I don't know if we can."' Ivan Nielsen is still dumbfounded when talking about the tempo of the game. He shakes his head. 'That was a stupid, stupid game. We were running and running and running and they just kept coming.'

Piontek realised he had to take some of the pace out of the game and shore up the right side where the technically gifted Jesper Olsen was being steamrollered by the powerful Russians. 'I was playing against two players,' says Berggreen. 'I was alone on the right side. I needed help.' Per Frimann, Anderlecht's busy, creative winger, came on to partner Berggreen and Piontek's calculations paid off.

The second half sparked a Groundhog Day for the strikers, but with a new headline act. Laudrup scored twice, in the sixteenth and nineteenth minutes – the same timings as Elkjær's goals in the first half. 'You start wishing a game had three halves,' said

Troelsen. Laudrup's goals displayed a footballing maturity baffling for his young age. He first pounced when Elkjær's touch on the edge of the Russian penalty area inadvertently turned into a pass. Laudrup faked to shoot with his left foot before lifting the ball above Dasaev into the top right corner. For the second, Lerby released Laudrup across the halfway line and followed through with a parallel run that transfixed the defenders. Laudrup, with impeccable vision and lucidity amid the gaggle of Soviet defenders hunting him down, controlled a low shot that sneaked inside the right-hand post.

The stadium turned into a giant beer garden with Danish fans swaying from side to side, arm in arm, singing along to the crowd classic '*Vi sejler op ad åen*' (We are sailing up the river). But Groundhog Day was still happening in Idrætsparken. As the song reached its high note, Gotsmanov's screamer from ten yards flew into the top left corner behind Qvist. This time the dog-tired Danes couldn't muster a steely reply, and they swayed like their supporters as the Soviet players pushed on for another goal.

Busk kept looking up at the clock on the scoreboard. 'The hands hardly moved during the last five to ten minutes,' he says. 'It's going absolutely nowhere and the game is getting longer and longer and longer and we are totally shattered. We are a bit like a groggy boxer whereas the bear keeps pushing on and on.'

In the final throes, it took a heroic last-gasp clearance from Berggreen to keep the score at 4-2. The Soviet players combined beautifully inside the Danish penalty area before Zygmantovich looked to have tapped in the simplest of goals. Berggreen emerged from the blind spot to play the ball out of danger and the pace of his run sent him tangling into the goal net. 'Even at the end when I cleared the ball off the line we could still lose,' says Berggreen. 'They didn't understand they had lost the match.' A couple of minutes later, after six seconds of extra-time, the greatest game ever played in Denmark was over.

Ib Thage and the rest of the crowd in the old concrete stand could hardly believe what they had witnessed. '*Grundlovsdag* is the one that changed it all,' says Thage. 'You were pissing yourself with nerves until the final whistle blew. They were so lightning quick, those Russians. Like bullets from a shotgun.' Outside the stadium after the game a group of Danish supporters cheered on their heroes and held up two fingers on one hand – and four on the other – as the Russian team coach passed by. In the middle of Copenhagen's central pedestrian street people jumped into a fountain. According to the Danish online encyclopaedia, it was the newspaper *B.T.* which that evening coined the word *roligans* after witnessing these scenes of jubilation.

Gehrs wrapped up the post-match analysis and jumped in a cab to go to Tivoli Gardens where the players were gathering for dinner. He only got as far as the City Hall square when the driver suggested he get out and walk the rest of the way. The sea of red and white had engulfed Copenhagen. Inside Tivoli, Elkjær left the dinner table and went down to unleash his final strikes of the day at a shooting gallery called *Bjørnegrotten* – the Bear Grotto.

It was only a few years ago that Sepp Piontek sat down to watch the whole USSR game on video for the first time. He might have thought he was watching a contemporary match; the pace of the game was from the 2010s, not the 1980s. 'I was completely astonished,' he says. 'I never remembered that we played such a good game. In the first half there was power, there was tempo. Fantastic! The Russians were good. They were so quick, they were boom-boom-boom.' He waves his hands around. 'I had not seen it in twenty-five years; we won!' Laudrup says it's the best Denmark game he ever played in. 'It could have been 5-5.' Like many players and fans, he refers to it simply as 'the game'.

Mention the match to anyone involved with the team and their eyes come alive. 'Have you ever seen it?' says Frimann. 'It's immense, isn't it? It's the basis of what we try to do today, and what we did in 1992 and 1998. Playing with confidence, despite being a small country, comes back to the fact that we played a great game against the Russian bear. That was the first time we said: "We can win the World Cup." It was like being on drugs. "Yeah, we can do everything, we can conquer the world." It was crazy.'

It was a day when football reached the high-water mark and sparked a rush of unrelenting joy and euphoria that reached well beyond the players and the swaying crowds in the stand. 'There are people who have had that game told to them,' says Gehrs. 'It will stand as one of the greatest games ever played in Denmark.'

Never mind in Denmark; it may be the greatest World Cup qualifier ever played.

Chapter 13

Gloria Dana

In the wake of that epic match with the USSR, there was an inevitable sense of 'after the Lord Mayor's show'. To tune up for the remaining World Cup qualifiers in the autumn of 1985, Denmark played Sweden in a friendly in Copenhagen in September, two weeks before the intimidating return fixture with the USSR in Moscow. Denmark were close to full strength with only Søren Lerby and Michael Laudrup missing. John Lauridsen stepped in to midfield and Sepp Piontek awarded a fiftieth international cap to Allan Simonsen. As a force in Scandinavian football, Sweden, who went to all three World Cups in the seventies, were now eclipsed by Denmark. They had not qualified for anything since 1978 and would not make it to Mexico; it was a good chance to limber up and assert some regional superiority.

Denmark were thumped 3-0, the final two goals the result of some slapstick defending and trickling into the net to an embarrassed silence around the stadium. Wildly contrasting international results were nothing new for Denmark, who had tanked for around six months between qualifying for the 1984 European Championship and the tournament itself, but nothing showcased the topsy-turvy nature of Piontek's team quite like 1985. The defeat by Sweden sparked a sudden and dramatic dip in form that threatened to scupper the Mexican adventure at the qualifying stage.

Their intended destination had problems of its own – just a week before the Danes resumed their qualifying bid, an 8.1-magnitude earthquake rocked Mexico City, killing at least 10,000 people and briefly casting doubt on Mexico's ability to host the tournament. Despite the billions of dollars of damage to the infrastructure of the country, the football stadiums were unaffected and the plans for the tournament continued. Whether these plans would include Denmark was soon put under close examination.

The return fixture with the USSR could scarcely have been more different from the festival of 5 June. Rain replaced sunshine in the Central Lenin Stadium, an enormous cavern of an arena built for the 1980 Moscow Olympics and packed with 103,000 spectators baying for victory. It was a world away from the beer-fuelled bonhomie of Copenhagen, and Denmark started encountering problems.

Ahead of the game Ole Qvist fell ill and Troels Rasmussen was promoted to the first team. Preben Elkjær, who had run wild and free in Copenhagen, started the match but was sporting a garish pair of cycling shorts to protect his hamstrings. After lashing a shot high and wide, he reached for the back of his right leg straight away and had to be replaced by Per Frimann after fourteen minutes. More trouble followed just after half-time when the seemingly indestructible Ivan Nielsen was forced off and replaced by Jan Mølby. With Denmark disorganised at the back, the Soviets scored immediately, swinging a free-kick into the area and smuggling in a goal at the back post by Oleg Protasov. That was the only goal of the game, and, but for some inspired goalkeeping by Rasmussen, the defeat could have been heavier. The game had a positive outcome for Rasmussen at least, as he supplanted Qvist as the number one choice in goal. It would be the most important game of his career with Denmark. 'I felt the backing of the media and also the backing of the players based on that performance,' he says.

Defeat in Moscow was a setback but there was the chance to get things back on track in the final home match of the qualifying series against Switzerland two weeks later. Piontek went for it in a big way – starting Lerby, Frank Arnesen, Laudrup, Simonsen and Elkjær – but must have wondered if the Swiss had popped over to Haiti to find a voodoo ritual to protect their goal. Both Klaus Berggreen and Arnesen hit the post for Denmark, and Arnesen missed a late penalty, which allowed Switzerland to escape with a goalless draw, Piontek's first with the national side since his opening game with Finland in 1979.

It wasn't the worst point in the world as it took Denmark to the top of the group on seven points, but you could separate the teams by a cigarette paper's width. Switzerland were also on seven points but had played a game more and had an inferior goal difference, with the USSR and then the Republic of Ireland both a point behind with two matches left, like Denmark. Even their next opponents, Norway, were not definitively out of it on four points but with a game in hand. There were few margins for error left now, not with the remaining matches with Norway and the Republic of Ireland away from home. As Denmark had beaten both comfortably earlier in the group, it didn't seem a problem.

However, in Oslo on 16 October 1985 it suddenly became a very real problem indeed. Just short of half-time a looping header from Tom Sundby sailed softly over Rasmussen and into the Danish net to give Norway the lead. As the players trudged off at half-time every team in the group was alive and kicking and Denmark were perilously close to losing control of their own destiny. What's more, Denmark had not scored a goal in international football for approaching six hours of play. Something had to give.

In the fifty-sixth minute Berggreen made a routine run to close down Åge Hareide as he was about to pass back to the goalkeeper. The pass was atrociously underhit and Berggreen raced on to it before going round the goalkeeper. Laudrup had followed the play, too, and came into his field of vision on the left. Berggreen couldn't have missed but Laudrup didn't give him the option, darting in to put the ball in the net and bring the game level.

'Before the match – and Michael knew this as we roomed together – I was 28-1 to score our first goal,' Berggreen jokes now. 'I had put a thousand kroner on myself to score the first goal for Denmark, and Michael stole the goal from me!' Berggreen understood that, in the middle of a vital fixture, all that mattered was that the team got the goal; he had 'stolen' one from Laudrup in similar circumstances against Yugoslavia at Euro 84. Besides, Berggreen could forgive him for the financial loss given how Laudrup would ignite the Danes in the next ten minutes. Seven minutes after the equaliser a gliding run and through pass by Laudrup released Arnesen, who was hauled down before he could shoot. The resulting penalty was dispatched with brutal efficiency by Lerby to put Denmark in front. Two minutes later Laudrup cut into the penalty area and crossed for Elkjær to give Denmark a 3-1 advantage.

Berggreen would have his moments, too. In the seventy-fifth minute Elkjær pulled off a sumptuous backheel turn – that same trick he had adapted for the professional game after seeing children practising it on the beach in Barbados – and crossed for Berggreen to chip the ball up and volley it into the net. It was the one thousandth goal in the history of the Denmark national team – a goal of historic and sentimental value, if not perhaps 29,000 kroner.

He doubled his tally three minutes later with a low left-foot strike under the goalkeeper. Denmark, having been 1-0 behind just twenty-three minutes earlier, were 5-1 in front. In that cathartic blast they had tapped back into the form they had shown against the Soviet Union and, more importantly, nailed down a qualifying place for the World Cup. *Ekstra Bladet*'s headline – NORGASME – captured the ecstatic rush of those minutes perfectly.

'Estamos en Mexico! I promise you now, estamos en Mexico!' Svend Gehrs had whooped with delight as Berggreen scored the fourth goal. The Soviet Union had beaten the Republic of Ireland earlier in the day, which meant only Switzerland could stop Denmark, and only the mathematicians were interested in their chances of qualifying. The Swiss needed to beat Norway in their final game; they also needed Denmark to lose in Dublin with a thirteen-goal swing. 'Never say never' was a redundant strand of hope. Denmark were going to Mexico.

There was euphoria in the stands of the Ulleval stadium, the *roligans* having arrived in huge numbers again after the overnight ferry trip across the water to Oslo. At the end of the match the Denmark players did a lap of honour to a huge crescendo, ending with them running over to the *roligans* and gleefully throwing their shirts over the barriers to the fans – just as they had in Greece when they qualified for Euro 84. The ferry journey home the next day would be equally memorable; they arrived back in Copenhagen with the same sense of triumph as when the Beatles returned to the UK after conquering America. The Gloria Dana ferry was decked out in red and white flags and scarves, with the *roligans* on deck singing the national anthem as the ship pulled into port.

Two weeks later the Soviet Union passed through Oslo for their final group match and won, meaning that Denmark would require only a draw to win the group on goal difference. With the pressure of qualification now off them, they could go for the win as the group concluded on the long grass of Lansdowne Road in November, which had been hosting international rugby not four weeks earlier. The Irish fans could only dream of having a football team to match their rugby equivalent, who had won the Triple Crown earlier in the year.

The Irish started well, with Frank Stapleton heading an early goal; Elkjær's equaliser, almost straight from the kick-off, was like an emphatic conversational putdown. The goal was created by the in-form right-back John Sivebæk, who played a couple of one-twos during a galloping run before beating Jim Beglin and crossing for Elkjær to volley in from close range. As the only outfield player based in Denmark, Sivebæk was something of an anomaly, but early in the second half he chanced upon a *carpe diem* moment that would change his entire future. By this point Laudrup had already put the Danes 2-1 in front with a fine goal, sprinting with David O'Leary into the area before cutting inside him to slot the ball home, but this was soon to be usurped by Sivebæk.

Sivebæk picked the ball up seventy yards from the Irish goal, played a quick give-and-go with Laudrup to get around Beglin and then raced into the Irish half. Elkjær made a dart to the right to drag defenders out of the way, and with Laudrup dumped to the ground when playing the return ball there was no one else in support. All that lay ahead of Sivebæk was green grass and green shirts. 'I looked around to find the guy to play it to,' he says, 'but nobody was there so I thought: "Okay, let's go on."'

Go on Sivebæk did, with a diagonal charge across Lansdowne Road. Beglin snapped at his heels but Sivebæk shook him off and then went past O'Leary and into the penalty area. With his weaker left foot he clipped a looping shot over Jim McDonagh for one of the most remarkable goals of the Piontek era.

Astonishment was the general consensus – from Gehrs in the commentary box ('Welcome to the scorers' club, John Sivebæk'), the crowd, the Danish players and mostly Sivebæk himself. His celebration passed into legend and was repeated in schoolyards in Denmark – hands in the air, a nonchalant shrug of the shoulders and a where-did-that-come-from look on his face, more embarrassed and self-deprecating than any Big I Am swagger. 'I was just surprised that I'd scored a goal, and the celebration was more like, "Oh, what's going on?"' he says. 'I just couldn't believe myself. That was the reason.'

It was a goal that sealed victory in the group for Denmark and also defined their whole philosophy. Every one of them was on close personal terms with the ball and could run it into other areas of the pitch without being paralysed by anxiety at leaving their comfort zone. For Sivebæk the moment instantly changed his life – as soon as the match was over the watching Ron Atkinson charged downstairs and cornered him in the changing rooms to negotiate an immediate transfer to Manchester United. That transfer would never quite work out, though he can at least claim to have scored the first goal in the reign of a certain Sir Alex Ferguson.

Denmark rounded off the match with another beautifully constructed goal in the seventy-sixth minute. Sivebæk played yet another quick one-two and escaped down the right, looping in a cross for Berggreen. With a beautifully disguised touch, Berggreen laid the ball into the path of Elkjær, who thrashed it past McDonagh. After a bout of the yips up to half-time in Oslo, Denmark had now scored nine times in a game and a half, confirming their place in Mexico in style. At the end of the game, the Irish fans gave Denmark a standing ovation, and the evisceration of their team was a warning of what Denmark could be capable of in the tournament proper. All things considered, a good day's work indeed.

For one man, however, it wasn't quite time to clock off. When Sivebæk's wonder goal landed in the back of the Irish net a signal went from the bench to the pitch that Lerby would be substituted. He trotted to the sidelines, exchanged a hug with his replacement, Jens Jørn Bertelsen, quickly shook hands with Piontek and then raced away down the tunnel. This was nothing to do with lounging into the loving embrace of a hot bath; Lerby had a plane to catch.

Plenty of people have done a double shift in a day before but the gap between the two is usually bridged by a dinner break or a strong coffee, not a plane trip of 736 miles. Bayern Munich were away at Vfl Bochum in the fourth round of the DFB Pokal, and, with an early evening kick-off in Dublin and a late kick-off in Germany leaving just enough of a window for a spot of continental jet-setting, Lerby agreed to fly back and play later in the evening; a ludicrous demand on the body and one subsequently outlawed. It had been privately agreed that Lerby would come off at half-time. Piontek held off for another twenty-four minutes, just to show Bayern who was in charge.

Uli Hoeness, the Bayern commercial manager, was at the match in Dublin and followed Lerby into the dressing room to hurry him along. The two then went to Dublin airport to catch a private jet laid on by Bayern to get Lerby to Dortmund, the nearest airport to Bochum. From there they caught a taxi to the stadium with a police escort attempting to clear the way. When this became stuck in human traffic a few kilometres from the ground, Lerby abandoned the taxi and took to his heels, bobbing and weaving through the mass of spectators to get to the game on time. To his annoyance, after all that effort he was named as a substitute – Bayern weren't that insane – but made it on for the second half. The game went into extra-time, meaning Lerby had pushed his body through more than two hours of competitive football in two different countries in one day. He wouldn't have wanted it any other way.

Lerby was a tremendous athlete, with his component parts seemingly carved from lumps of granite and wired together with steel cables. In tandem with his physique he possessed a will to win that bordered on the obscene. 'He was a big fighter for the team,' remembers Berggreen. Where others wanted to win, Lerby needed to win. Anyone who failed to meet his exacting standards was at risk of a serious earful, and he wasn't exactly deferential when he felt one was justified. At Wembley in 1983 he launched a tirade at Simonsen after a misplaced pass ruined a breakaway chance for Denmark. 'Football,' Lerby has said, 'is not for the silent.'

It was never personal. Lerby disappeared so far into the zone during matches that it was incredible he ever found his way out.

He would berate his colleagues with a devastating fury only to return to the dressing room oblivious of having said anything at all. 'When he was shouting,' says Per Frimann, 'you needed to close your ears.' Morten Olsen, for whom the highest professional standards are the norm, dubbed him Dr Jekyll and Mr Hyde. 'Football is a game of survival,' Olsen says. 'You don't need only nice people, you need people on the pitch who are winners. Søren was one of these types. You couldn't recognise him on the field – he was a nice guy off the field.' Lerby was the ultimate white-line player. When the game started his sole focus was on winning and he would not allow anything or anyone to get in the way.

Even by the measure of the day he was seriously, ludicrously, hard and had his own unique way of expressing it. Where others flexed their muscles Lerby showed you his shins, playing almost all his career with his socks rolled down and no shin guards to protect his tibia and fibula. Playing without shin pads is illegal now; in the eighties it bordered on lunacy. Lerby didn't care. As with Viv Richards strolling out to bat without a helmet, or Muhammad Ali dancing around the ring with his arms by his side and his chin stuck out, the message was clear. Think you can hurt me? Just try it.

'I think it was just to show that he was a He-Man,' says Berggreen. It was a look also adopted on occasion by Søren Busk. In Danish football, Søren seemed to be the hardest word. Where Busk toyed with the fashion, Lerby lived it. 'I don't know why,' says Piontek. 'It was some kind of "I'm-so-strong, I-need-not-protect-my-legs." But he was very hard; it was no problem.'

Lerby was certainly hard in the tackle. As a ball winner he was relentless, and although he was not as much of a dribbler as some of his team-mates he often dragged his team away from danger by picking up the ball and galloping forty yards with it to reset the game in a more suitable position. Beyond that he could really play, and possessed a left foot with numerous settings. He could pass accurately to any range – short, mid and particularly long – and had a murderous shot, best exemplified for Bayern Munich against Werder Bremen in 1984 when he smashed in two free-kicks and a twenty-yard volley for a hat-trick of the highest quality.

As Ajax, Bayern Munich and PSV Eindhoven will attest, if you recruited Lerby he invariably hunted down the league title like a tracker dog. In the thirteen seasons between 1976 and 1989 he won an astonishing nine league championships with those three clubs. With Ajax in the 1979–80 season he was the top scorer in the European Cup with ten goals, including five in one match against Omonia Nicosia, a tournament record he still jointly holds today. At twenty-three Ajax made him club captain and when Bayern Munich needed to replace Paul Breitner in 1983 they made a beeline for his door.

Although his brooding intensity would suggest a professional entirely consumed by his trade, away from the pitch Lerby had a lighter side. When asked who the biggest jokers were in the Denmark team, Gehrs confirms: 'Lerby. He was talking all the time, laughing all the time.' Gehrs would know, having chaired the recording of an end-of-year TV round-up of Denmark games in 1986 with Lerby, Arnesen, Sivebæk and others that had frequently to be paused due to continuous giggling. When playing in Holland he was even caught out on television with a Jeremy Beadle-style prank on his car, which he took in markedly good humour when it wouldn't be difficult to imagine other hard men of the time lamping the perpetrators for holding up their day.

He also became one half of a celebrity couple when he married his first wife, the Dutch actress and singer Willeke Alberti, giving him a higher profile off the pitch than most of his team-mates. Lerby's ability to combine being a great player with three other sub-divisions of footballer – the hard man, the joker and the celebrity – made him one of the more enigmatic characters in

Piontek's side. Above all, though, it was his drive, determination and relentless work ethic that characterised him. They would be useful qualities, as Denmark were about to walk through the valley of the Group of Death.

Chapter 14

'Re-Sepp-Ten'

It was shortly after midnight when Sepp Piontek got through on the phone from Mexico City. By that stage his players sported sombreros and were raising their champagne glasses after receiving the 'Gold' sports award at a ceremony in Copenhagen. While his stars were hobnobbing with the culture secretary and showbiz glitterati, Piontek had already begun his reconnaissance mission in Mexico after overseeing the previous day's World Cup finals draw. 'They have started calling it the Group of Death here,' Piontek said on the phone, according to the newspaper *B.T.* 'Franz Beckenbauer is walking around looking pretty worried.'

Group E: West Germany, Uruguay, Scotland, Denmark.

The Danish papers splashed their sports sections with headlines about a 'Dynamite Group', but it was Uruguay's manager, Omar Borrás, who popularised the phrase that would go on to become a ubiquitous feature of any team competition. *El grupo de la muerte* – the Group of Death. These days that label seems so ubiquitous that it has lost its impact. Even Norway's 2012 veterans handball championship had its Group of Death. But Borrás's observation was astute and fully justified at the time. World Cups had seen superpowers bundled together before – Italy, France, Argentina and Hungary slugged it out in the opening round in 1978, for example – but Group E in Mexico was a perfect storm of talent, history and momentum.

All West Germany, Uruguay and Scotland needed from the lowest ranked pot in the draw was a World Cup novice to act as the whipping boy of the group. They might have ended up with Canada, Iraq, Algeria, Morocco or South Korea. Instead they were dealt Denmark, who were grouped in the lowest tier due to their status as virgins in the competition and a seeding system that didn't take their rising Euro stock into account. Denmark didn't care. They would laugh in the face of the Group of Death.

The countdown back home had started during the Norway game when Svend Gehrs promised the viewers a summer in Mexico. If the build-up to France 84 had been overwhelming, Mexico 86 took hype and excitement to a new level. This time around there wasn't any room left on the bandwagon. Any magazine, drinks retailer, travel agent or wheeler-dealer found their hook, draped it in red and white stripes and slung it out to an adoring public. Even the readers of *Ugens Rapport* were treated to a 'Mexico Sexico' supplement, featuring a topless model wearing a *roligan* cap.

Money-spinning imaginations knew no boundaries. A shopping mall in the Copenhagen suburb of Ballerup became 'The Dynamite mall of 86'. An Ole Qvist lookalike launched the 'Easy Dane' reclining chair for TV viewers (tagline: Olé, Olé, Olé). Carlsberg re-dressed the label on their classic pilsner bottle from green to red. Supermarkets sold *roligans* kitchen roll embossed with Danish flags. The kitchen roll was designed for 'when the sweat needs wiping off the forehead, when you tip over the glass. In short, when you need a kitchen roll you can trust.'

Then there was the kit. It is hard to tell whether the sportswear brand Hummel tried to channel the team's free-flowing aesthetics or simply got caught up in the moment, but the strip produced for the Mexico team transcended design and style; it was a sartorial manifestation of the Danish Dynamite culture. For the 1984 tournament, Hummel had veered away from a traditional

141

monotone design by adding white sleeves embroidered with red chevrons. Later that summer, Hummel's outfits for the Danish handball team caused a stir at the Olympics in Los Angeles when the diagonal candy-coloured stripes on the tops and skimpy shorts earned the team the nickname *bolsjedrengene* (the bonbon boys).

Yet nothing quite prepared the assembled journalists for what they had in store when Morten Olsen, Frank Arnesen and Per Frimann premiered the Mexico collection in Copenhagen in February 1986. The shirt was split into two contrasting striped panels: one half with red and white stripes and the other in dark shades of red. The panels on the sleeves and shorts matched the strangely futuristic design. 'I think it's ... different,' Olsen told Danish TV after he had been playing keepie-uppie on a checkerboard floor, 'but I think it's a breath of fresh air.' Arnesen pulled the edge of the shorts with his fingertips to show how the lightness of the fabric was similar to the type used in athletics. 'They have a very loose fit,' he said, 'and I think that's a big advantage because you are going to be sweating a lot.'

Olsen suggested that football associations sometimes had a conservative view as to how their teams should dress. That was certainly true of the Danish journalists. The kit was labelled the carnival suit, with *Tipsbladet*'s cartoonist depicting the players wearing Batman and court jester costumes. The journalist Per Høyer Hansen said the shirts were an insult to the team and described them as 'cutesy, as if they were for babies with a rattle and pacifier. Others would use such rags as kitchen drapes.'

Even if it had the Marmite effect on people, it was good business. The managing director of Hummel, who appeared at the launch in a cardigan version of the Mexico shirt, reckoned domestic sales alone could bring in ten million kroner (£1 million). 'It was a marketing triumph,' says Klaus Berggreen, who would go on to work in the fashion industry. 'It was totally awful when you look at it now, but as a piece of publicity it was fantastic.' When asked by a magazine to rank the shirts Denmark had played in over the years, Berggreen put the 1986 version top of the list.

A delegation from Hummel had travelled around the world looking for ideas at a time when block-coloured patterns were starting to make inroads. Birgit Leitner, who worked on the design for Denmark's Mexico collection, said the innovation was to introduce the striped panels and use a thin blue stitch to enhance the colour combination. 'It wasn't that the players contributed to the design,' says Leitner, 'but they were a bunch of exuberant and fun boys. Working with them could only lift your spirits.'

Hummel's initial concern wasn't fan or press reaction but, rather, how the shirt, particularly the thin stripes, would look on TV. Rumour had it that the company was prepared to stage a match in the national stadium so that the kit could be seen in action. It never got that far. Fifa approved the shirts but ordered Hummel to redesign the shorts as monochrome. Denmark were left with plain red or white shorts to go with their red or white halved shirts, and the team used each permutation in their four games in Mexico.

Journalists who got shirty at the launch would have done quite well for themselves if they had stashed away the kit. Today it regularly fetches north of £200 on eBay, and twenty-four years after Mexico – and after the Danish national team had switched to Adidas – Hummel relaunched replicas of both the 84 and 86 strip ahead of the World Cup in South Africa. In other countries the kit became the definitive symbol of Danish football's golden age; few if any experimental kits are as recognisable. The legacy also resonates with fans of Coventry, Aston Villa and Southampton who adopted the pinstripe design, but without the same kitsch currency.

The Danish team stuck to the 1984 fashion range when they faced Bulgaria in a friendly two months before the World Cup. Søren Lerby had to deputise as libero while most of the usual starting XI were busy filling their clubs' trophy cabinets around Europe. The 3-0 defeat had echoes of the team's calamitous build-up for the 1984 European Championship. 'There you have your world champions,' Piontek said after the game. 'The ones you praise to the skies, right? Stop all the praise. We played like we did during our amateur days.'

Among those in the crosshairs of his scathing assessment was John Lauridsen, who, despite being a star in Spain with Espanyol, never quite won over Piontek. The manager's Mexico-bound squad was virtually a done deal. The only question mark was whether two of the brightest stars from the Danish first division would be blooded on the world stage: Flemming Povlsen and a young goalkeeper called Peter Schmeichel. Povlsen, a prodigiously gifted striker who lit up Borussia Dortmund's attack in the early nineties, eventually stayed at home to finish his exams. With Lauridsen out of favour, there was room for Feyenoord's John Eriksen and a swansong for Allan Simonsen.

Schmeichel had guided Hvidovre to promotion from the Danish second division, but Piontek opted for experience in the shape of Lars Høgh, a formidable shot-stopper who spent twenty-three seasons with his hometown club, Odense Boldklub. Høgh upped his training in the year before the tournament. He went swimming every morning throughout the winter before his day job at a shipping company and then trained in the evening with his club. 'It was a tough time,' says Høgh, 'but I invested a little bit in this.' Whether or not his son was going to play in Mexico, Høgh's father had already invested his bit for the team by organising the shipment of some of their clothing to Latin America.

Even with the squad decided, Piontek was cutting it fine with the deadline for his players to arrive. When training kicked off at Hotel Marina in Vedbæk in early May only seven players were there to don the striped kit, because the domestic leagues around Europe didn't finish until later that month. When the rest of the team had turned up ten days later, they included league winners from Italy, West Germany, England, Holland and Belgium – but none from Denmark.

One of the late arrivals was Frank Arnesen, who had to stay in Eindhoven and help PSV clinch the Eredivisie title with an 8-2 win over Go Ahead Eagles. A few days before the title decider, Arnesen jetted into Copenhagen for a four-hour visit to lay down the lead vocals on the Danish World Cup song, 'Re-Sepp-Ten'. The title was a pun on the word for medical prescription (*recept*) and their manager's talismanic effect. When asked by the record's producer, Morten Olsen had singled out Arnesen as the outstanding musical talent of the group. As a kid growing up in Copenhagen's Christianshavn area, Arnesen sang in the school choir and had his rock-and-roll education at the local youth club. He was nicknamed Frankie Boy.

'I know I have a good voice, but that the whole country now has to listen to it for years honestly made me a bit nervous,' he said after the recording of 'Re-Sepp-Ten'. Little did he know that the song would become the fastest and biggest selling single in Danish pop history. Arnesen landed himself another gig that year when he recorded a song for the Danish railways, DSB. In an advert featuring the song '*Vi Er På Banen*' (We are on track), he wore his Denmark kit – with the uncensored striped shorts – and juggled an empty milk carton with his feet from the filthy floors of a train carriage to a rubbish bin.

The newspaper *Ekstra Bladet* had asked its readers to contribute the lyrics for 'Re-Sepp-Ten', offering a trip to Mexico and match tickets for the winning songwriter. Some of the early entries were as baffling as they were poor ('It's red and white, it's yours and mine, and it's tax free'). The best suggestion came from Grethe Larsen, the fifty-six-year-old *roligan* who won the prize. The opening game against Scotland would be the twenty-fifth Denmark game she had watched. 'Before the trip to Mexico I had travelled

25,000 kilometres to follow the Danish team, and I have no idea what it has cost me,' Larsen told the magazine *Se og Hør.* 'Too bad I got started so late. But I was scared of flying. I conquered that fear in 1979 and then I was hooked.'

The comedian Jarl Friis-Mikkelsen, one-half of the duo Øb og Bøv who had played a joke on Simonsen on primetime TV before the 1984 tournament, was charged with stitching the words together. He managed to turn the lyrics for 'Re-Sepp-Ten' into a catchy concoction of patriotic gibberish, fairy-tale characters and risqué double entendres. There were nods to the Ugly Duckling and Mother Denmark who loves to see her boys bang... the football. And then the chorus: 'We are red, we are white, we stand together side by side.'

One reader suggestion had sparked the idea of linking the national team with Hans Christian Andersen's fairy tales. Friis-Mikkelsen decided to run with the theme. 'If you had to make a tribute song then it couldn't be opulent enough,' he says. 'It's typically Danish so it needs a bit of humour on top.' Friis-Mikkelsen had also conjured up an idea for a B-side, but it didn't find favour with the DBU. 'We wanted to make a different chorus which said "we are red, we are white, we are really deep in shite". You sing when you win and you sing when you lose.'

While Arnesen was the consummate pro in a studio, it was amateur hour when the rest of the team turned up to record the chorus. They readjusted the balance of the squad according to their vocal prowess and added in a few ringers from a band who were recording next door. The lead singer of that band, Maria Charlotte 'Dodo' Gad, would go on to become a bona fide pop star, but her place in Danish cultural history was cemented when she was offered the chance to sing on 'Re-Sepp-Ten'.

'I was deeply fascinated,' says Dodo. 'I wasn't anybody there, it was the national team who were the main attraction. I was completely squeezed up into the corner and saw this team of men who I had only seen on TV.' The players were equally fascinated by her. 'Everybody liked Dodo because she was good-looking,' says Berggreen. 'And when she started to sing we fell in love with her even more.' Dodo and her bandmates say Berggreen was one of the few players who had a decent voice and that Preben Elkjær couldn't hold a note if his life depended on it.

Once the music had been recorded, they shot a video where Piontek played the role of record producer and the team hammed it up Live Aid-style in multi-coloured tracksuits that resembled cards from the game Uno. Elkjær was standing behind Dodo grinning like a Cheshire cat and flipping his headphones around ninety degrees so that they were planted on his nose and neck. 'It was only when I saw the video that I noticed they were taking the mickey,' says Dodo.

The song struck a far greater chord than its simple structure and synth-horn arrangement suggested. Within four days of premiering on TV, 35,000 copies had been sold. Halfway through the group stages in Mexico sales had passed 118,000 copies. The record company suggested that Dodo, who was about to put out her group's debut album, fib about being on holiday so as to avoid media attention.

'Re-Sepp-Ten' is still only rivalled by the national anthem for most popular song choice when Denmark play at home. 'They are still singing it today,' says Piontek with a mixture of disbelief and pride. 'Every time we qualify they make a new song, but never like this one – they even play it at handball games.'

Piontek told the producers they had only ninety minutes to wrap up the recording and video shoot before the bus headed back to the training camp. The studio sessions were a much-needed break for the players who were being put through their paces at the training facilities in Vedbæk. They were all individually taken through a fitness test at the August Krogh institute in Copenhagen, a department of the university named after a Nobel prize-winner who championed the study of the capillary motor regulating mechanism.

In an attempt to adjust to the high altitudes in Mexico, Piontek had taken a tip from a race-walking coach who recommended a somewhat unorthodox method for coping with the thin air. Oxygen tanks were strapped to the players' backs while they breathed through what looked like spacemen's masks that replicated oxygen levels for running at an altitude of 2,300 metres. They shared five of these units, and the schedule was designed for each player to complete twenty minutes of steady jogging before a series of short sprints.

At the time Berggreen described the feeling as like having sandpaper in the mouth. He now admits that some players found a way of sneaking in a cheeky bit of fresh air on the side. 'Sepp did it just to show us that it was going to be hard. I was doing it right but I could see Michael and Preben pulling it to one side and not doing it properly.' The rumour that Elkjær even found a way to have a puff on his cigarette through the side of the mask was one urban myth too far. The obsession with altitude training and the impact of atmospheric conditions got to the point where *Ekstra Bladet*'s sports editor asked whether the nation had become obsessed with the 'thin air' in Mexico. But Piontek was meticulous in his quest to maximise the potential for this group of players. His training schedule was straight out of the concrete book of coaching:

8.30 a.m.: breakfast
9.30 a.m.: altitude training
10.30 a.m.: training
1 p.m.: lunch
2 p.m.: rest and massage
5.30 p.m.: training
7.30 p.m.: dinner
8.30 p.m.: free time or massage
Midnight: bedtime

In between training sessions the team found time for a warm-up game in Norway, which they lost 1-0, and a visit to the Danish royal family. Elkjær had suggested in an interview that the team didn't receive the recognition it deserved from Denmark's Queen Margrethe. The royal court duly obliged at a time when the football team were marketing gold dust. The players swapped their kit for cobalt-blue dinner jackets, striped ties and dark trousers, and lined up on the steps outside the palace alongside the queen and her family. They brought tracksuits and boots for the two young princes. 'Nice lady, Margrethe,' Elkjær told reporters. 'She didn't even tell me off.'

The next day, Denmark played their final warm-up game against World Cup-bound Poland before a packed stadium in Copenhagen. Rod Stewart, dressed in Mob-style trench coat and *Borsalino* fedora, watched Denmark win 1-0. He claimed Scotland would come out on top three weeks later in Mexico. Stewart's flight to Denmark was delayed so he missed the first half and the spirited crowd who sang the Danish national anthem with such force that it drowned out the accompanying band. Most of those fans wouldn't get the chance to follow their team all the way to the World Cup. For those who did, there was no shortage of ingenuity.

Some fans sold their cars and homes to raise the money necessary for the trip. Others used up work sabbaticals or auctioned off prized farm animals. For one group of football enthusiasts working for Scandinavian Airlines (SAS), the journey to Mexico had already started on the way home from the final qualifying game in Ireland. Most of them had been following the team home and away for years, but they needed to find a way of getting to the promised land together, in style, and without breaking the bank. The answer was a beaten-up double-decker bus, which had been running as a tour bus in Los Angeles. A delegation went over to the US to purchase the bus before SAS staff at LAX airport decorated it with horizontal red and white stripes. The hubcaps were also painted red and white, and the bus was christened *Roliganexpressen*.

The group of twenty-five departed for Los Angeles – travelling first class – wearing matching harlequin-style suits and jesters' hats. They had befriended a Danish businessman called Andy who threw a party near his plant nursery before the merry *roligan* pranksters embarked on their journey to Mexico. When the bus returned to LA at the end of the World Cup – with the aid of a tow truck – Andy bought the bus from the SAS employees and converted it into a greenhouse.

Most of the group slept on the top floor of the bus while a few followed behind in a Dodge van also decorated with candy stripes. The organisers sent a letter to the group before the trip, reminding them that they had to leave their private lives at the bus door: 'Those who have a Walkman are asked to bring it along in the likely case that somebody wants a bit of privacy on the trip – and that is the only way you can get that.'

Lars Møller, who worked at the check-in counter at Copenhagen airport, says they were greeted like kings and queens wherever the bus went in Mexico. They would normally book a few rooms at a motel so they could park there for the night, but their arrival often turned into a huge party. Sometimes the local mayor even joined in.

Roliganexpressen was offered a police escort to the stadium amid the heavy traffic before games, and their exploits brought them to the attention of Mexican TV where the bus featured in a montage before the World Cup broadcasts started. 'Every time we came to a new village we had to sign autographs,' says Møller. 'It was completely crazy. We couldn't work out whether they thought we were playing football or what.'

If a bus full of tequila-guzzling *roligans* could charm the Mexican crowds, it was nothing compared to what the players were about to achieve on the pitch.

Chapter 15

For Denmark

Denmark set out for their first World Cup from Copenhagen airport at 3 p.m. on Saturday 17 May 1986, two weeks before the start of the tournament. It took them almost twenty-four hours to get to their training camp in Colombia, including stop-offs in Paris, Madrid and Caracas. 'It's scandalous that we haven't been able to find a more direct route to Bogotá,' Klaus Berggreen told the newspaper *B.T.* Preben Elkjær had only one thing in mind, and it wasn't the day job. 'Nobody is going to make me touch a ball for the first day. Now Elkjær wants to hit the sack.'

The mattresses were fine, there were phones in the room and nobody had concrete illness. There was luxury but in spirit the Hilton Hotel in Bogotá might have been a cousin of Idrættens Hus. Sepp Piontek, desperate for Denmark to maximise their ability and conscious that many of these players would never play in a World Cup again, set up a regime of work, rest and play in which most of the play took place on the field.

The work in Colombia was particularly intense. 'If this is a pro's life, it's pretty drab,' the midfielder Jan Bartram told Danish TV. 'At home you can grab a beer, but I think I've had two here. And I miss my girlfriend.' Piontek severely restricted the amount of beer his players could have, although some had access to a Carlsberg stash within the hotel. 'Sepp was trying to win the World Cup,' says Ivan Nielsen before giving a familiar snigger. 'We just wanted a beer!'

Nielsen is one of the players who thinks that, in hindsight, the training was too much, the Danish/German balance seriously out of whack for the first time since the early days of Piontek's reign. 'Normally I was ninety kilos,' he says. 'When I came back from Mexico I was eighty-two. We stayed in a hotel but you could not use the swimming pool. Around the hotel there were guards with guns. You could not get a beer, nothing. You were imprisoned! We were training and training and training and training, it was so stupid. I've never trained so hard in my whole life.'

The players bounded into the training with their usual innocent enthusiasm. Aches and pains are easy to bear when you are at your first World Cup. 'We trained too hard,' agrees Berggreen. 'That was the biggest mistake we made. When we arrived at that World Cup we were in 100 per cent condition. That's too early – everybody knows that now – but we just wanted to be prepared. We were so happy to do it. Sepp couldn't even stop us; we were like wild horses. Train, train, train, even at two kilometres high. We couldn't breathe; we were just running and training. The problem was that we couldn't stop it.'

On the first day of training, Berggreen couldn't stop the ball; the thin air caused it to run away from him like something out of a comedy sketch. There was a kind of comedy, too, when an errant shot from Elkjær smacked a local journalist in the face and gave him a nosebleed. Nobody could control the ball. The back-up goalkeeper Lars Høgh said he barely saved a shot for three days as he got used to how quickly the ball moved in the air. The blistering heat was also an issue. On one occasion, Berggreen and Elkjær jumped for a corner in training. Elkjær's arm landed on Berggreen's shoulder and removed a layer of sunburned skin. Three decades later, Berggreen sucks on a lemon as he recalls the pain.

The intense training was augmented by warm-up matches against local sides and also Paraguay, against whom Frank Arnesen was sent off. The match was played with cars parked around the pitch, and the players separated from spectators only by a length of string. Denmark's patience with the referee soon snapped. He missed two bad tackles on Michael Laudrup and then Jesper Olsen before giving a free-kick on the edge of the Danish area for no apparent reason. Søren Lerby lost it and, amid the burgeoning chaos, Arnesen – the only Spanish speaker in the Denmark side – had a go at the referee. *B.T.* said the gist of his words were: 'Stop that crap, it's only training, you idiot.' The referee sent Arnesen off and stuck to his decision despite the appeals of both sides, who wanted to practice eleven against eleven in the thin air. Laudrup, who had been getting a rough treatment from the Paraguayan defenders, was booked after he told the referee to 'vamos'.

Laudrup might have told his team-mates to 'vamos' after a few minutes of the next game against local side Cristal . They were 2-0 down amid defending that Piontek described as 'almost criminal'. At half-time Denmark, irked by another referee they considered inadequate as well as by the opposition turning up twenty minutes late for the game, resolved to put on a show. They did just that, winning 5-2, with Laudrup at his bewildering best.

The warm-up games changed Piontek's plans for the opening World Cup match against Scotland. Jan Mølby was struggling after a long season with Liverpool and was under renewed pressure from Jens Jørn Bertelsen, whose defensive protection was increasingly missed, while the form of Per Frimann was a serious threat to Arnesen's previously guaranteed place.

In the last game in Colombia, however, Frimann suffered a dreadful ankle injury against Atletico Junior in Baranquilla. 'I think we made a mistake in that we were playing so well and maybe we were a bit too cocky,' he says. 'I remember Søren Lerby saying, "Don't do too much, just play, let the ball do the work."' When you are twenty-three, perhaps in the form of your life and tantalisingly close to a starting place in the World Cup, that is not so easy to do. Frimann went on another solo run and was caught by a bad tackle. He suffered ligament damage and a broken ankle, with the joint structure also affected. He stayed with the team for a fortnight before flying to Holland for an operation. 'You think you can recover, and you have new goals immediately, but of course it was shit to go home from Mexico.' Frimann never did truly recover: he developed an infection in the ankle joint after the operation and had regular ankle problems before eventually retiring at the age of twenty-eight. 'I'm not bitter. I was lucky enough to play in a great team and have lots of great experiences. If you play six or seven years of good football you think: okay.'

Frimann's injury overshadowed an eventful match. An audacious volley on the turn from Elkjær hit the bar with such force that it rebounded as far as the centre circle, prompting *olés* from a large crowd. Bertelsen did not always stand out in the crowd, but his superb performance clinched his World Cup place ahead of Mølby.

As Mølby lost his place, so two of the players lost over five kilos during the game. They almost lost a few more in nervous sweat during a horrible plane journey, when they were swerving between mountains like something out of a computer game. That was one of a number of incidents that engendered a sense of unease during the trip to Colombia. And even before it. 'We had been told Bogotá was the wildest city in the world,' says Høgh. 'We couldn't go out of the hotel.'

The players had been told not to leave the Hilton without security even before a representative from Hummel was mugged on the front steps. The hotel's head of security hardly settled the nerves by describing the Danish team as 'immensely attractive kidnapping victims'. The level of security, with guards waving machine guns all over the place, and the poverty was a serious shock to the Danes.

Their mood did not improve when there was a fatal car crash outside the team hotel, with one of the victims, a woman, lying dead for hours before her body was finally removed. The whole trip had a strange atmosphere. When the players went for a walk one day, flanked inevitably by security, Elkjær almost punched one of his team-mates after feeling a hand in his pocket.

'Bogotá was a unique experience,' says Bertelsen. 'We also went on a bus ride where we saw the downside of it all. They were terrifying, poor and dangerous conditions to move around in. So we didn't.' The lack of freedom, totally alien – shocking even – to the Danes, left many of the players struggling with boredom. Things were far more relaxed in Mexico, but there was still little to do apart from training and playing darts, chess or cards. The latter was always a popular pastime but now even those who did not usually play were drawn in. The back-up striker Flemming Christensen went along just to listen to the chat between the players. Piontek did not want the players to gamble for money. When they did during one flight, with thousand-kroner bills flying around like confetti, he started ranting about how, as a child, he used to eat dry bread dipped in water. Later he disgustedly shoved a huge pot of money into a bag just as one player was about to claim his winnings.

Health rather than wealth was more of a concern for most of the players. More than half the twenty-two-man squad had Montezuma's revenge even before the tournament started. The players brushed their teeth with mineral water and showered with bowed heads and closed mouths so as not to inadvertently swallow water. There were other problems. Nielsen twisted an ankle; Troels Rasmussen was recovering from tonsillitis. Ole Qvist had a strange ear infection that affected his balance and ruled him out of the group stages.

The physio, Rasmus Bach Andersen, turned his eight-room suite into a hospital. The masseur, Thure Johnson, had a video installed so the players could watch films and TV shows while being treated, with *Fawlty Towers* a particular favourite.

Denmark had brought their own off-field team, including the chef, Flemming Larsen, from Hotel Marina. His supplies, according to the magazine *Se og Hør*, included four boxes of miniature flags, baking powder, poppy seeds and meat extracts. The most important order was for fifty kilos of flour for making traditional Danish rye bread. He also cooked pork roast with red cabbage, meatballs, fried fish and roast beef, as well as a traditional Danish layer cake with strawberries and cream. Larsen even planned a victory dinner should they win the tournament: prawn cocktails, steaks with Béarnaise sauce and ice cream with fruit.

Such preparation was pragmatic rather than hubristic. The whole football world agreed that Denmark were one of the favourites to win the tournament. Despite being drawn in the Group of Death, they were seen as Europe's likeliest winners along with France. The climate meant that the South American heavyweights – Brazil, Argentina and the South American champions Uruguay – were favourites, along with the hosts Mexico, but Denmark were joint-fifth favourites at 12-1. Pelé said they were the best team in the Group of Death; Alex Ferguson and Ossie Ardiles were among those who said they were the best team in Europe.

'An outside seed was never so fancied,' said *The Times*, who tipped them to finish runners-up in the tournament. 'Denmark arrive at this World Cup as the most talented debutants in the history of the competition.' And one of the most popular. 'If the 1986 World Cup is to capture the imagination then it is in everyone's interest for Denmark to make substantial progress,' said the *Guardian*. It was not just in England that they were fancied. OF COURSE WE SHOULD LOVE THESE UGLY DUCKLINGS was the headline in *Expressen*, Sweden's second biggest tabloid, which went on to make a cute land grab by hailing Laudrup as 'the Nordic Maradona'.

Their first match was against Scotland. Like Spain, the Scots were a different side in the 1980s – although their fortunes have gone in opposite directions since. Mexico was their fourth consecutive World Cup, and they had only gone out of the previous three on goal difference to Brazil, Holland and the USSR. They were managed by Ferguson, put in temporary charge when Jock Stein died of a heart attack after their dramatic World Cup qualifier against Wales the previous September. Ferguson controversially omitted Alan Hansen, after which Hansen's clubmate Kenny Dalglish pulled out, but his was still a strong squad. Only three of the twenty-two players were at the Glasgow clubs, Rangers and Celtic, a reflection of the depth of Scottish football in those days. The squad had representatives from Manchester United, Liverpool, Arsenal, Barcelona and Sampdoria, not to mention seven from the New Firm of Aberdeen and Dundee United.

The match was built up in some quarters as a contest between Graeme Souness and Mølby, Souness' replacement at Liverpool who a month earlier had lorded it over Everton in the FA Cup final as his team completed their first Double, but in reality he was never likely to start now that Bertelsen had reminded everyone of his worth. Henrik Andersen missed out through illness but Morten Olsen was passed fit.

Denmark made their World Cup debut on 4 June 1986. It was the second fixture of the day; earlier, Uruguay and West Germany had drawn 1-1. There was a long wait for the kick-off: the players were out on the field for eight minutes before the whistle was blown. After fifty-six years, a few more minutes wouldn't hurt. The team turned en masse to wave to the *roligans* before the national anthems.

Denmark had more of the ball and showed the classier touches in the first half, yet Scotland had the better chances. Søren Busk made a magnificent block with his instep from Charlie Nicholas, and the marauding right-back Richard Gough lofted a great chance over the bar after going past the keeper Rasmussen.

Rasmussen, who had been vomiting for forty-eight hours in the build-up, was a nervous figure throughout: he missed a number of crosses, handled the ball outside the area and almost bundled a Gordon Strachan cross into his own net in the second half. 'I don't want to use the illness as an excuse,' says Rasmussen. 'My performance wasn't good. I was not ill when I went into the game, I just hadn't had the best preparation.'

Ferguson was well aware of the threat posed by Denmark. When the draw was made he thought, 'One bloody burst of that Laudrup and we're in big trouble.' That burst came early in the game. After a long passing move, a thrilling solo run from Laudrup ended with a vicious long-range shot just over the bar. Denmark swaggered through the first half, mixing patient passing moves with sudden bursts of dribbling. Few sides have ever had such a devastating change of pace both individually and collectively. Denmark used possession as hypnosis before punishing opponents with a sudden increase in tempo. 'Nobody looks a mug on the ball,' said Brian Clough during the tournament. 'Everybody's comfortable with it. They just coax it and handle it and want to keep it – that's what you do when you've got something you love.'

Piontek had created a framework in which all Denmark's footballers could express themselves. Frimann says they were able 'to play with a lot of pleasure'. It was shiny, happy football – just like when they were children. 'In the seventies and eighties Denmark had very good street footballers who had a very good vision of the game and were very good technically, but we needed the hard hand, and he [Piontek] came with that,' says Morten Olsen. 'Nevertheless, he also saw that we couldn't play German football – we had to play with our vision of football, we needed some freedom in our play.'

Souness had also learned a few things from the street, as he demonstrated when he floored Jesper Olsen with an unpunished elbow. Much of the game ran through Arnesen, although he was as edgy as he was excellent: two outbursts at the referee hinted at what was to follow later in the tournament.

It was obvious what was to follow after half-time, when Denmark imposed their class to devastating effect. In a nine-minute spell they might have scored five times. Denmark's first World Cup goal was not so much in the post as sent by recorded delivery. Elkjær scored it in the fifty-eighth minute.

Before the game, Ferguson had told his centre-backs about Elkjær's ability to use the shins of opposing defenders; he would kick the ball off them, pick up the ricochet and run clear on goal. Forewarned was not forearmed, however. The goal was a languid relay run right through the centre of the pitch: Morten Olsen, Laudrup, Arnesen and finally Elkjær, who ran straight through Willie Miller before clipping an expert shot in off the far post. 'It was a good goal,' the Scotland defender Alex McLeish told the *Scotsman* in 2002, 'not a lucky one as people thought at the time.'

Denmark were fairly comfortable thereafter – Rasmussen, for all his jitters, did not actually have a save to make – but were fortunate when Roy Aitken had a goal wrongly disallowed for offside. Elkjær and Souness missed half-chances at either end, Frank McAvennie lobbed an overhead kick that looped over Rasmussen and just wide.

By far the most notable incident of the game's denouement was Berggreen's dreadful foul on Nicholas, for which he was booked. Berggreen's motive was simply to stop Nicholas, who was breaking dangerously, but he caught him so badly that he might have broken his ankle. Nicholas had to be carried off the pitch, with Scotland finishing the match with ten men. After the match Berggreen apologised but said he would 'have been an amateur' if he had not made the tackle. 'I did what any professional player would have done.' This was 1986, not 1978. Denmark were not the happy amateurs any more.

Nicholas was not happy either. He said it was 'the worst tackle I have ever received in my career. Really criminal.' Thirty years later, Berggreen continues the metaphor. 'Today I would get two years in prison for doing it. I did it for Denmark. He was free, so I had to stop him. That's the way we played in Italy. It's in the war. In those days that tackle was not so unusual, but of course I feel sorry for hurting him.'

Ferguson said Scotland were 'thoroughly unfortunate' to lose; a stretch, perhaps, but a reflection of a classy, open game to which they contributed fully. The consensus among the international media was that the last game of the first round of fixtures had probably been the best. Piontek takes great pleasure in teasing Ferguson about the result whenever he sees him.

There was a different kind of teasing going on after the game. In Mexico the Danish players had only spoken to their wives and girlfriends through the fence at training; now they were allowed some time alone. But first they had to sit through a formal dinner at the wives' hotel, with a mariachi band and local folk dancers laid on. 'There were,' laughs Elkjær, 'a lot of speeches.'

The players, who were sharing rooms, filled the time by bargaining over who would go first and who would have the most time. 'They thought more about their wives than the food,' says Frits Ahlstrøm. 'Some of them didn't even get to the starter.'

As the squad became increasingly impatient, the two single players, Berggreen and Andersen, decided to lighten the mood. 'We could feel this tension, so to make everyone a little bit more relaxed we took each other's hand and walked off towards the lifts,' says Berggreen. 'We were standing by the lifts laughing, and within two and a half seconds Ivan Nielsen arrived with his wife. "Come on, Ivan!" It was so funny.'

A few days later, the joy of six would be on Denmark's mind.

Chapter 16

A public fiesta of football

Uruguay weren't just World Cup opponents, they were World Cup legends. In 1930 they won Jules Rimet's inaugural competition, which they hosted in Montevideo. After refusing to enter the pre-war editions in Europe in the 1930s, they silenced the Maracanã and sent a nation into mourning when they beat Brazil to win the 1950 World Cup. It needed extra-time for the Magical Magyars of Hungary finally to loosen Uruguay's grip on the tournament in the semi-finals of 1954. In the first Mexico World Cup in 1970 they finished third and, after a brief hiatus, returned to the greatest competition on earth in 1986 as one of the favourites to win the trophy.

There was good reason. Uruguay were reigning South American champions, having outmanoeuvred Brazil over two legs in 1983, and considered one of the teams likeliest to win in 1986. The inability of any European side to register a World Cup win across the Atlantic was no fluke as the likes of Uruguay provided a formidable barrier in the Americas. The architect of their team was Enzo Francescoli, a player so captivating that Zinedine Zidane – who watched Francescoli at Marseilles – would name his first-born after him. He completed a huge transfer from River Plate in Argentina to Racing Club of Paris on the eve of the tournament and was expected to showcase to a world audience the gifts that made him a South American Footballer of the Year. Yet at the

1986 World Cup the Uruguayan team didn't do football, they just did players.

Many teams have claimed to be prepared to do whatever it takes to win a match but seldom has the elasticity of this maxim been so tested. At times it seemed as if Uruguay took the Group of Death literally, almost as if they were being paid by the corpse. Quite what prompted the change in emphasis from artistic expression to sadistic intention no one knows – perhaps a solitary win against Canada in their eight previous warm-up matches drained their confidence. Uruguay left the World Cup with their manager banished to the stands, several of their players disgraced and suspended and the Scottish Football Association chief Ernie Walker labelling them 'the scum of world football'.

The warning signs were there against West Germany in their opening game, the dour 1-1 draw in Querétaro. Uruguay held on to an early lead until Klaus Allofs stole a grubby equaliser five minutes from time. In between the goals they defended their advantage with a ferocity that prompted Fifa to send a warning letter to the Uruguayan Federation over incidents in the game. Somehow they only picked up two yellow cards, but the tone of Uruguay's tournament had been set. There was definitely a whiff of menace about them but it had precious little to do with their football – and it would soon get worse.

In Francescoli they at least had someone who could offer a potent threat with the ball, and Sepp Piontek knew it. If Denmark could put the shackles on him they could control the match. The man-marking duty was given to Ivan Nielsen, under clear instructions to cling to Francescoli like a barnacle to the underside of a boat. After years of man-to-man marking the likes of Marco van Basten in the Dutch league this kind of assignment was second nature. Any thought that his treatment of Francescoli might provoke some retribution from some of the more spiky characters in the Uruguay side was unlikely to make Nielsen lose sleep. 'I don't take, I give,' he says of his playing style, accompanied by both a childlike giggle and a stern glint in the eye that suggests only a fool would test that statement. Henrik Andersen came into the side in place of Jesper Olsen but otherwise Denmark were unchanged from the Scotland game.

The teams walked out on to the pitch at Neza knowing that the dynamics of the group had shifted earlier in the day. After conceding an early goal, West Germany bounced back to beat Scotland 2-1 in Querétaro and gain control of the group. A win would see Denmark back in charge, a draw would put them second at the least, but a defeat would put them in third place, opening the group back up for Scotland and with West Germany to face in the final game. In most World Cups an opening-game victory allows a team to relax. Not here. That was the beauty of the Group of Death; there was danger at every turn.

Piontek left the team in no doubt that they were playing for more than just two points. 'You have won the first game and that was well done, but have you got any idea what the world will say if we beat Uruguay, the South American champions?' he told his players. This was Denmark's first ever professional match against South American opposition, arguably the highest-profile game in their entire history, and as such an occasion befitting something special. One teacher at Hvalsø school near Roskilde even declared an unofficial school holiday. 'I don't want to see you on Monday' was her parting message as she sent her pupils away for the weekend. It meant they could stay up to watch a match that kicked off at midnight on Sunday. Those children enjoyed a different kind of midnight feast.

When the match began, it was immediately evident that the Uruguayans had a plan that would make that tempestuous game between Denmark and Belgium in Strasbourg look like port and cigars at a gentleman's club. In the fourth minute Michael Laudrup, on the floor after sliding in to regain the ball in a tackle, was kicked in the face by Miguel Bossio while the unknowing referee, Jan Keizer, followed the play.

If the intention was to kick Laudrup into hiding it didn't work. In the eleventh minute he set off on one of the gliding and effortless runs that would be a feature of his World Cup, going away from Francescoli and over a scything lunge from Eduardo Acevedo before releasing Elkjær into the penalty area. Elkjær drilled a merciless left-foot shot underneath the goalkeeper, Fernando Alvez, to put Denmark in front. Back home in Aalborg, one fan punched a table so hard in celebration that he fractured a metacarpal in his hand. He waited until the end of the game before driving to hospital, and his story appeared in *Ekstra Bladet* a few days later. The doctor's report of the injury reflected a country that was on first-name terms with its heroes: 'Banged right hand down on table during Denmark–Uruguay game when Preben scored the first goal.'

The goal had been signposted since kick-off. There was a fluidity to Denmark's movement on and off the ball that made it seem certain that there was more to come. Laudrup was wreaking havoc in the oasis between the midfield and the forwards. Two minutes after the goal, Bossio opted to wallop him off the ball again, but this time Keizer caught it and showed a yellow card. That wasn't the first card of the afternoon; Nielsen was booked for a mistimed tackle on Francescoli, his first ever yellow card for Denmark and one of only two in fifty-one appearances for his country. He also fouled Francescoli on several other occasions during the match, much to the Uruguayans' annoyance. Nielsen's fouls, however, were fairly innocuous, and no one could make the case that he was quite so keen to be dismissed as Bossio. Six minutes after his caution for the foul on Laudrup, Bossio flew into a ludicrously late challenge on Frank Arnesen and was sent off. On ITV John Helm sought his co-commentator Billy McNeill's verdict. 'The man's a head case, John, isn't he?' McNeill replied. Playing against ten men is not always easy – there were seven other red cards at the 1986 World Cup, and in the 215 minutes of those games the team with the numerical advantage failed to score. Five days later, Uruguay would play eighty-nine minutes against Scotland with ten players and keep a clean sheet. Denmark had the lead, though, and only had to sit on it by keeping the ball away from Francescoli and seeing the game out.

That was about as likely as Bossio receiving an honorary doctorate for humanitarianism. Denmark poured forward at every opportunity looking for more goals, having one by Elkjær disallowed and also two good penalty appeals turned down. Uruguay cracked five minutes before half-time. Søren Lerby led a breakaway from his own half and shifted the ball out to Elkjær on the right wing. Elkjær sized up his marker and burst past him before hooking a low cross into the penalty area. Lerby had continued running and made the classic late arrival of the goalscoring midfielder, burying the ball in the Uruguayan net with his left foot. With the game seemingly now dead in the water, Francescoli went to ground to win a generous penalty in the final minute of the half, which he converted to just about keep Uruguay's hopes alive.

It was the briefest stay of execution. Early in the second half Laudrup ended the match as a contest with a bewitching moment of genius. It would resonate through the 1986 World Cup and beyond. 'Laudrup is, quite simply, a magnificent player,' Graeme Souness said prior to Mexico, 'he goes past players better than anyone I have seen.' Uruguay were about to get a demonstration of this.

There didn't seem anything on when Laudrup picked up the ball from Lerby around thirty yards from goal, but a quick spin and shake of the hips took him past Mario Saralegui. Laudrup swayed to the right to avoid Nelson Gutierrez, who was also distracted by a dynamic off-the-ball dart from Lerby. As he had done four years earlier for Jesper Olsen against England, Lerby's selfless running created the space for one of the most famous goals in Danish football.

Laudrup cut back to his left and surged into the area and away from Victor Diogo. All of a sudden he was bearing down on Alvez in goal. Alvez was out quickly but Laudrup went around him and rolled the ball between the posts. Acevedo reached it but could only help it over the line; only the most miserable pedant could have awarded an own goal.

Incredibly, the scorer of one of the best goals in the 1986 or indeed any World Cup doesn't even rate it particularly highly. 'I think it was really easy,' Laudrup says now. 'I just took the ball and ran, I only had to change direction once. I really don't think it was anything special.' There is no sense of false modesty; it is simply that genius sees football through different eyes. Few agreed with Laudrup's verdict. In isolation, but in unison, both Helm and Svend Gehrs called him a genius.

Few players have received the kind of lavish praise that Laudrup would get from the true greats of the game. Johan Cruyff and Franz Beckenbauer have both given gushing testimonies to his greatness, and his peers such as Michel Platini, Romário, Raúl, Luis Figo and Hristo Stoichkov all bear witness to just how special he was to play either with or against. A modern master like Andrés Iniesta is prepared to go all the way with his praise. When asked who was the best player in history he replied: 'Laudrup.'

After Mexico, in a glittering career with Juventus, Barcelona, Real Madrid and Ajax, he would become one of the greatest football players the world has ever seen. His rate of goalscoring would slow down through his twenties as he adopted the more selfless role of loading the gun for the world's best strikers rather than firing it himself. Laudrup became the king of assists. He utilised all the conventional methods and honed others to perfection, like the delicate scooped ball over the top of a packed defence or the blind pass that went in a different direction from his line of vision and could hoodwink an entire team. 'To do a thing that nobody expects and it ends in a goal, that's a bigger satisfaction than to score a great goal myself,' says Laudrup. It's arguable that no other player has elevated the assist into such an art form. Every now and then, and seemingly on a whim, Laudrup would provide a reminder of that moment of inspiration in Neza with a little solo riff of his own.

At 3-1 he and his team-mates were turning the game into a carnival of free expression, though it wasn't exactly going down well with the opposition. Shortly after the goal, Jorge Da Silva sent Jens Jørn Bertelsen crashing to the floor in the same clinically precise manner with which a lumberjack fells a pine tree with a chainsaw, writing off any interest in the ball and landing a sickening stamp halfway up Bertelsen's leg while it was planted on the floor. The Danish players, fearing another Allan Simonsen incident, rushed to their stricken comrade. They alternated between desperately calling for a stretcher and remonstrating with the referee to take action.

Da Silva had already been booked, yet even by the standards of 1986 the sheer sociopathic nature of such a challenge warranted a straight red card. Incredibly, Da Silva wasn't even pulled to one side by the referee and asked to turn it down a notch. If Klaus Berggreen's tackle on Charlie Nicholas would get you two years in prison these days then Da Silva's was life with no parole. Jan Mølby came on to replace Bertelsen, who now had a huge doubt over his future participation in the tournament.

After the savagery towards their colleague, Denmark turned the remainder of the game into a righteous infliction of retributive justice. With the game won, an advisable policy might have been to ease off, given the numbing heat and with the games coming thick and fast, but it seemed that a subconscious, collective decision had been made to give Uruguay a beating. 'If we could have beaten them 10-1 we would have done,' says Berggreen. 'We couldn't stop. It was our way of playing.' As with the pre-tournament training, they were like wild horses. Even Uruguay couldn't tame them. Gehrs says that Piontek told the team before the game that they should eschew the dribbling because of Uruguay's thuggishness – 'and what they did was dribble more than ever'.

At the heart of everything was Laudrup, who was quite simply unplayable. In the sixty-ninth minute he set off on another meandering saunter through the Uruguayan defence, bouncing through challenges only to see his shot saved by Alvez. Elkjær raced in to gobble up the rebound and make it 4-1. There were eighteen consecutive passes between Danish players in the build-up to the goal, interspersed with a defiantly arrogant cameo from Morten Olsen, who dribbled around Francescoli on the edge of the Danish penalty area when he was the last man.

Ten minutes later Elkjær completed his hat-trick after being sent clear by Mølby, and raced fifty yards with the ball to glide effortlessly past Alvez and tuck the ball away. Even Brian Clough, who spent most of his stint as an ITV pundit for the World Cup being distinctly underwhelmed by what he was seeing, dropped the act for a second. 'That,' he exclaimed in the post-match assessment, 'was gorgeous.' Laudrup was booted to the floor again as he ran with Elkjær to offer support to the attack but the referee took no action. Such was the determination coursing through the Danish players that it scarcely mattered any more.

Uruguay were punch-drunk and the *roligans* loved every second. Each pass was met with an *olé* and the song '*Og Det Var Danmark*' rang out loud and clear in the stands. There is a clip in *Hero!*, the brilliantly awful official film of the tournament, of the whites of the devastated Francescoli's eyes as he looks back down the pitch at his team being ripped apart. In the face of their opponents' aggression, Denmark could have met fire with fire; instead, they met it with flair, and blew the Uruguayans away. Two minutes from time, Elkjær escaped down the right wing and crossed the ball for Jesper Olsen, who had come on as a substitute. He duly shot through the beleaguered Alvez to complete the rout – 6-1, the heaviest World Cup defeat in Uruguay's illustrious history. 'It's the smartest football I have ever seen any national team play,' Gehrs says now, 'but it wasn't a game. It was a show.'

The crowd roared their approval and several Danish fans made their way on to the pitch. One handed Elkjær a bouquet of flowers. Another, wearing only the tiniest pair of pants – red and white, of course – waved the Danish national flag in the centre circle and bowed at his heroes as they left the field. Elkjær punched the air as he left the pitch, and with good reason. It had been one of the most exhilarating slaughters of a team in the history of the World Cup. The Mexican TV commentator caught the mood in one line: 'Señores, Señores, you have just witnessed a public fiesta of football.' The joy was catching outside the stadium too.

'I remember after the Uruguay match it was a very poor area in which we were playing,' says Berggreen twenty years on. 'When we left the stadium and went out on to the street there were people applauding all over, just for us.' Back in Denmark in the still of the night a group of pilots at the military base at Karup found tins of white and red paint and sprayed a Draken jet in the colours of the Danish flag. The lieutenant colonel in charge allowed one of the pilots to take the jet on a round trip to the other bases in the country.

Praise flowed from César Luis Menotti, one of the standard-bearers of the attacking game and coach of the stylish Argentinian team that won the 1978 World Cup under the black cloud of the military junta. 'An example to boys everywhere,' he told the English press. 'They don't stall, they go out to play and shame the others.' The sight of base cynicism being so skilfully humiliated in Neza had warmed hearts all over the world. 'There are players true to the spirit of the game who can still delight the crowd,' Menotti continued on his kindred spirits, 'like Denmark.'

The media joined in the swooning the next day. DENMARK'S FIRE SETS FINALS ALIGHT was the headline in the *Guardian*, with David Lacey memorably summarising the game as 'a sort of Pamplona in reverse, with the bulls running away from the daring young men'. In Italy, *La Gazzetta dello Sport* captured the magic in two words: FAVOLOSA DINAMARCA, and Norwegian newspaper *VG* argued that Denmark had become the favourites for the World Cup overnight. In *The Times*, Clive White went for the greatest comparison of all. 'The arrival of these Danish princes is reminiscent of Brazil's reclamation of their crown at the last World Cup here sixteen years ago.' In the same paper, Simon Barnes went for a more familiar reference. 'Uruguay had cast themselves as the Draculas of the tournament, so how pleasant it was to see them get thumped – and thumped by a side who played the loveliest football I have seen since the Dutch of 1974,' he wrote. 'That moment when Elkjær faked left and then *went* left to score ... for once it was a moment worth being replayed seventy-eight times. It is the kind of thing that gives football a good name.'

It was the combination at the head of Denmark's team that was really getting people excited. The Swedish author Per Olov Enquist wrote in the Danish newspaper *Politiken* that there ought to be a green field in heaven reserved for Laudrup and Elkjær. 'We – the spectators – will also come and join the game on this heavenly evening,' he said. The potency of Denmark's front two had illuminated the opening week of the tournament and they were by far and away the most dangerous strike force in the World Cup. In the Ballon d'Or voting at the end of 1985, Elkjær finished second and Laudrup fourth; Elkjær's World Cup hat-trick took his tally for Denmark to 37 in 58 games, whereas Laudrup's wonder goal took him to 18 in 32.

It was debatable who had the better game of the two. Elkjær could rightly lay claim to one of the best individual performances in World Cup history. 'I think people remember that I participated in five goals in that game,' he laughs. 'I certainly do!' With four goals in two games already, he was reaching for the laces to tie up the golden boot. Yet the general consensus is that he was marginally eclipsed by Laudrup, who set up two of Elkjær's goals as well as adorning the game with a brilliant individual goal of his own. In his recollection of the game years later, Jesper Olsen's first memory is that 'Laudrup was fantastic in that game'.

With a strike force in such devastating form, the dream – that Denmark could actually win the World Cup at their first attempt – was starting to look possible. Elsewhere in Mexico only the USSR had so far managed a performance of similar magnitude when they larruped Hungary 6-0. The prospect of replicating the Constitution Day spectacular across the Atlantic in the knockout rounds was mouth-watering. Denmark's preparation was paying off – with two games gone in the tournament they were flying and looked the best team in it, already through to the knockout stages.

Not that they were without problems. With Frimann's injury ahead of the Scotland game Denmark had already lost one player, and Da Silva's assault on Bertelsen put him out of the third group match against West Germany with badly damaged ligaments. It would need round-the-clock treatment of icing down the injury and gentle jogs to try and get him ready for the knockout rounds, but he could scarcely be expected to be fully fit. As one of the first names on Piontek's team sheet Bertelsen was vital. There were problems in goal, too. Troels Rasmussen's first two games had been marked by indecision and Ole Qvist was still sick, opening up the possibility of seeing that rarest of birds at the World Cup: the third-choice goalkeeper, in this case Lars Høgh. It also opened up an interesting stick-or-twist dilemma for the West Germany game. With Denmark now so much in charge of their own fortunes they could weigh up alternatives of opponents and altitude for the second round. Those worries, however, were for another day.

When the players returned to the hotel a party had been arranged to celebrate the victory. Also in the foyer were the Scotland squad, who had just arrived to prepare themselves for the special attention of the Uruguayans in a few days' time. Few Danish players decided to hang around, though a curious Piontek did stay to observe proceedings. Fascinated by the refuelling habits of the Scottish players, he ended up serving their drinks.

That one afternoon of kaleidoscopic movement, lightning pace and dead-eyed finishing imprinted the Denmark team on the consciousness of lovers of the beautiful game for ever. That it was such a one-sided hiding largely excludes it from those lists of greatest ever World Cup matches dredged up when the tournament comes around every four years, but it stands as a peerless demonstration of superiority by one tournament favourite over another. It has become the main exhibit in the case for the enduring greatness of Piontek's team. The 6-1 in Neza is as evocative a memory of the 1986 World Cup as Diego Maradona, Panini stickers and that odd, spider-shaped patch of dark grass in the centre circle at the Azteca stadium.

Chapter 17

Pyrrhic victory

On the map they were neighbours, but there were oceans between Denmark and West Germany on Planet Football. The two sides had met just five times since the Second World War, with Denmark's sole win coming in a friendly in which West Germany lined up with a team of amateur players. During the early years of Sepp Piontek's reign, the West Germans had been reluctant to play friendlies against Denmark. When Mexico 86 came around they were anything but indifferent to their neighbours from the north. 'For years, Denmark's main exports have been porn and cheese,' noted a German TV reporter. 'But since the arrival of the German manager, football is Denmark's main brand.'

When the Group of Death was picked out of the bowls in Mexico City, the 14 June clash against the Germans was targeted by many Danes as their crucial game. Piontek was facing his countrymen while Søren Lerby was going up against Lothar Matthäus and the Bayern Munich team-mates he had only just bid farewell to after switching to Monaco. These two match-ups hadn't gone unnoticed in either country. *Der Nordschleswiger*, a newspaper for the German minority living in southern Denmark, printed a full-page ad with pictures of Franz Beckenbauer and Piontek. THERE IS A GERMAN BEHIND EVERY SUCCESS read the headline. The Danish newspaper *Jydske Tidende* responded by running a picture of Lerby and the text: 'There is a Dane behind every championship'.

In Italy there was a further sub-plot. Here it was billed as Preben Elkjær against Hans-Peter Briegel: the chain-smoking star striker and the decathlete-turned-defender who had been an inspirational duo during Hellas Verona's *Scudetto*-winning season. They had been team-mates and friends, sharing the swimming pool by their house in Bardolino near Lake Garda, and the thirty-kilometre car journey to Verona's training facility. 'Of course I'm going to give Briegel a kicking,' Elkjær joked when a Danish reporter met the two players in Italy. It was indicative of how their national teams' stock had fluctuated in the early eighties that Briegel wasn't going to cast West Germany as the favourites. 'I think expectations are higher in Denmark, where everybody expects at least to see the team in the last sixteen and probably go even further.'

After the first two group games in Mexico, Briegel's assessment of the Danes had only gained more traction; maximum points, seven goals and the adoration of the world press bestowed on them. But one thing didn't fit the script. The game against West Germany – the game Elkjær, Piontek, Lerby and most of Denmark had been talking about for six months – was no longer a battle for qualification but merely a decider for first place in the group. Both teams had already reached the second stage, and thanks to the Danes' 6-1 thrashing of Uruguay, West Germany were virtually guaranteed second place even if they lost the final game.

A win against the Germans initially looked an attractive proposition for Denmark – landmark victory, top the Group of Death, stay in Querétaro and have an extra day's rest. They would also stay in what on paper looked the easier side of the draw (Brazil, Italy, France and Mexico were in the other – favourites, world champions, European champions and hosts respectively). There was only one flaw in the equation: Spain awaited the winner of their group while the second-placed team faced Morocco.

To the loser belonged the spoils. This strange scenario clouded the build-up to the game in some tension and confusion. Memories of the Disgrace of Gijón at the 1982 World Cup in Spain were still raw. With the other last-round game of their group played the previous day, West Germany beat Austria 1-0 in a match in which any semblance of football ceased after eleven minutes, when the goal was scored. Both teams knew that scoreline would put them through at Algeria's expense. In Mexico, pride and prestige prevented the Danes from ever considering such conspiratorial mischief. 'Normally we should not win against West Germany,' says Piontek. 'But to go to my team and tell them to lose the game? That I will not do. It's not the soul of football.'

Jesper Olsen says the thought of playing for a draw or defeat never crossed the players' minds. A win against West Germany would be a further confidence boost for the squad, and getting one over on his countrymen was too important for their manager. 'Piontek would love to beat the Germans, and also because it's such a great footballing nation I don't think you ever go out and say "let's get a draw". It was just not in our team.'

If his record as Bundesliga manager had been found wanting, Piontek's tenure in Denmark had earned him the respect of his peers. In April he had gone to the West German embassy in Copenhagen to receive his *Bundesverdienstkreuz*, the German federal order of merit. Among previous recipients were footballing greats Sepp Herberger, Fritz Walter and Helmut Schön, the very manager who had cut Piontek from the 1966 squad. Knowing that Beckenbauer planned to quit as manager after Euro 88, the head of the German Football Association, Hermann Neuberger, suggested before Mexico that Piontek was among the candidates to take over as their next coach.

Not that the prospect of swapping sides looked particularly attractive at this stage. On top of losing their first ever World Cup qualifier, against Portugal in October 1985, West Germany had suffered the ignominy of playing six games in a row without a win – the first time this had happened since the Second World War. In

175

June 1985, Beckenbauer and his team travelled to Mexico to play two friendlies against England and the World Cup hosts. Less than two days after their fifteen-hour journey via Dallas, West Germany turned in a lethargic performance against England in a half-empty Azteca stadium. They lost 3-0 and hardly improved three days later with a 2-0 defeat against Mexico.

Beckenbauer had failed in trying to talk Bernd Schuster into a return to the national team, and the manager didn't think he had the talent available to go all the way in Mexico. Blaming the long domestic season, he told reporters before his team's departure that he wasn't sure whether it was even worth making the journey: 'With this team we cannot even get close to winning the world championship.' The turmoil continued when they arrived in Mexico. The tabloid *Bild* ran lurid stories about late-night shenanigans, while Dieter Hoeness and the unused sub Olaf Thon rowed with their manager; the reserve keeper Uli Stein was sent home after calling Beckenbauer a laughing stock. Years later it was Beckenbauer who was laughing when, according to the book *Tor!*, he told a journalist: 'Well, can you believe we reached the final of a World Cup with these players?'

Beckenbauer had vowed to fight tooth and nail for victory in the Denmark game, but his desire was tempered with pragmatism when he decided to leave Pierre Littbarski and Karl-Heinz Rummenigge on the bench. Piontek also made four changes from the previous game, more out of necessity than with a view to sparing his star players. The creative axis of Elkjær, Michael Laudrup, Frank Arnesen and Lerby was still in the starting XI. He rested Klaus Berggreen and Ivan Nielsen, both of whom were one yellow card away from suspension, introduced Jan Mølby in place of the injured Jens Jørn Bertelsen and gave Lars Høgh a chance in goal.

'The weather was insanely hot,' remembers Søren Busk about a game that kicked off at midday on Friday 13 June in Querétaro.

While Busk had to run to the touchline to get water during breaks in play, he watched bemused as the German players had tiny plastic bags thrown on to the pitch. 'Then they bit a hole and got liquid. It was clever, something we hadn't thought of. It was just something that made you think, well, they have tried this before.' For all Denmark's talent and meticulous preparations, experience was a rare commodity that proved all too valuable during this World Cup.

In the early exchanges, German ambition seemed as thin as the air the players were gasping for. Morten Olsen commanded the Danish box and darted out to intercept any advances. The Danes were a last-man clearance away from the lead in the seventh minute after right-back John Sivebæk again demonstrated the team's freewheeling approach. He won the ball near the halfway line and continued his run into the penalty area while Elkjær played Laudrup down the right wing. Laudrup found Sivebæk, who went past the German keeper, Harald Schumacher, before directing a diagonal shot back at goal, only for Karlheinz Förster to make the block. One minute later, Lerby's goalbound shot from twenty-five yards forced the German keeper to save at full stretch. If there had ever been a memo about backing off in this game, it never made it to the Danish dressing room.

Not that the Germans were reluctant to take part either once the game got going. Klaus Allofs and Matthäus both forced brilliant stops from Høgh, before Andreas Brehme unleashed a cannonball of a shot after half an hour. Only the bar saved Denmark, the force of the strike sending the German wing-back to ground so that he required medical treatment to his back.

As if pre-ordained, Morten Olsen gave one of his finest performances in the libero position with the master himself, Beckenbauer, watching from the German dugout. After a botched Denmark corner, Völler got an open run down the left touchline but Olsen raced back from the halfway circle to time his sliding tackle to perfection. 'You have to read the game,' Olsen says. 'You have to control it but you also have to coach the other players. It's a lot easier when you are in your thirties and you have a lot of experience.'

The crowning glory came two minutes before the end of the first half. Olsen picked up the ball in the centre circle, hesitated for a split second while he scanned the field ahead, and then set off on a breathtaking run towards the German penalty area. He edged past Wolfgang Rolff whose feeble attempt to keep up the pace caused him only to trip Olsen. Penalty. When Olsen arrived at Cologne after the World Cup, he heard from his team-mates that Beckenbauer had told the German team not to worry about Olsen's raids because he wasn't quick enough. 'So he was wrong there,' laughs Olsen. 'Mostly Beckenbauer is never wrong.'

The other Olsen, Jesper, calmly placed the ball in the bottom left corner and Arnesen was the first to throw his arms around the goalscorer.

Arnesen had been booked earlier in the half. It looked as if Dietmar Jakobs had committed a clear foul on the edge of the German penalty area, but the Belgian referee, Alexis Ponnet, decided that Arnesen had dived. Ponnet, who had awarded the penalty to Allan Simonsen at Wembley in 1983, said before the game that he wouldn't tolerate any players 'trying to have me on'. Arnesen was seething after the yellow card, folding his hands behind his back as he remonstrated with Ponnet before walking away shaking his head.

With hindsight it's easy to see why a player who had been kicked about and unjustly booked was on the edge of combusting. At the time, most people were simply in awe of another stupendous display from Arnesen, whose twists, turns and bursts down the touchline kept unlocking space behind the German defenders. Then again, most people at the time had no idea that Arnesen hadn't slept for almost two days in the build-up to the game because he was keeping a vigil by his wife's bedside.

Kate Arnesen had fallen ill while staying with the other players' wives in Mexico. When she was taken to hospital in Querétaro, doctors discovered that she had a brain infection. It wasn't sunstroke, as had been suggested. It was meningitis. 'It was awful,' Arnesen told the magazine *Billed-Bladet* after Kate had made a full recovery. 'Never have I seen somebody so ill. Kate just lay there. She couldn't even speak. It was terribly draining.' Arnesen went ahead and played the game but his mind never quite left the hospital bed during the game against West Germany.

Jakobs was at it again in the second half after a glorious piece of skill from Arnesen, who picked up the ball on the edge of his own area and ran almost the length of the field. He played a double one-two with John Eriksen, on as a substitute for the injured Elkjær, and approached Jakobs on the edge of the German penalty area. Wingers usually beat their man with either change of direction or change of pace; Arnesen combined the two in a unique and exhilarating speed-shuffle. He slowed down and started to go left, then almost instantaneously moved right and burst past Jakobs, whose desperate lunge earned him a booking. Arnesen was left pounding the ground in pain and frustration. The Danish marking had started to slip on the hour mark when Matthäus found himself with acres of space in the Danish box with only Høgh to beat. The Danish keeper, undeterred and unwavering in his commitment, rushed out and parried the ball with both hands.

Those in the German camp who thought goalkeeping was the weak position in the Danish side hadn't paid much attention to the shot-stopping ability of third-choice keeper Høgh, who produced one of the great goalkeeping World Cup debuts. Peter Schmeichel, the player Høgh had pipped to the post for a place in the squad, would go on to monopolise Denmark's number one shirt in the nineties, but Høgh got his moment in the sun. 'When you look back on it it's like a movie,' says Høgh. 'You're just part of it. It was a great time.' The greatest time for Høgh came eight years later when he kept a clean sheet in his club Odense's astonishing win over Real Madrid in the 1994 Uefa Cup.

At the other end of the pitch, Denmark found another heroic debutant after one of the most audacious moves in the tournament. Henrik Andersen's chipped goal kick was picked up by Lerby in the middle of the Danish half. He brought the ball forward and laid it off parallel to Mølby, who found Arnesen wide open on the right edge of the German box. Arnesen squared a fizzing pass in front of goal where Eriksen powered the ball high into the net. The build-up was a study in delicious simplicity, accentuated by the devastating change of pace that had created the assist. And it had all started with a chipped goal kick.

For all the headline-grabbing stars surrounding him, Eriksen was one of the most natural goal scorers the Dynamite era ever saw. 'The forgotten man of top Danish football has been anonymous for too long,' wrote *B.T.* when Piontek picked Eriksen for the 1986 squad. Whereas others happily hogged the limelight, Eriksen thrived in the relative anonymity of the smaller clubs. But there was nothing modest about his goalscoring. His thirty-six goals for Swiss side Servette in the 1987–8 season earned him second place in the European Golden Shoe award. Nielsen played alongside him for a year at Feyenoord. 'He was always standing there when the ball dropped,' he says. 'I don't know how he did it. It was the same in training. A special, special guy.'

The Germans never looked like threatening the Danes' lead after Eriksen's goal. A few minutes later, Piontek sent on Allan Simonsen to replace Jesper Olsen. Two years on from his broken leg in Paris, Simonsen got his curtain call on the biggest stage. It was to be his only appearance in a World Cup and his final competitive match for Denmark. 'It was a gift,' says Piontek. 'A thank you.' As the stadium announcer read out Simonsen's name, the *roligans* in Estadio La Corregidro erupted with a rousing cheer. Few of them would have noticed that Rummenigge, another former European Footballer of the Year, was also getting ready on the touchline to make his entrance.

It was Simonsen's penultimate appearance for Denmark; he retired from international football after a farewell appearance, also against West Germany, at the start of the following season. 'It took longer than I expected to recover but I'm very happy I played at the World Cup,' he says. 'It was a good time to step down after that.'

With a few minutes to go, Ponnet looked at his watch. He had no intention of prolonging a game in which the tempo had ground to a comedy slow motion. Most of the players' thoughts were already in the next round when Arnesen received the ball and made his most fateful contribution in a Denmark shirt. The other German players around him were technically walking by this stage but Matthäus took it upon himself to chase down the ball. Arnesen turned around. Morten Olsen was wide open ten yards in front of him. All he had to do was lay the ball back, Olsen would pass it back to Høgh, another few seconds would run off the clock and the game was over.

Instead, the pair got tangled up and Matthäus tackled Arnesen, going in on his left ankle. Arnesen tried to move away, but Matthäus's raking challenge brought him down. Then the fuse blew. Arnesen later described it as a 'reflex move'. On his knees and looking away from Matthäus, Arnesen kicked back with his right foot. It looked like a hundred-metres sprinter kicking out to feel the starter blocks. Matthäus reacted as if he had been hit by a train.

Arnesen quickly picked up the ball and tried to get on with his free-kick, but Ponnet had seen everything. He presented the red card with a conductor's flourish of the hand, and Arnesen clutched his knees before rolling over backwards. Then he knelt down holding his head. He somehow found the grace to get up and shake Matthäus's hand. Then came the long walk. 'Damn, it was as if it was buzzing inside my head,' Arnesen told Danmarks Radio in 1989. 'I didn't hear anything.' When he crossed the touchline,

Hoeness looked at him in bewilderment: 'Why did you do something like that?'

The referee restarted the game, then blew the final whistle thirty-five seconds later.

Arnesen had been substituted in five of the seven games he played at France 84 and in Mexico. When there was nothing on the line against West Germany he played until the all-too-bitter end. 'Arnesen was never a player who got two yellow cards,' says Piontek. 'He was a player who was always technical.'

Nielsen reckons Arnesen should have been substituted after the first booking. Their wives roomed together so he knew how severe Kate Arnesen's illness had been. 'Of course it would have been on his mind before the game,' says Nielsen.

If leaving Arnesen on the pitch seemed a strange decision, nobody could argue with Denmark's intention to win the game. Piontek says that while on paper Spain were more daunting opposition, victory against Morocco in the next game was no foregone conclusion. Morocco, who knew a thing or two about playing in the heat, had topped their group and conceded only one goal. 'Who says we would have won?' says Piontek. 'I would do the same if I was coach today.'

Elkjær says there has been lots of talk over the years about whether they should have lost the game, but nobody mentioned it back then. 'It's not the Danish way,' says Elkjær. 'The manager didn't say anything about that. If he had we would have said "are you crazy?" It was important to win this group, because it was a very tough group – the Group of Death – and we were fairly sure that we would beat Spain, because we were a better team than Spain.'

Chapter 18

The worst time

Sepp Piontek was walking through the team hotel in Querétaro when he heard some of his players confirm what his instincts told him: that they were starting to become homesick. Denmark had won the Group of Death – almost a tournament within a tournament – in stunning style. What more could any self-respecting Dane ask for? 'I heard them say they had done very well,' says Piontek, 'and if they now had problems it was not so bad and they could go home and have holidays.'

Trust is good but control is better. Piontek tried to regain control by giving a speech that was pitched somewhere between Churchill and Hollywood. For some of the players the memory is vivid. 'I remember it very well because it is something you can really use as a manager,' says Michael Laudrup. 'He said, "I know some of you are tired. You want to win tomorrow, but if you don't, well, you are tired. Some of you are tired physically and all of you are tired mentally. I want to tell you one thing: we are Denmark, we are not West Germany, we are not Italy, we are not Brazil. For some of you, maybe for all of you, this will be the first and the last time you will ever participate in a World Cup."

'I remember that, because the next time Denmark played a World Cup, twelve years later, there was only one player left: me.' It stayed with Laudrup; he gave a similar speech to his own Swansea players before their Capital One Cup final victory over Bradford in 2013.

Laudrup had been the centre of attention before the game against Spain. He had turned twenty-two three days earlier. Two years before, Denmark had beaten Yugoslavia 5-0 the day after his twentieth birthday. 'It would be fantastic if we could do that again when we play Spain,' he said. 'But the present I would really love most, of course, is the World Cup.'

His comments reflected the mood around the world, not just among the Danish squad. A banner on the streets of Querétaro needed no translation: *Dinamarca Dinamita Roja! Proxima Victima España!* They were huge favourites to beat Spain – Ladbrokes gave them odds of 4-6, Spain 7-2 – and nobody really cared that they were playing Spain rather than Morocco. 'After the group stage,' says Laudrup, 'we thought: "Phwoar, we're good, we're *good*."' Their potential quarter-final opponents, Belgium, who had beaten the USSR 4-3 in a controversial second-round thriller, were little to worry about.

During the build-up Spain's Ramón Calderé was fined £8,000 for failing a drugs test but was not banned, with Fifa accepting his explanation that he was given medication in hospital for food poisoning. Piontek was not happy with that, or with a Fifa mix-up that meant both sides were staying in the same hotel in Querétaro. Despite an official complaint, both teams remained in the hotel; Klaus Berggreen recalls waving to the Spanish players by the pool as Denmark went off for yet another training session. Spain were pretty relaxed despite their formidable opponents. 'Denmark play very well,' said Emilio Butragueño, 'but they also let you play.' Some Denmark fans travelled home before the game, either because they had run out of money or because they had not expected Denmark to get through the group stage and had already made plans to do so.

There were the usual fitness problems before the game. Ole Qvist had recovered from dizziness but was only on the bench, Preben Elkjær needed extensive treatment for the injury he had sustained against West Germany, Jens Jørn Bertelsen played even though he was not 100 per cent fit after his bad injury against Uruguay and John Sivebæk was ruled out of the game with a stomach bug. He had been fine when he went to bed the night before, a young man high on the prospect of a World Cup knockout match. Overnight his stomach was so bad that he told Piontek he was not sure he could play. Piontek left the decision up to Sivebæk. After much soul-searching, he pulled out. His place was taken by Henrik Andersen, which meant Jesper Olsen would move from the left wing to the right. He was in the side in place of the suspended Frank Arnesen, whom many, including Piontek, felt had been Denmark's best player in the group stage.

Jesper Olsen, Andersen and the goalkeeper Lars Høgh were the only players who had not started against Spain in the Euro 84 semi-final. Spain had four survivors. 'It's incredible to be Danish in Mexico these days,' said Svend Gehrs before the game. 'Everyone comes up to you and says Denmark will make the final.' Denmark were the better side in the first half without being quite at their best, due in part to the almost incessant Spanish pressing. They created chances nonetheless; Elkjær and Laudrup failed to force in Berggreen's dangerous cross after an exhilarating surge and stepover from Morten Olsen; Elkjær's arrowing long-range drive was fingertipped wide by Andoni Zubizarreta; and Elkjær hit a tired shot straight at Zubizarreta after a superb run and one-two with Laudrup.

Spain's threat came largely on the counter-attack. Julio Alberto slashed a vicious cross on to the roof of the net and Míchel, twenty yards out, dragged an inviting square pass from Butragueño well wide.

Denmark took the lead in the thirty-third minute. Berggreen found Elkjær, who changed direction superbly, waited for the run and then returned the ball to Berggreen on the edge of the box. As he played the ball, Elkjær was clobbered by Andoni Goikoetxea, who had already been booked. But the referee's eyes were on the ball: Berggreen fell over a clumsy challenge from Ricardo Gallego and a penalty was given. 'It was the Italian way of falling,' says Berggreen. 'I am from the Italian school.'

Jesper Olsen sauntered up to the ball, waited for Zubizarreta to dive and passed it insouciantly the other way. Olsen was the best player in the first half, troubling Spain with a number of sinuous dribbles. One ended with a dangerous cross that was held by Zubizarreta, another with a sliced shot wide from fifteen yards. He had scored in three consecutive World Cup games, was on top of his game and looked set to keep his place even if Arnesen returned for the quarter-final.

Shortly after the goal he received a throw from Høgh on the right edge of the penalty area and, through typical sleight of hip, beat Julio Alberto without touching the ball. It was a deliciously arrogant piece of play. Høgh, like all Danish keepers in the 1980s, eschewed the long goal kick 95 per cent of the time. This time, unfortunately, when Høgh prepared to take a goal kick with a couple of minutes to half-time, Olsen again came short to receive the ball. Høgh's plan was to play a one-two, pick up the backpass – which was permitted in those days – and waste a little more time before the interval. As he rolled it out to the right of the area, Julio Salinas came to press Olsen, who swaggered past him with a stepover and began to move upfield. Høgh stayed where he was, thinking Olsen would play the ball down the wing, and all the Danish defenders started to trot upfield.

Olsen, thinking Høgh had moved back to a central position, played a blind square pass across the face of the penalty area. There was a man there, but it wasn't Høgh; it was Butragueño, who had smelt something. As Høgh ran desperately across the face of the goal, Butragueño opened up his body to slip the ball through Høgh's legs and into the net. Svend Gehrs's commentary captured the national mood: 'Jesper, Jesper, Jesper, that one is lethal.' Busk, who had been running the other way before hearing the alarm call from his teammates, wondered: 'What the hell just happened?'

'I would never have done anything else,' says Olsen. 'I already knew before the ball came what I was going to do. It's just one of those things. The manner in which it happened maybe sucked it out of the team a little bit.'

Two of the strengths of the team – short goal kicks and players expressing themselves with the ball – had become a weakness at the most important time. Had Spain's Tomas not drilled one of the worst crosses of the entire World Cup miles over the bar, Denmark would not have had a goal kick. Had Arnesen not been suspended, Jesper Olsen would not have been playing. Had Sivebæk not gone down with sickness, Olsen would not have been on that side of the pitch to receive the ball from Høgh. 'I take my share of the blame,' says Høgh. 'Once Jesper went past Salinas I didn't expect him to play the ball back, but I should have been more alert to the situation.'

The manner of the goal winded Denmark, yet by the end of the half-time break they were ready to go again. 'At that point,' says Berggreen, 'I was still 100 per cent sure we would win the match.' Early in the second half Elkjær had two wonderful chances in the space of forty-five seconds. The first might have been the defining goal of his career. He set off on a diagonal run from the halfway line in which he beat Tomas twice, first with strength and then with balance, roared past Goikoetxea, dismissed Gallego with a hand to the throat and finally, from the edge of the area, smashed a shot that got stuck between Zubizarreta's legs.

Elkjær was still panting moments later when he ran through on goal, despite looking offside, after a fine long pass from Søren Lerby. The ball bounced like an off-break on the poor Querétaro pitch but Elkjær should probably still have scored. He sliced his shot wide of the near post from six yards.

Those chances looked even more important when Spain scored soon after. An outswinging corner from the right was flicked across goal and headed in by the unmarked Butragueño. The defending was diabolical. Laudrup mistimed his jump at the near post; then, when the ball was flicked across goal, a number of the Danish defenders started running away from goal, allowing Butragueño to move into space six yards out.

Denmark were behind in the World Cup for the first time. Piontek went to his tried-and-trusted book of substitutions, bringing on a striker, John Eriksen, for a defender, Andersen. A similar switch had worked instantly against Belgium two years earlier; it almost did again when, after a patient eleven-pass move and a blistering run from Laudrup, Eriksen hammered a twenty-yard shot straight at Zubizarreta.

Another classy run from Laudrup suggested Denmark had nothing to panic about. But when they did not equalise immediately they did begin to panic. Bertelsen gave the ball away in a dangerous area to Butragueño; he played the ball through to the onrushing Míchel, whose shot was saved by Høgh. From that moment, Denmark lost the plot: what was ostensibly a 3-4-3 formation was more like a 3-2-5 or a 2-3-5. Spain had a series of four-on-three or three-on-two breaks, the kind that usually only occur with two minutes remaining, not twenty-five.

One such break led to a killer third goal in the sixty-eighth minute. Denmark had five men ahead of the ball when an attack broke down, and Spain sliced them open with one long pass from Míchel to Butragueño. He was up against the last man, Busk, with nobody else within twenty-five yards of them. As Butragueño moved away from him on the right of the box, Busk fell over and inadvertently brought Butragueño down as he fell. It was a clear penalty. Goikoetxea rammed it in. 'He falls easily, which is fair enough,' says Busk. 'I just shouldn't have touched him. At 2-1 we threw Morten up ahead of the defence and I remember all of a sudden it's bloody quick with those counters. We gambled it all going forward way too early.'

Denmark's street footballers lacked the necessary street wisdom. In a sense it adds to the charm. 'We were a little naive,' says Morten Olsen, 'but that was the way we played.' Just as they might have declared at 3-1 against Uruguay, so they might have declared and saved face at 1-3 against Spain. 'At 3-1 it's over,' says Ivan Nielsen. 'You know it's over, so it doesn't matter.'

It unravelled quickly and embarrassingly, and Denmark were spanked. Busk, Nielsen and Olsen had a combined age of ninety-eight; Spain's three attackers – the two forwards Butragueño and Eloy, and the attacking midfielder Míchel – had a combined age of sixty-six. Those thirty-two years were compounded by the furious heat. Factor in weary limbs (Busk and Morten Olsen were two of only three Danes to play every minute in the tournament) and the lack of protection, and Denmark's defenders had no chance, especially as Spain were thoroughly ruthless. 'We have to acknowledge,' says Bertelsen, 'that Spain were frustratingly good at punishing us.'

There were half-chances for the substitute Jan Mølby and Elkjær, whose frustration manifested itself in a dreadful over-the-top-of-the-ball challenge on Goikoetxea for which he wasn't even booked. Denmark played the last twenty-five minutes with the naivety of soldiers going over the top, and they were punished again when Butragueño completed his hat-trick after another four-on-three break. He was probably offside; it barely mattered.

There was no question about the penalty decision for the fifth, when Butragueño Cruyff-turned Morten Olsen and was taken down. Even though it was a clear foul, the usually calm Olsen gesticulated at the referee. Denmark's heads had gone. So had their bodies.

'The problem came once we went behind,' says Berggreen. 'We were playing at midday, you couldn't breathe and you had trained so hard. You were so tired you couldn't feel your legs.' Butragueño swept home the penalty to become only the sixth man to score four goals in a World Cup match. There were thirty-one seconds remaining. The rest was silence.

There is a British TV archive page that lists the result as 'Spain 1-5 Denmark'. At the time those who had not seen the game nodded sagely when they were told the score. Then they were told which side had actually won. It was football's saddest, maddest thrashing. 'It annoys me tremendously still today, because it's ridiculous,' says Elkjær. 'We were the better team, but we lost our heads and that's crazy.' Yet in a sense it was also in the spirit of Danish Dynamite. This was a team who could win 6-1 one week and lose 5-1 the next – and at Mexico 86 they became the only team since the 1950s to score and concede at least five at the same World Cup.

Spain, not for the first time, were kryptonite to Danish Dynamite. Opta stats show that Denmark had more shots and much more of the ball. Spain had 43 per cent of the possession and scored five goals. This truly was a different era of Spanish football.

The Danish dressing room was a combination of shock and trauma. Some players focused on a spot a thousand yards in the distance; others wept. 'There was a really sad atmosphere,' says Bertelsen. 'All the good football, all the goodwill and all that euphoria there was around us, all of a sudden we had to live without that. It died.' It was not just the Mexico adventure that was gone. Nobody knew it at the time, but something died in the team that day.

Elkjær tried to console Busk by telling him that he and the team had played well; that some things weren't meant to be. Busk's response was as heartfelt as it was concise. 'My man scored four goals.' Thirty years on, Busk can see the funny side. 'We were faced with these quick strikers, Eloy and ... eh ... oh, what's the other guy's name. I almost can't remember. Butragueño? Yes, I almost can't remember him.'

The Spanish newspaper *El País* said 'Spain go the quarter-finals with the prestige of the man who shot Liberty Valance'. Neutrals who had fallen in love with Denmark felt as if Spain had shot Bambi. When the players returned to the hotel after the game, many of the staff were in tears. Back in Denmark, Dodo wasn't far from tears either: the defeat had cost her a trip to Mexico, as she was scheduled to sing 'Re-Sepp-Ten' before the quarter-final. 'I was watching the games with all my friends,' she says. '"You guys know, that if we win then I'm going to Mexico to sing." Everybody got really excited, and then we lost. I was very disappointed and I had to drink away my sorrows.'

She wasn't alone in that. As they waited for the bus to Mexico City the following day, Denmark soothed weary limbs by drinking orange juice with champagne. It was somewhere between a party and a wake. In *Tipsbladet*, Per Høyer Hansen wrote that Jesper Olsen played 'Re-Sepp-Ten' on repeat on a ghettoblaster and made a speech to the hotel manager before giving him the ghettoblaster as a present. Ivan Nielsen, the only man with Danish cigarettes, sat puffing away on the quiet table. Lerby's son Kaj christened Olsen *Jesper Julemand* (Jesper Santa Claus). The staff sang *Viva Dinamarca* as the players set off.

'I was drunk for four days,' sniggers Nielsen. 'We were up the whole night. The next day we went on the bus to Mexico City. We filled the bus with beers from Carlsberg and were singing "Re-Sepp-Ten". Then we got there, we went to a nightclub, and the day after we took the plane. We had a few drinks during the flight. Look at the pictures when we come back to Copenhagen, we all have sunglasses. We hadn't slept for three days.'

The players returned as heroes, but a defeat so shocking demanded an explanation, both in Denmark and around the world. Victory has a thousand fathers but defeat is an orphan. In the immediate aftermath the majority went for the obvious: Olsen's backpass, even if the tape told a different tale, that Denmark were much the better side at the start of the second half.

There was no particular backlash against Olsen, no effigies or hate mail, but it did define his memory. The backpass has cast a shadow over an outstanding career. 'Youngsters only see YouTube,' says Michael Laudrup. 'If they hear the name Jesper Olsen they only think of the backpass. If there's a player who deserves much more credit for what he did for Danish football, it's Jesper Olsen.'

Many footballers have had moves named after them: the Cruyff turn, the Panenka penalty. Not so many have had a description that extends into popular culture. A *rigtig Jesper Olsen* (a real Jesper Olsen) is used in Denmark to describe a mistake in any walk of life – even in politics. At a conference for the Social-Liberal party in 2001, the term was bandied about to chastise a former leader who publicly criticised the incumbent.

'If we won 3-1 then nobody would have really said anything,' says Olsen. 'It was emphasised because we lost 5-1 and their way back into that game was that goal from Butragueño. It depends: where do you look in a game, where did it change? I suppose that was probably the moment, even though you can regroup.'

To many Olsen book-ended the era of Danish Dynamite with his glorious solo goal against England in 1982 and his backpass against Spain four years later. He eventually moved to Australia. 'It doesn't bother me now, but obviously it did for a while,' says Olsen. 'Not living in Denmark was probably a good thing because it was one of those things where you think, "Oh, bloody hell …" I also think I learned a lot from it about how to deal with stuff. It was very good personally to have to get through that, and with people too. I never heard anything really bad said but it was a real process to get through.'

There was far more to Denmark's defeat than a bad backpass from Jesper Olsen. Even Diego Maradona had a theory; in his autobiography he said, 'the manager went mad'. Three decades later there is no shared discourse. Those involved cite various factors: the Danish mentality, the training, the heat, the tactical naivety, the absence of Arnesen, the substitution of Eriksen for Andersen. The truth, as ever, is somewhere in the middle.

'If Danish players thought they needed a holiday or if it was being dragged out too long for some, then that has something to do with the mentality,' says Piontek. 'I don't think we trained too hard. We were in top shape. You don't win 6-1 against Uruguay if you are not in shape. We had energy left in the first half against Spain. Of course when you concede a stupid goal like the one Jesper Olsen did then you lose some of the atmosphere and it can seem a bit depressing.'

Gehrs has a similar view. 'I had expected much clearer disappointment from the players than I saw. I think that somehow they thought they had done what everybody could expect of them by winning the Group of Death and playing the best football of the tournament. As Sepp used to say, that was the old Danish mentality coming to the surface.'

Most of the players reject the notion that they had the keys to the kingdom and a subconscious that told them they were trespassing. 'Most of this discussion came after the match, because we had a big party,' says Berggreen. 'It wasn't because we were happy. After being in a training camp for two months you start to have some alcohol and you get drunk very, very easily. Two beers and you are starting with the jokes. So we looked happy, and that went into Sepp's head: "Ah, they are not so unhappy at being knocked out."

'We were totally finished physically, there was nothing more in us. Also because of the concentration, you have to be focused, it's very hard. You play at midday, running like crazy and fighting like crazy. It was total soccer, something totally new, a fantastic level, but you can only play it when you are running twice as much as the other teams. There was no more in us. We were kaput.'

It was difficult for Denmark to stop themselves on the field when their natural instinct was to attack with abandon. That approach went too far as soon as they fell behind to Spain. 'It still hurts me that we lost,' says Laudrup. 'Not because it was 5-1, but because it was stupid to lose the way we did. I think it was a lack of experience in this kind of competition.' In a post-mortem in the *Observer*, Hugh McIlvanney slammed their performance with liberal use of a word that was no longer supposed to apply to Danish football. 'Denmark's swashbuckling marauders lost a stunningly amateur equaliser to Spain and continued to perform so amateurishly thereafter that the intelligently deployed, hungrily competitive Spaniards buried them like paupers.'

Even though they went out in the last sixteen – the same as entirely forgettable sides from Italy, Morocco, Paraguay, Bulgaria, Poland and Uruguay – they are forever associated with the tournament. Only the winners, Argentina, left a more indelible impression on Mexico 86. Fifa's technical report of that World Cup said they 'played the most spectacular football during the tournament ... their readiness to risk something, linked to a full physical commitment, provided the Danish game with an exceptional dynamism'.

In a strange way, Denmark went out on their terms. 'We showed that football can be played in a way which is fun, but which ultimately is not always effective,' said Piontek. 'We gave European football a new dimension and that's some consolation.'

In the next round they would have played Belgium, then Argentina, then West Germany in the final. Could they have won the tournament?

'Noooo,' says Laudrup. 'Winning competitions is not only about quality. It's about experience. There is a reason the big teams always go on to the quarter- and semi-finals. We had the quality to go far – I think we had more quality than Spain and Belgium – but we would have played Maradona in the semi-final and we would have lost to him, like everybody did.'

Bertelsen offers a different view. 'Both in France and in Mexico the championship was within reach. We could have been European champions, we could have been' – he exhales, almost unable to say the words – 'world champions.'

Chapter 19

The binary boys

Querétaro would have been a good-looking corpse. It was more in the spirit of Danish Dynamite for the team to burn out rather than fade away, but they did the latter over the next four years. There was still enough residual power in Sepp Piontek's fallen heroes for them to pick up the pieces ahead of the qualifying campaign for Euro 88. Wales, Czechoslovakia and Finland was a benevolent draw; Denmark's biggest problem was coping with the transformation of their own team as the stars from 1984 and 1986 faced retirement.

The Serie A trio of Michael Laudrup, Preben Elkjær and Klaus Berggreen were not available for Denmark's first qualifier against Finland but the line-up still counted ten players who had been integral in Mexico. 'If there is anything in football that can lie, then it's these numbers right here,' said Svend Gehrs at half-time when the 0-0 scoreline came up. Denmark had controlled the game and laid siege to the Finnish goal, but this was hardly a fiesta of football. The only goal was indicative of the struggles they endured. After Jens Jørn Bertelsen's inspired run into the penalty area, it took two deflections off Finnish defenders before his ball crossed the line.

'Are we on our way to West Germany?' The newspaper *Berlingske Tidende* spelled out the question most people were asking throughout the qualification campaign. Troels Rasmussen regained his place in goal and enjoyed his best spell during the qualifiers, where Denmark only let in two goals in six games. The problem was that their results read like binary code. They only scored four times themselves: Bertelsen's against the Finns – which could have been given as an own goal – two from Jan Mølby set pieces and one goal from Elkjær. The numbers on the backs of their shirts matched the names from Mexico but the spellbinding exploits of the World Cup were starting to look like the fossilised remains of a bygone era.

When Denmark reached the final group game at home against Wales, qualification was no longer in their own hands. Before the corresponding fixture in Cardiff, Juventus had voiced their concern with Piontek over introducing Laudrup, who was coming back from injury. 'I cannot promise you he will not suffer another injury,' Piontek said in *The Times*. 'The Welsh are very strong. If you are frightened he will break his nose or something perhaps you should put him behind glass in a museum and say "this is Michael Laudrup, he was a footballer."' Laudrup was furious when Piontek pulled him off at half-time in a tempestuous affair that Wales won 1-0.

John Sivebæk said he expected Wales to try to intimidate the Danes again in Copenhagen. This time inadvertent intimidation came courtesy of Idrætsparken's orchestra. As soon as the first bars of 'God Save The Queen' rang out behind the Welsh players, a confused Ian Rush, expecting to hear the Welsh national anthem, turned around to the band leader and waved his hand in disgust. The tension was even greater on the pitch where the Danes struggled to pick their way through the Welsh defence. When the winning goal came early in the second half, it had all the hallmarks of the team's heyday. Morten Olsen shook off two Welsh strikers in his own area before storming through the middle of the pitch and laying it off to Per Frimann. Flemming Povlsen cut to the right and found the deep gap that so often had been prised open by Frank Arnesen. Povlsen's cross into the box bounced off two Welsh defenders before Elkjær tapped in from six yards. Wales claimed it was offside – their manager Mike England said they had been 'conned good and proper' – but replays showed Povlsen timed his return perfectly.

The tension on the pitch spilled into the stands when a not-so-*rolig* fan threw a bottle onto the pitch, hitting the Romanian referee on the left shoulder. The referee picked up the bottle, handed it to a steward and instructed the stadium announcer to issue a warning to the fans. Having received fines after incidents in previous home games against Finland and the Czechs, the DBU could breathe a sigh of relief that the referee kept his cool and the repercussions weren't more severe.

Denmark's qualification wasn't secure until the Czechs beat Wales 2-0 four weeks later. Piontek's team had only scored as many goals as Finland, who were last in their group, yet they had somehow reached a third international tournament on the trot. This was a remarkable return on the money that had been invested in order to bring the national team to a new plateau. Now that the team had built themselves an even higher level, it became a challenge to cling on.

Arnesen returned to the microphone for the team's Euro 88 song '*En For Alle*' (One for all). If 'Re-Sepp-Ten' had delivered giddy optimism, these lyrics hinted at the uncertainty ahead: 'We have a secret plan which nobody knows.' Whatever the plan was, Arnesen was no longer part of it. The home qualifier against Czechoslovakia in June 1987 was his last international, the injuries he had battled throughout his career finally catching up with him. When Denmark once again faced the Czechs in a friendly before their departure for Germany, Arnesen made his way to the pitch on crutches with his left foot in a cast. His team-mates stood behind him as they sang their new theme song in front of an adoring crowd.

Bertelsen had called time on his Denmark career at the age of thirty-five but Jesper Olsen made the twenty-man squad after going on a short-term loan from Manchester United to his childhood club, Næstved, to prove his fitness. Morten Olsen, who had only missed one game since Mexico, was still the bedrock of the Danish defence. In the final warm-up game for Euro 88 against Belgium he scored his third goal for Denmark – seventeen years after his second goal.

Denmark needed the leadership qualities of their captain to stand any chance. Spain, West Germany and Italy weren't so much a Group of Death as a European Mount Rushmore of football. 'That's an insane group,' says Søren Busk. Piontek puts his hands over his head when he recalls the names of the opponents.

Spain, Danish misery's favourite company, were first up in Hanover. They hadn't won in six games, and the Danes could take further solace from that year's European Cup semi-final between PSV and Real Madrid where Ivan Nielsen had kept Emilio Butragueño in check and Denmark's Jan Heintze had held his own against the Spanish conductor Míchel. But the team from Madrid hadn't been wearing red and blue.

The 30,000 Danish fans in the stands sang 'Re-Sepp-Ten' before the game and did their best to create a home advantage. The fans were still red and white and standing side by side, but Spain were ruthlessly skilled in exploiting an overzealous Denmark side who attacked the game as if Querétaro had never happened. The first half ended 1-1 after Rasmussen had saved a Míchel penalty, but Butragueño put Spain back in front when the Danes mistimed their offside trap. The game ended 3-2. *Tipsbladet* wrote that Spain had won 'as usual'.

West Germany reversed the 2-0 scoreline from Mexico and effectively dumped the Danes out of the tournament in the second group game. The inevitable introspection and cull began before the final game against Italy. In the starting line-up there were now more players who had taken part in the 1988 Olympic qualifiers than had been on the pitch in Mexico. 'Our team was already on the way down,' Piontek says about the tournament.

Michael Laudrup is not sure whether he would have prioritised any differently had he been in charge. 'Put yourself in the same situation. You are a manager; you have these six, seven, eight, nine players, they have done so much for you, for the team, for the country. You have your doubts if they are at the same level. Then you have a new generation. Are they good enough? They have talent, they have potential, but are they good enough now?'

At the end of the Italy game, another 2-0 defeat, Klaus Berggreen came on as a substitute in his final appearance for Denmark. He saw it as a goodwill gesture – a final 'present' from Piontek – to honour his commitment. Berggreen says the challenges Danish football faced in the late eighties were not just a question of new players coming in to fill the gaps. It was a wider culture clash where you also saw the increasing influence of the assistant manager, Richard Møller Nielsen. 'When you have two generations, and two coaches, you have to have the old system with the old people or the new system with the new people,' he says. 'It was difficult.' The defeat against Spain in Mexico marked the end of an era for Danish football; Euro 88 merely spelled this out and paved the way for a new era to begin.

While the Danish national team had to get used to a new reality, things couldn't get more unreal for the supporters at Vejle Boldklub in the Danish first division. Close to 15,000 fans climbed the trees and floodlights around the stadium when their new number ten ran out on the pitch in August 1988 for a game against Odense. The Vejle supporters still couldn't quite believe what was happening when the stadium announcer read out the name: Preben Elkjær. Not since Bobby Moore played nine games for Herning Fremad in 1978 had Danish league football seen anything like this.

When Elkjær was released by Verona, a group of local businessmen in the eastern Jutland city of Vejle pooled together money for the most unlikely comeback. Elkjær's old friend and Denmark team-mate Allan Simonsen also played for the club and put on the charm offensive which sealed the deal. The other first division clubs were grateful for the spike in ticket sales whenever Elkjær turned out, but his spell with Vejle was marred by injuries and attracted headlines for the wrong reasons. At one stage the team's defensive problems forced the manager to recast Elkjær as libero. 'Our manager said: "We are letting too many goals in, we need somebody with experience",' says Elkjær. 'I did that and it went fantastic. But after nine games or ten games we had a problem – we couldn't score. "Can you change again?" The next match I scored twice.'

Vejle ended in a play-off to avoid relegation in 1990. When the team celebrated their win after penalties, Elkjær had already left. In his last competitive football game – fifteen years after he had seen red in the youth cup final and taken his frustration out on a car bumper – Elkjær was sent off. He gave the referee an earful before leaving the stadium and driving off. Even if he didn't bow out in style, Elkjær never lost the unpredictability and fury that made him the most mesmerising player to watch.

Berggreen and Laudrup also joined the Danish exodus from Italy. Berggreen was released by Roma and returned to Lyngby in Denmark, while Laudrup left for Spain, where his club career would reach new levels. In the national team, Laudrup was now playing alongside his brother Brian, who was part of the next generation.

Møller Nielsen had presided over the Olympic team that racked up twenty-five goals in a remarkable campaign to qualify for the 1988 games in Seoul. Five days after the team had beaten Poland 2-0 in Szczecin, Fifa found out Frimann had played in three of the qualifying games for Mexico 86 and was therefore ineligible. It kick-started an omnishambles where Denmark had two points deducted, lost out on qualification and the head of the DBU resigned. But the groundwork wasn't all in vain. Several members of that team formed the backbone of the Denmark squad that would try to qualify for the World Cup in 1990. Among these were Peter Schmeichel, Lars Olsen, Kent Nielsen, John 'Faxe' Jensen, Kim Vilfort and Povlsen.

While the campaign for Euro 88 had been marked by a dearth of goals, Denmark enjoyed a dead-cat bounce during the summer of 1989. Both Laudrup brothers were on the scoresheet when Denmark went on a scoring rampage against Greece in a home qualifier. The 7-1 win sparked headlines about the 'good old days', but Michael Laudrup told reporters after the game to stop dwelling on the past. This team had to write their own stories.

The Greece qualifier was Morten Olsen's final competitive game for Denmark at the age of thirty-nine, and it severed one of the last ties with the Dynamite era. With the score at 6-1, Denmark were awarded a penalty. The new captain, Lars Olsen, asked his predecessor if he wanted to take it. Morten refused. Sentimentality wasn't going to cloud his consummate professionalism. 'I remember my miss in the penalty shootout when Anderlecht met Tottenham in the Uefa Cup final in 1984,' he told *Ekstra Bladet*. 'I wouldn't want to make a mistake since the goals can become crucial for us making it to the World Cup in Italy.'

Morten Olsen only had to wait another month before he scored the fourth goal of his international career in what was his last Denmark game. Some people end their career on a whimper, while others are rewarded with the glory of beating Brazil with Pelé watching from the sidelines. The DBU marked its centenary by inviting Sweden and Brazil for a tournament, and the greedy hosts cleaned up the party by beating Sweden 6-0 before Morten Olsen got the first goal in a 4-0 win against Brazil. It was his 102nd international for Denmark.

Qualification for Italia 90 came down to the final two games against Romania. After faltering in friendlies against Belgium and a Dutch B side, pundits called on Piontek to bring back Busk, Søren Lerby or even Morten Olsen, who had only just taken his celebratory flowers out of the vase. For the home game against Romania, Piontek stuck by the new guard, and they rewarded him with a 3-0 win that put Denmark on the cusp of qualification. Brian Laudrup channelled his brother's weaving style by scoring the second after an audacious run through the Romanian penalty area. Praise was also lavished on the Danish defenders who kept Gheorghe Hagi – the 'Maradona of the Carpathians' – in check.

Even after their accomplished performance at home, Piontek couldn't help tinkering ahead of Bucharest. He brought Lerby – who hadn't played for Denmark since Euro 88 – back for a game which the Danes had to draw to qualify. 'Wednesday is judgement day,' wrote *Tipsbladet* ahead of the game. 'From 1 p.m. a large part of Danish society will come to a standstill.' The teachers and schoolchildren who gathered in auditoriums across Denmark to watch the game on big screens got a lesson in how not to defend a lead. After Povlsen had scored inside ten minutes, the Danish midfield and defence collapsed when Hagi took control and led Romania to a 3-1 win and the World Cup.

In the stands of the Steaua stadium was Valentin Ceauşescu who cheered on the Romanian team. The following month his father, Nicolae Ceauşescu, the Romanian dictator, was put on trial and executed as the revolution grabbed hold of Bucharest. The Danes would soon find out why sport and politics could never really be separated.

The Romania defeat came only three years after Mexico but almost the entire team from the World Cup were now gone. As the eighties turned into the nineties, the following had all played their last game for Denmark: Morten Olsen, Ivan Nielsen, Søren Busk, Klaus Berggreen, Jens Jørn Bertelsen, Frank Arnesen, Søren Lerby, Per Frimann and Preben Elkjær. Some of them were relatively young – in their early thirties – but they had all given so much physically that their mileage rendered them much older in real terms.

There was no real suggestion that Piontek would follow them. A new deal was said to have been sealed on the way home from Bucharest, with some suggesting Piontek had committed the rest of his career to Denmark. But tensions were brewing between the manager and the press as the draw for the Euro 92 qualification approached. After serving the country for eleven years, Piontek had learned to understand and appreciate the Danish mentality, even if he thought that everything often reminded him a bit too much of the small town of Jante in Aksel Sandemose's novel; the place where nobody ought to have ambitions beyond the common good. When Piontek started out as Denmark manager and had to get his residence permit extended, the office staff would marvel at the numbers when he wrote down his salary. He explained that his salary reflected the fact that there was only one national manager. 'This is Denmark,' says Piontek. 'If there is one who earns a bit more, then people think "how can we bring him down?"'

On the day of the Euro 92 qualifying draw, *Ekstra Bladet* splashed the headline: SEPP HAS ACCOUNT IN TAX HAVEN. The story didn't spell out any specific illegalities on Piontek's behalf but alluded to an account he kept in Liechtenstein for his advertising engagements. The story tipped the scales for Piontek. The day the story was published, 2 February 1990, he announced he was stepping down as Denmark manager.

'I have never deceived others,' he told *Ekstra Bladet*. 'Neither with tax nor anything else. So when people now raise questions about whether I pay tax on this and that, how much I save when I eat a meatball on a DBU trip, or whether my phone bill is taxed, then I don't want to be part of it any more. I also have a dignity that I want to preserve.' Piontek's 115th and last game in charge of Denmark was a friendly against his future employers, Turkey. Before the game, a group of *roligans* presented him with a fez that had been fitted with clapping hands, in the style of their famous headgear.

Most people agreed that the DBU wouldn't have to look far for Piontek's successor. Møller Nielsen had been a faithful lieutenant for Piontek, coached the under-21s and taken the Olympic team to the brink of qualification. But nothing was obvious as the quest to replace Piontek evolved into a farce. Møller Nielsen had his detractors in the DBU – most notably one member who said that his grandmother could have done just as good a job with the Olympic team. After a board meeting, the DBU announced that they needed a manager with sufficient international experience and were therefore looking abroad for their new coach.

According to *Berlingske Tidende*, the DBU short list included established names such as Tomislav Ivić, Jupp Heynckes, Sven-Göran Eriksson and Otto Rehhagel. Instead, it was Horst Wohlers from Bayer Uerdingen who was wheeled out in front of the Danish media in a hastily organised press conference. Wohlers, a forty-year-old German, had only been manager at Uerdingen for one year and was now about to take charge of Denmark's national team. If the DBU had been looking for international experience, all they could point to was a passport that was not Danish.

At the press conference Wohlers was flanked by the president of the DBU and Frits Ahlstrøm, who was head of press for the association. They were all caught in the headlights, their dazed and confused expressions revealing the calamitous state of affairs that was about to surface. 'I may write the true story about it one day,' says Ahlstrøm. 'Only three people know the real story. The details are very, very interesting.'

It quickly transpired that Wohlers was not going to be the next Denmark manager. Despite his talks with the DBU, Uerdingen were not going to release their manager, at least not without a sizeable payoff. Some reports suggested that the DBU had not even spoken to Uerdingen, but Ahlstrøm says both parties were in contact. His problem was that the story about Wohlers broke too early and the DBU got rushed into an unveiling that never should have taken place. 'I should just have been tough and said we don't do anything,' says Ahlstrøm. 'Tell the media to wait. I would have done that today.'

For all the drama that happened around Wohlers's bizarre twenty-four hours as Denmark manager, few people would want to change anything about the next chapter in the country's football history.

Chapter 20

Glory

The DBU swallowed their pride and went back to Richard Møller Nielsen, who was appointed as the national manager and saved them any further embarrassment. With doubters and detractors inside and outside the DBU, he faced an uphill struggle to prove he was more than just Sepp Piontek-lite. He decided on some quirky innovations to create his brave new world, one of which was Piggy, an old ballgame that the players would have done in training as kids. The idea is to keep the ball in the air and whoever lets it drop to the floor gets a letter – a P, then an I, then a G and so on. Whoever has the fewest letters at the end of the game wins a soft drink.

When he was asked about Møller Nielsen's introduction of this game to national team training, Michael Laudrup burst out laughing. 'What the hell,' he told Danish TV. 'It's one of the new things.' Cans of pop weren't the only things being contested; friction between the coach and senior players over tactics and team selection would cast a large shadow over Denmark's attempts to qualify for the 1992 European Championship.

The campaign did not start well. In the opening game at home against the Faroe Islands, an archipelago of the kingdom of Denmark playing only their second competitive international, Denmark were embarrassed as the minnows came back from a goal down to hold their hosts and overlords at 1-1 for a further sixteen minutes before caving in to a 4-1 defeat. In Belfast they could only draw 1-1 with Northern Ireland, a game in which Møller Nielsen controversially substituted both Laudrup brothers when in search of a winning goal. Things got worse against the key group rivals and dynamic rising force, Yugoslavia. Denmark were outplayed, outfought and out-thought at the national stadium and lost 2-0. Michael Laudrup wasn't finding this funny any more. He retired from international football at the age of twenty-six.

A year earlier Johan Cruyff had recruited Laudrup for his Barcelona revolution that would result in the famous Dream Team of the early nineties, of which Laudrup was the fulcrum. His impact was so profound that when he announced he was leaving in 1995 his team-mate Pep Guardiola was reduced to tears. With all of the stars of Piontek's team bar Laudrup now retired, a nation was also looking to him to do it all. It was too much. 'I'd been changing,' he reflects now. 'In 1984 I was the youngest, and then in 1990 I was the last from that generation left so I was suddenly alone. Because of who I was they said, "Everybody is on the shoulders of Michael". I had the same in Barcelona, so I said, "I cannot do both things". Two completely different ways of playing football as well. I thought, "No, I have to concentrate only on Barcelona. I cannot do both things".' And, like that, he was gone.

It was difficult to see where Møller Nielsen could go from here. Not only had one of the best players in the world walked away from the squad but Laudrup's brother Brian also turned his back on the national team. To lose one Laudrup could be considered unfortunate; to lose two was just plain careless. The brothers who had been earmarked to guide the team through the nineties were gone, and beyond them the squad was short on quality. As if that wasn't enough, Piontek's team overshadowed everything Møller Nielsen did – many of them, like Preben Elkjær and Frank Arnesen, were working in the media and casting a critical eye over the failings of the new team. Denmark managed to win their remaining five qualifiers, including the away match in Yugoslavia, but they could not make up the ground after such a poor start.

Yugoslavia had picked up the baton that Denmark took from Holland to become the most eye-catching team on the Continent. The generation that had won the 1987 World Youth Cup put in a creditable showing at the 1990 World Cup, succumbing to Diego Maradona and Argentina on penalties in the quarter-finals. A year later, Red Star Belgrade, where many of those players earned their wages, won the European Cup. Having bested Denmark by a point in the qualifiers, they looked a mouth-watering prospect for the European Championship in Sweden in 1992, packed with gorgeous, ball-literate players who, like the Danish players a decade earlier, would become stars at the very best clubs on the Continent. The Yugoslavian players' migration was forced by tragedy though: early in 1992 Yugoslavia collapsed internally and was plunged into the bloodiest conflict in Europe since the Second World War.

As the full horror unfolded it soon became clear that a team could not be sent to represent Yugoslavia under the circumstances and UN sanctions eventually decreed it so. On 31 May 1992, eleven days before Yugoslavia's scheduled opening match with England, Denmark were confirmed as their replacements, having finished second in the qualifying group. With many of his players already on holiday and in varying degrees of post-season slumber, Møller Nielsen abandoned plans to refurbish his kitchen and dragged the squad together for a last-minute crack at the European Championship.

They could scarcely have been more different from Piontek's tournament squads, which felt as if they were from an eternity ago. Everything was different, from the training and expectations to the make-up of the squad itself. Only John Sivebæk and Henrik Andersen remained from those who had played in Mexico. Around three-quarters of Denmark's tournament squads under Piontek were made up of overseas-based players; thirteen of Møller Nielsen's twenty earned their living in Denmark. Brian Laudrup had returned in the months before the tournament but there was no place for Michael, who had just helped Barcelona win their first European Cup.

'People asked me if I wanted to go,' he says now. 'I said, "No I don't think it's fair, I have not played for two years, I don't want to come in now just because they are playing in the European Championship".' Without Michael Laudrup the squad was thin on world-class talent. Flemming Povlsen was the pick of the outfield players and there was the bulletproof-confident Peter Schmeichel, who was at Manchester United and one of the finest goalkeepers in the world. The anticipation was that, given the squad and the short notice, Schmeichel might be a busy man. The tactics Møller Nielsen had to employ – soak up the pressure and hit on the break – were anathema to the free-form attacking of Piontek's side but the best option given the available personnel.

Initially it didn't seem as if Denmark would be hanging around for long. A tepid 0-0 draw with England was followed by a defeat to the hosts, Sweden, leaving them with the daunting task of beating France to make the semi-finals. The French had qualified flawlessly by winning all of their matches, but were under pressure to perform whereas Denmark were not. 'We played without nerves because we thought we'd be going home,' the midfielder Kim Vilfort told BBC Sport. Implausibly, Denmark won the game with a late goal from Lars Elstrup, a striker whose summer in Sweden was preceded by a stint at Luton Town and followed by him quitting the game, joining a religious sect and changing his name to Darando. Denmark advanced to the semi-finals.

They now faced Holland, the reigning European champions, resplendent with Marco van Basten, Ronald Koeman, Frank Rijkaard and Ruud Gullit. Surely the road would end here. Twice

Denmark went in front through Henrik Larsen; twice they were pegged back, the second time with four minutes of normal time remaining. Things didn't go all Denmark's way. Andersen's match and tournament finished early when he fractured his kneecap, to the soundtrack of his own blood-curdling screams.

The game went to a penalty shootout, hardly the forte of the Dutch, and Schmeichel saved van Basten's effort to give Denmark the edge. Hans van Breukelen got a good hand on two of the Danish penalties but couldn't keep them out before centre-back Kim Christofte, with one of the shortest run-ups in history, sent him the wrong way to put Denmark into the final.

If any team could be guaranteed to ruin this story it would be Germany, the reigning world champions and the Grim Reaper of late twentieth-century football. It looked as if Denmark didn't have a prayer, with Germany having as many registered footballers as Denmark had inhabitants and a fearsome squad of world-class players. With Schmeichel having one of the games of his life, they didn't need one. He made three stunning saves in the match, two from a flabbergasted Jürgen Klinsmann, and rounded off his evening with a spectacular one-handed catch from a looping cross. Down at the other end, amazing things were happening too.

John Jensen's shooting during the tournament had been wildly erratic, a series of yahoos that either trickled miserably to the goalkeeper or were launched into neighbouring postal districts. After eighteen minutes in the final he drew back for another one, located the hitherto undetected sweet spot and thrashed a twenty-yard piledriver past Bodo Illgner. Denmark were clinging on when, with twelve minutes remaining, the ball dropped to Vilfort. He had been playing under intense personal pressure as he had been travelling home during the tournament to tend to his daughter, who was suffering from leukaemia. With a hint of an arm, he controlled a bouncing ball on the edge of the German penalty area and clipped a left-foot shot in off the post, sealing one of the great fairy tales of international football.

It didn't make sense then and it doesn't now. Nor should it. Denmark conquered Europe in the same month the country voted in a referendum not to enter the European Union. 'If you can't join them,' the foreign secretary Uffe Ellemann-Jensen famously said, 'beat them.'

Euphoria would be a rather feeble word to describe how the victory was received in Denmark, but when the dust had settled it did throw up an intriguing and enduring question. Usually small countries only get one golden generation of players, if at all, and Denmark have never had as many gifted players of world renown in their national team as they had under Piontek. Nor have any of their teams played with anything like the same panache and flair. Yet Piontek's team didn't win, and their opposites in almost every way, Møller Nielsen's team, pulled off that extraordinary triumph in Sweden. Who, or what, is better?

It can't be disputed that Møller Nielsen's team were materially more successful than that of Piontek. They still couldn't get the better of Spain, missing out on the 1994 World Cup when they lost their final qualifier in Seville despite Andoni Zubizarreta being sent off after ten minutes. In 1995, though, they won the King Fahd Cup, a forerunner of the Confederations Cup, beating Argentina in the final. It is also in the record books that the quarter-final defeat to Brazil in the 1998 World Cup in France, where Michael Laudrup brought down the curtain on his incredible career, is Denmark's best finish at the World Cup, an excellent campaign guided by the Swede Bo Johansson.

Just as facts can't be argued neither can taste be dictated. Piontek's team have left an indelible mark on a generation of fans, a victory over hearts and minds that few teams in football history, never mind the 1992 European Championship-winning side, have achieved. In football as in life many of the most fascinating and enduring characters are those who fall short despite seemingly having all the ingredients for success.

Cruyff has always maintained that his Holland team of the 1970s were immortalised precisely because they didn't win the World Cup, a failure that has also shrouded in greatness the Puskas-led Hungarians of 1954. The Brazil team at the 1982 World Cup of Socrates, Zico and Falcao were knocked out in the second round group phase by Paolo Rossi and Italy. Prior to that they had buried the USSR, Scotland, New Zealand and Argentina under an avalanche of goals so sublime that many consider them the most 'Brazilian' Brazil team in history. Their subsequent victories in 1994 and 2002 mean relatively little in comparison.

Despite their failure to win, all three teams were in the top ten when a panel of experts was invited in 2007 by World Soccer to compile a list of the greatest football teams of all time. Also on that list at number sixteen (ninth among international teams) were the Denmark World Cup team from 1986. When coupled with their run to the semi-finals of the 1984 European Championship it might, at first glance, seem a ludicrous claim to call Denmark one of football's greatest teams on the evidence of a relatively scant body of work. That only applies, however, if the yardstick is success alone. 'The great fallacy is that the game is first and foremost about winning,' runs former Tottenham captain Danny Blanchflower's memorable quote. 'It's nothing of the kind. The game is about glory. It's about doing things in style, with a flourish, about going out and beating the other lot, not waiting for them to die of boredom.' Møller Nielsen's necessity-driven run of sucker punches on France, Holland and Germany in 1992 was impressive, but stylistically it stood in contrast to what Piontek believed in.

The Dynamite team are still held in the highest regard around the world for their uncompromising commitment to stylish and attacking football, beliefs which were unshakeable. When pressed on whether he'd have preferred to have the experience in Mexico or the against-the-odds victory under Møller Nielsen in Sweden, Klaus Berggreen is unequivocal. '1986, no doubt about it. I'm proud of the soccer we played.'

'The most important thing is to win,' Michael Laudrup says. 'But there's nobody who can guarantee that doing it in one way or another you will win. There are a lot of ways of winning trophies. You have to stick to what you believe – not to change because you lose some games or because one year things are not going so well.' Piontek transmitted that philosophy to his players and they carried it with them in all situations. The phenomena of game management, killing time, shutting up shop or damage limitation were not for them – not when they were 3-1 up against Uruguay, nor when they were falling further and further behind to Spain in Querétaro. Attack at all costs, come what may.

In Argentina they summarise the debate of aesthetics versus results with the philosophies of two radically different coaches. Are you a stylish and attacking Menottista or a more pragmatic and defensive Bilardista? Picking between the two is not exactly a hardship for Argentines as both César Luis Menotti and Carlos Bilardo delivered a World Cup triumph for the nation. It speaks volumes of the reverence felt for Piontek's team, however, that they can burn so brightly in the memory despite never even having won a knockout stage game at any tournament under him. Something about the team took hold in people's imaginations. Maybe it was the element of surprise that helped tip the balance.

Once upon a time you could turn on your television for an international tournament and know pretty much nothing about many of the teams involved, but the saturation of football coverage has killed the air of mystique that used to go hand in hand with international football. There are hardly any revelatory players at an international tournament any more, let alone an entire team. A goal scored now by an emerging young talent in any top-flight league in the world can be uploaded as a Gif or a YouTube link and go viral on Twitter before they can be pulled to one side to describe it in the post-match interview. Ahead of 1984 and 1986, in Europe particularly, there would have been some who had seen a few Danish players in their league or perhaps the odd Denmark game. For the rest of the Continent, and then the world, they were a gloriously refreshing assault on the senses.

If Denmark appeared to come from nowhere it's because they did exactly that. The distance they covered in just seven years is staggering. Piontek took over a Denmark team in 1979 that would be nailed to the bottom of their European Championship qualifying group and yet in the next edition in 1984 they were within a penalty shootout of reaching the final; two years later, they flattened the Group of Death at their first World Cup before their spectacular defeat at the hands of Spain. Unless Albania is secretly harvesting a generation of players to shake the world in the next decade, it seems impossible for such a small country, from Europe at least, to rise from anonymity to prominence in such a short time again. Arguably only the Dutch can claim a comparable achievement when reaching the 1974 and 1978 World Cup finals, though this was built on a decade of solid improvement through the 1960s and supplemented by Feyenoord and Ajax establishing a monopoly on the European Cup from 1970 to 1973.

It is the Dutch team of the seventies to whom Piontek's team are so often compared, not just in terms of the football they played but also their charisma. The football had echoes of the Dutch side but it was distinctly Danish, and the same applied to their characteristics. Both the Dutch and Danish players were almost effortlessly cool, drinking and smoking around international fixtures like a touring rock band. There was always something detached and unreachable about Cruyff, Johnny Rep and their colleagues. Piontek's players were equally life-affirming but sourced their appeal from self-deprecation and everyman normality. When the floating fan was looking for someone to get behind in 1984 and 1986, there was really only one team they could identify with.

Time has not been kind to the fashion sense of anyone from the eighties and this is clearly one area where the Danish team cannot compete with the Dutch. The long hair and love beads that the Dutch players sported regularly come back in and out of fashion but it's safe to assume there will be another Ice Age before the thick moustaches and cock-rock mullets paraded by Piontek's squad are deemed even close to acceptable again. The shirt from Mexico is the one acceptable item from the era – it is far more popular now than when it was first launched just before the World Cup – and the fact that the almost identical Southampton version (albeit with their own badge, and Draper Tools splashed across the chest) isn't as sought-after by the memorabilia geeks of football speaks volumes. As iconic as the design might be it would be worthless without its association with the Danish players who wore it.

Morten Olsen was asked how a group of players who individually earned their living at Europe's most ruthless clubs could collectively play with such joyous abandon for their national side. 'When we come together to play for Denmark football becomes our hobby again,' he told a throng of international reporters in Mexico. 'A happy thing to do together, like when we were all young boys.' The innocence in that statement from Denmark's most experienced player reveals both their huge appeal and also the root of their downfall.

Their overly attacking style of play was always a double-edged sword and ultimately the one they died by, a cinematic ending but not the happy one. The numbing defeat in Querétaro was a fitting conclusion to their story, pouring forward with an almost childlike naivety in that final half-hour only to be repeatedly picked off by a savvy Spanish team. It was magnificent but obviously doomed, yet their refusal to compromise on their principles only served to make them seem even more human.

They stayed true to themselves right up until the end, an increasingly rare quality that everyone desires but few actively try to develop, and worth more than any trophy. Long after the medals have been handed out and the tournaments have been condensed into a short collection of memories, that is the detail that stays with everyone who saw them. To the victors went the spoils. The glory went to Denmark.

Chapter 21

When we should have been world champions

Danish Dynamite isn't cult in Denmark; it's culture. The players, the manager, France and Mexico all share a place in the national consciousness. When a DJ on national radio introduces a song from 1986 as 'the year when we should have been world champions' no listener is left in doubt. When Michael Laudrup signs a deal with Swansea, a Danish tabloid uses the headline THAT'S GENIUS, THAT – the same words Svend Gehrs famously said when Laudrup danced his way through the Uruguayan defenders in Mexico. The Dynamite vernacular has become shorthand for a nation.

Gehrs's co-commentator Tommy Troelsen summed it up before the match against the Soviet Union on Constitution Day in 1985: 'It's nice for all the fans that we now have a team which we can support and which we can call our own, as opposed to earlier when we had to adopt favourites from other places.' The Danes still call that team their own; they call them heroes. Many people have an easier time listing the starting XI against USSR or Uruguay than the one that played in the most recent international.

Some of these names – Laudrup, Frank Arnesen, Søren Lerby – still play their part in international football. After an unsuccessful stint as manager of Bayern Munich in the early nineties, Lerby started a meat exporting business before he became a players' agent. Arnesen, his old friend from Fremad Amager and Ajax, has roamed the higher echelons of club football at Tottenham, Chelsea and Hamburg. The image of cheeky Frankie Boy has been supplanted by that of a top-level executive who made his name by discovering the likes of Ronaldo and Ruud van Nistelrooy.

Morten Olsen went on to manage Ajax, but eventually returned home to oversee a new generation of Denmark players. He holds one of the most remarkable records in football; in 2009 he became the first person ever to reach one hundred games for his country as both player and manager. Allan Simonsen also served as international manager – for the Faroe Islands and then Luxembourg – before returning to club football in Denmark. He also appeared on *Vild Med Dans*, the Danish version of Strictly Come Dancing ("What's there to sell out of as a 60-year-old?" Simonsen told *Ekstra Bladet*).

For others, life after football started a long time ago. Klaus Berggreen, the *Dottore*, learned more in Italy than just football. He used his business degree and Italian fashion connections to set up a women's clothing label (the name, Piro, links two of his Italian clubs, Pisa and Roma). Jens Jørn Bertelsen, who for so many years provided high-risk cover in Piontek's squad, is back working in the insurance business where he got his apprenticeship. He also ran a group of high-street steakhouses for seventeen years. 'I'm no wizard in the kitchen', says Bertelsen, 'but the desire was there to make it in the business world.' He still socialises with John Lauridsen and Ole Kjær but doesn't lace up his boots when the old boys' team in Esbjerg – the 'fat bellies club' – take to the pitch.

Ivan Nielsen might be football's only European Cup-winning plumber. When he is interviewed for this book he sits on an upturned black plastic bucket in a garage in Copenhagen's Amager district. 'Ivan and Thomas Nielsen VVS' reads the lettering on the breast pocket of his blue jumper, where he keeps his cigarettes and glasses. He gets up, pats his paunch and runs a finger over the moustache. His fellow defensive bouncer Søren Busk – who these days sells footballs as director of the Danish sports company Select – has now shaved off *sneglen* (the snail), but Nielsen's trademark 'tache is going nowhere. It has only got the chop once since he was seventeen, but when his wife remarked how much younger it made him look Nielsen immediately grew it back. His bowl-cut has also stood the test of time, but the weary eyes and lived-in face tell the story of a man who has done many a hard day's work – many sour metres, in the words of his old friend Busk – on and off the field.

After ending his international career, Nielsen returned to club football in Denmark. He won the championship with FC Copenhagen in 1993, but after two short stints as manager with smaller clubs there was nothing. 'At one point after football I was so sick and tired of coming home and doing nothing. I couldn't keep doing it. I couldn't do it.' Instead he turned to the trade he had been taught before his football career and launched a plumbing business with his son Thomas.

In 2002, Nielsen attended the funeral of John Eriksen. His former Denmark and Feyenoord team-mate suffered from dementia and died at the age of forty-four. Jesper Olsen and Per Røntved both suffered brain haemorrhages in the years after their Denmark careers. Olsen's recovery was quick – 'One of those lucky things I suppose' – while Røntved used his fearless tenacity to battle through four years of rehabilitation after part of the left side of his body was paralysed. The accident happened in 1984 after a playful skipping rope contest at his summer house. Twenty years later, Røntved hit a hole in one at his local golf course. Today, his eyes light up and the stories flow as he watches YouTube highlights from his Denmark games.

The memories of Idrætsparken, Wembley and Neza are a long time ago. But only if you measure it in terms of years. *Firserholdet* (the eighties team) were inducted into the Danish Football Hall of Fame in 2009, an event which has effectively turned into an annual reunion party where Denmark's golden generation enjoy another third half and kick around memories of old times. Two years after the team's induction, Sepp Piontek was back on the podium as one of two individuals honoured. The other was Røntved. Richard Møller Nielsen died at the age of 76 in February 2014, a few weeks before he was due to receive his award.

That Danish football wanted to bestow on Piontek an individual recognition of his achievements is as much about the results on the pitch as it is a tribute to his transformational effect on the country to which he moved. 'The German who made us be Danes' read the strapline on a 1990 biography by the writer Knud Esmann. Piontek was greeted in 1979 with a mixture of fear, awe, stereotypes and respect. He ruffled the feathers of the Establishment and unlocked the potential that the Danes were too blinded by old habits to realise. Not only did he bring them the results, he did it in a breathtaking manner that made the rest of the world hold them in the highest regard. The Danes took Piontek to heart and vice versa. Even when he quit their national team he never left them.

Piontek's fingers race across a red tablecloth in between coffee cups, spoons and dictaphones as he relives the highlights of a career that has been defined by an ability to mine footballing success in a barren landscape. 'There are no expectations,' Piontek says of his career choices. 'If you build them up, you'll be the king.' He managed chaos and voodoo in Haiti, ignited the dynamite in Denmark and has widely been credited with transforming the fortunes of Turkey. Even if Turkey's biggest international results were recorded in the years after Piontek's departure, his three years as manager laid the foundation and tapped into a potential that, just like the one he found in Denmark, had been unfulfilled.

Piontek managed clubs in Turkey and Denmark, but had to pack away the pipe after suffering a coronary thrombosis. He scaled down his career but didn't shy away from a challenge when he took on a coaching job with Greenland, even if their football association had no money to pay him. Instead, the seafood company Royal Greenland came by his house in Denmark every three weeks and let him fill his freezer with lobster which usually ended up on the queen's dinner table. Twenty-five years on from Baby Doc's money machine, Piontek was once again paid in damp wages.

In recent years he has divided his time between public-speaking engagements and helping out a small lower-league football team; if his right knee allows, he fits in a round of golf on the neighbouring course. It's thirty-five years since he first arrived in Denmark and he still calls it his home. He realised he was never going to leave the country after marrying his wife Gitte in 1988. 'I feel fine about being in Denmark,' says Piontek. 'People are nice to me and they haven't forgotten the eighties so I couldn't have it any better. The only thing that annoys me is the high car prices and that we have to pay so much in tax.'

Piontek has been trying to convince his good friend Preben Elkjær to spend some time at his summer house in Turkey; their family holidays together have included trips to the Indian Ocean. Their lasting friendship would have been the most unlikely storyline in 1979, but it is because of that common ground between the German yin and Danish yang that Piontek and his players edged closer throughout the eighties. 'We needed somebody,' said Elkjær. 'Not only us, but Danish football needed somebody who was really professional, who took things seriously, who also taught the DBU how to conduct business.'

After a stint managing the club Silkeborg, Elkjær learned how to conduct business the hard way when he became head of an ambitious new sports TV channel. The channel shut down within a year, but Elkjær stuck to the screen. Together with Brian Laudrup, Jan Mølby and Per Frimann, he has been part of an all-star line-up that presents Champions League coverage in Denmark.

One of Elkjær's most prized pieces of memorabilia is not from the world of football. It's a framed photograph depicting a young boy standing in a refugee camp in Goma. The boy is wearing a 1986 Denmark shirt with the name Elkjær on the back. The picture was taken by the Danish photographer Henrik Saxgren who posted it to Elkjær. 'It's a very strong photograph,' says Elkjær. 'It's a beautiful photograph.'

The shirt in the photograph is a replica. It even has the wrong number – nine – printed on the back. It wouldn't fetch much on eBay. Elkjær thinks it must have been a charity donation. 'Somebody got tired of Elkjær and thought: what can I do with this shirt?'

Back on the Isle of Man Dave Bignell's friends from football weren't tired of Elkjær. Some of them specifically asked to be seated at his table for the wedding. There were guests who probably couldn't tell the difference between one table name and the other, and were happy as long as they got a good view of the bride and groom. For those who had stayed up those late nights in 1986 or still had the old VHS tapes, the names on the tables were shorthand for one of the greatest stories football ever told.

Bibliography

Andersen, Jens, *Frankie Boy*, People's Press, Copenhagen, 2008

Ankerdal, Steen, *Landsholdet*, Aschehoug, Oslo, 2006

Ankerdal, Steen, Lassen, Kurt, Sloth, Peter *Chefen,* Ekstra Bladet, Copenhagen, 2009

Bartram, Jan, *Løb for livet,* Aschehoug, Oslo,1998

Boisen, Axel, Christian Mohr Boisen and Henrik Nordskilde, *Laudrup – et fodbolddynasti,* Lindhardt og Ringhof, Copenhagen, 2008

Elkjær, Preben, *Guldkjær*, Aller, Copenhagen, 1985

Elkjær, Preben, *Målkjær*, Aller, Copenhagen, 1980

Elkjær, Preben, *Mit liv som Elkjær,* Politiken, Copenhagen, 2012

Ellegaard, Lasse, *Fodbold er ikke for de stumme*, Gonzo, Copenhagen, 1986

Esmann, Knud, *Sepp*, Hovedland, Gjern, Denmark,1990

Freddi, Cris, *Complete Book of the World Cup,* HarperSport, London, 2006

Gandil, Johannes, *Dansk Fodbold,* DBU, Copenhagen 1939

Jakobsen, Joakim, *Tynd luft*, Gyldendal, Copenhagen, 2008

Jørgensen, Palle 'Banks', *Landsholdets 2198 spillerprofiler,* Tipsbladet, Copenhagen, 2004

Jørgensen, Palle 'Banks', *Landsholdet – i medgang og modgang*, Tipsbladet, Copenhagen, 2000

Krabbe, Hans and Sørensen, Dan Hirsch, *Drengene fra Wembley,* Lindhardt og Ringhof, Copenhagen, 2008

Laursen, Thomas and Sønnichsen, Ole, *Danish Dynamite: spillernes egne historier om 80'er-holdet*, Gyldendal, Copenhagen, 2008

Lundberg, Knud, *Dansk Fodbold 1–3*, Rhodos, Copenhagen, 1986–1988

Hesse-Lichtenberger, Uli, *Tor!: The Story of German Football*, WSC Books Limited, London, 2003

Molby, Jan, *Jan The Man: From Anfield to Vetch Field*, Gollancz, London, 2000

Mønster, Flemming, *Vejen til Mexico*, Hovedland, Gjern, Denmark,1985

Peitersen, Birger, *Dem der ikke hopper*, Ekstra Bladet, Copenhagen, 2004

Robson, Bobby, *World Cup Diary*, HarperCollins, London, 1986

Robson, Bobby, *Farewell but not Goodbye: My Autobiography*, Hodder & Stoughton, London, 2005

Various, *Det bedste de gav os*, Haase, Copenhagen, 1990

Newspapers and magazines

Ekstra Bladet, Billed-Bladet, Se og Hør, Jyllands-Posten, Aktuelt, Politiken, Berlingske Tidende, B.T., Alt om Sport, Tipsbladet, Ud & Se, Weekendavisen, Sabotage Times, The Blizzard, The Guardian, The Observer, The Daily Express, The Times and Sunday Times, The Daily and Sunday Telegraph, The Daily Mirror, The Sun, The Daily Mail, World Soccer, FourFourTwo.

Film and TV archives

Og Det Var Danmark (Carsten Søsted and Mads Kamp Thulstrup)
Landsholdets Legender (Frits Ahlstrøm)
Footage from: Danmarks Radio, TV2, TV3+, BBC, ITV, SVT

Acknowledgements

A number of people were extremely helpful in supplying contacts, support, inspiration and even steak. We'd like to thank Kalle-Weis Fogh, Kim Rotbøl at Hummel, James Dart, Tom Adams, Jan Madsen (and his friends from France 84), Lars Møller Nygaard (and everybody onboard Roliganexpressen), Gavin Hamilton, Jonathan Wilson, Duncan Alexander, Dave Bignell, Cris Freddi, Per and Helle Kjærbye, Paul Doyle, Scott Murray, Alex Netherton, Daniel Harris, Jacob Steinberg, Leander Schaerlaeckens, Lars Berendt and the DBU, Stine Riis at Polfoto, Jonathan Wilsher, Malene Thomsen, Bashir and Ayo, Charlotte Sørensen, Mike Alderson, Peter Kjær and Mathias Buch Jensen.

We'd like to offer special thanks to those who ran the extra *sure meter* to help us: Christian Mohr Boisen, Janus Køster-Rasmussen, Frits Ahlstrøm and our agent Ed Wilson, and of course everyone at Bloomsbury: the publisher Charlotte Atyeo, editors Jane Lawes and Nick Humphrey, copy-editor Richard Collins, designer Steve Leard and publicist Eleanor Weil.

Thanks to the interviewees who were polite, engaging and generous with their time – and who proved sometimes it is safe to meet your heroes, even if you're sitting on upturned buckets in a smoke-filled garage or surrounded by the retro kitsch and Twin Peaks vibe of Motel Brasilia: Sepp Piontek, "King" Klaus Berggreen, Jens Jørn Bertelsen, Michael Laudrup, Preben Elkjær, Allan Simonsen, Ivan Nielsen, Søren Busk, Morten Olsen, Jesper Olsen, Troels Rasmussen, Ole Kjær, Ole Qvist, Lars Høgh, John Sivebæk, John Lauridsen, Per Frimann, Steen Thychosen, Kenneth

227

Brylle, Henrik Eigenbrod, Flemming Christensen, Per Røntved, Jan Sørensen, Steve Nicol, Eoin Hand, Horst Wohlers, Svend Gehrs, Frits Ahlstrøm, Martin Tyler, Simon Kuper, Dodo and her band, Jarl Friis Mikkelsen, Birgit Leitner, Carl Peter Mysager and Dave Bignell.

Finally, thanks to our friends and families for being so helpful and understanding when our minds and hearts were occupied by the endeavours of a football team from the past.

And here's to Eik Rocky Nordquist Eriksen one day wearing the no 10 shirt for Denmark and capturing the spirit of our heroes.

Index

World Cup 2, 17, 213
  1930 6
  1938 20
  1950 161
  1954 213
  1958 6–7, 8–9
  1966 22
  1970 88, 161, 161–2
  1974 24, 215
  1978 13, 16, 215
World Cup, 1982 25, 26, 40,
    175, 213
  qualification campaign 29,
    31, 33, 34–6
World Cup, 1986 3, 43, 112,
    141, 156, 160, 179, 182,
    184, 194, 213, 213–14
  altitude training 148
  Bronze Ball 38
  Danish World Cup song
    145–7
  Group of Death 140–1
  health concerns 155–6
  homesickness 183
  Danish World Cup kit 141–3
  red cards 165, 181–2
  supporters 149–50
  training 148–9, 151–5
  warm-up games 149, 152–4
World Cup, 1986 qualification
    campaign 113–15, 129–36
  Soviet Union match 116–28,
    130

Norway match 131–3
Republic of Ireland match
    133–5
group victory 134–5
World Cup, 1986 group stage
  Scotland 156–60
  Uruguay 157, 161–72, 214
  West Germany 157, 173–82
World Cup, 1986 Spain match
    182, 183–94, 184, 185–
    90
  fitness problems 184–5
  Olsen's goal 186
  Olsen's backpass 186–7,
    191–3
  second-half Denmark
    collapse 187–90
  post-mortem 190–4
World Cup, 1990 202–4, 209
World Cup, 1994 212
World Cup, 1998 212
World Soccer 1, 65, 213

Yugoslavia 25, 31, 34, 209
Yugoslavia national team
    82–6, 88, 208, 209

Zidane, Zinedine 161
Zoff, Dino 24, 35
zombies 25–6
Zubizarreta, Andoni 185, 186,
    187, 212
Zygmantovich, Andrei 124, 126